The Social Health of the Nation

The Social Health of the Nation

How America is Really Doing

Marc Miringoff

Marque-Luisa Miringoff

Contributing Author

Sandra Opdycke

New York / Oxford

Oxford University Press

1999

For Helen and Hy Miringoff
Who Together Could Always Gauge The Indicators

Oxford University Press

Oxford   New York
Athens   Auckland   Bangkok   Bogotá   Buenos Aires   Calcutta
Cape Town   Chennai   Dar es Salaam   Delhi   Florence   Hong Kong   Istanbul
Karachi   Kuala Lumpur   Madrid   Melbourne   Mexico City   Mumbai
Nairobi   Paris   São Paulo   Singapore   Taipei   Tokyo   Toronto   Warsaw

and associated companies in
Berlin   Ibadan

Library of Congress Cataloging-in-Publication Data is available

ISBN 0-19-513348-X (cloth)
ISBN 0-19-513349-8 (paper)

9 8 7 6 5 4 3 2 1
Printed in the United States of America
on acid-free paper

Foreword

A democratic society must continuously seek ways to understand its progress. Yet, the question of how to determine real progress is a difficult one. What is viewed by the economist as positive movement may not seem so to the poet. This book is about a new perspective, which we call social health.

We at the Fordham Institute for Innovation in Social Policy have been engaged in studying and reporting on the social health of America for more than a decade. We began in 1987, with the first annual publication of the Index of Social Health. Since that time, the Index has become a nationally recognized yearly barometer, reporting information and trends on family income, education, health, housing, child poverty, drug use, and other social indicators that reflect the conditions of our national life.

As the Index and instruments like it have developed, they have come to represent a compelling idea—that it is necessary to monitor our social health in the same way we monitor other aspects of our society, such as the economy, politics, or even weather and sports. It is both the advancement of this idea, and the ways that it can be publicly portrayed, that compose the subject of *The Social Health of the Nation*.

A vital source of assistance and inspiration for us has been the vision of the Ford Foundation. In the summer of 1996, Lance Lindblom, Program Officer at Ford, contacted us and requested that we plan a project. He inquired, "What is needed to advance the field of social indicators and deepen its impact?" The result was the formation of the Working Group on Social Indicators. This group, convened by the Fordham Institute, consisted of twenty-two members representing a variety of disciplines, including medicine, economics, education, law, sociology, psychology, demography, and public health. They had a diverse range of research interests, including children, women, minorities, the aging, poverty, and hunger. They came from universities, research institutes, foundations, the media, government, business, and local community organizations. Each was concerned with increasing the public awareness of social conditions.

At its first meeting, in the spring of 1997, the Working Group considered its charge: to create an agenda that would advance the language, tools, and impact of social indicators. Task groups were formed to examine a number of areas, including improving the current governmental system of social statistics, enhancing the impact of the community indicators movement now emerging across the nation, and enriching the ways in which the media cover social conditions. Further, the group agreed to consider the kinds of social conditions that might be included in a national social report for the United States, a yearly official document that could portray the nation's social health. One participant, Ralph Smith of the Annie E. Casey Foundation, summed up the ultimate goal, noting, "if, in future presidential campaigns, the nominees have three debates—one on the economy, one on foreign policy, and one on social health—we will have achieved something."

The process that unfolded over the next eighteen months stimulated a wide diversity of views. There were agreements, disagreements, discussions, and debates. Running through it all was the bond of common intent. By the time the group concluded its work, the ideas were sharper, the visions clearer, and the next steps more certain. Although responsibility for the content of this book lies solely with the authors, we are deeply indebted to the members of the Working Group for their time and their talent.

As the meetings of the Working Group on Social Indicators moved ahead in 1997 and 1998, another source of energy and support came forward. Joan Shigekawa, of The Rockefeller Foundation, called and asked us, "Do you think your concept of social health should incorporate the perspectives of the arts and the humanities?" The question resulted in the formation of the Working Group on the Arts and the Humanities. This Group's task was to develop a series of indicators that reflected how the arts and humanities contribute to social health. Artists, philosophers, and humanities scholars convened to consider this issue. Together, we are seeking a new view of indicators designed to complement and enrich the contributions of the social sciences. This group, too, has served to inform the ideas of this book.

The Social Health of the Nation is divided into three parts. In Part One we argue that the United States needs a fuller and more meaningful view of the nation's progress than is portrayed by traditional economic and business indicators. We show how this view would enhance the public discourse by bringing sustained attention to the daily concerns of the public. Finally, we describe how this perspective has been advanced by initiatives in the United States, in other countries, and through multinational organizations.

Part Two begins an exploration of the social health of the nation. It presents sixteen major social indicators that convey the conditions of children and youth, adults and families, the aging, and some that affect the society as a whole, expanding the discussion with related information that informs the larger picture. In addition, it provides comparisons between the United States and other industrial countries. This section then frames this data in the context of social performance, showing how current performance can be judged and future performance anticipated, in order to provide a fuller understanding of the nation's progress.

In Part Three, we propose a set of initiatives that would further broaden and deepen the concept of social health and the ways it can be reported to the public. These initiatives include new concepts and tools for the field, more accessible means to report social data, and new ways for the media, both electronic and print, to portray the nation's social conditions.

It is our hope that this book will be of assistance to those in government, the academy, the media, the world of business, and most importantly the general public, who are interested in new ways to understand and to assess the state of the nation. If it can help to provide a deeper view of the everyday conditions that affect the daily lives of the people of this society, it will have achieved an important objective.

The Working Group on Social Indicators

J. Larry Brown, M.D. Director, National Center on Hunger, Poverty, and Nutrition Policy, Tufts University

Blondina Cardenas, Ph.D. University of Texas, Department of Education; former member, U.S. Commission on Civil Rights

Beverley Carlson Social Affairs Officer, United Nations Economic Commission for Latin America and the Caribbean

Anna Maria Cugliari Vice-President, Advertising Council

Christine Dwyer Senior Vice-President, RMC Research, Inc.

Patrice Flynn, Ph.D. President, Flynn Research, Inc.

Leo Goldstone Director, World Statistics, Ltd.

Mary Elizabeth Guinan, M.D. Chief of the Urban Research Center, Centers for Disease Control

Heidi Hartmann, Ph.D. Director, Institute for Women's Policy Research

Ichiro Kawachi, M.D., Ph.D. Department of Health and Social Behavior, Harvard School of Public Health

Jon Lickerman   Director for Social Investment Research, The
                                       Calvert Group

Jeffrey Madrick   Editor, *Challenge: The Magazine of Economic
                                       Affairs*

Judy Milestone   Director of Research, Vice-President of Network
                                       Booking, CNN

W. Henry Mosley, M.D., M.P.H.   Professor of Population Dynamics, International
                                       Health, Immunology, and Infectious Diseases,
                                       Johns Hopkins University School of Hygiene and
                                       Public Health

Harold A. Richman, Ph.D.   Director of Chapin Hall Center for Children,
                                       University of Chicago, and Herman Dunlop
                                       Smith Professor of Social Welfare Policy, School
                                       of Social Service Administration, University of
                                       Chicago

Julius Richmond, M.D.   John D. MacArthur Professor of Health Policy,
                                       Emeritus, Department of Social Medicine,
                                       Harvard University Medical School; former
                                       Surgeon General of the United States

Earl Shorris   Contributing editor, *Harper's Magazine*; Author

Ralph Smith, J.D.   Vice-President, Annie E. Casey Foundation

Frances Stewart, Ph.D.   Economist, Fellow, Somerville College, England;
                                       Senior Research Officer, Queen Elizabeth House,
                                       Oxford University

Alvin R. Tarlov, M.D.   Executive Director, Health Institute, New
                                       England Medical School; Professor, Tufts
                                       University, Harvard University

Daniel Yankelovich   President, Public Agenda Foundation

Edward Zigler, Ph.D.	Sterling Professor of Psychology, Yale University; Director, Bush Center for Child Development and Social Policy

Affiliate Member:

Alan AtKisson	Former Executive Director, Redefining Progress, Inc.

Project Directors:

Marc Miringoff, Ph.D.	Director, Fordham Institute for Innovation in Social Policy, Fordham University; Associate Professor of Social Policy, Fordham University Graduate School of Social Services
Marque-Luisa Miringoff, Ph.D.	Professor of Sociology, Vassar College; Consultant, Fordham Institute for Innovation in Social Policy
Sandra Opdycke, Ph.D.	Associate Director, Fordham Institute for Innovation in Social Policy

Project Associates:

William Hoynes, Ph.D.	Associate Professor of Sociology, Vassar College
Eunice Matthews, Ph.D.	Assistant Professor, Fordham University, Graduate School of Social Services

Acknowledgments

Many people contributed to the work and to the ideas that went into the preparation of this book. At Fordham University, home to the Fordham Institute for Innovation in Social Policy, numerous people have made our work on social indicators possible. Amy Miller, Assistant Director of the Institute, has contributed her time, effort, and remarkable wisdom from the beginning. Two additional people have been vital: Dean Mary Ann Quaranta of the School of Social Service, of which the Institute is a part, and Father Patrick Sullivan, Administrator of the Tarrytown Campus,where the Institute is located. We are also grateful for the formidable organizational abilities of Marcy Maggio of the Institute staff.

At Vassar College, George Laws has contributed his talent to the graphic design and layout of all of our publications, including this book. Much of our effort would have been impossible without his vision. William Hoynes, colleague and friend, assisted us with both the Ford and Rockefeller Working Groups, helped further our efforts on *The Social State of Connecticut,* and reviewed the statistical content of this book.

Over the years, many individuals have been important to the progress of the work. During the 1980s, we were both inspired and supported by Sol Levine and Al Tarlov of the Health Institute of the Harvard School of Public Health, who helped us with the early conceptualization of the Index of Social Health. At the United Nations, Richard Jolly, then Deputy Director of UNICEF, supported the creation of the Index of Social Health of Children of Industrial Countries. In Connecticut, Elaine Zimmerman, Director of the Connecticut Commission on Children; David Nee, Executive Director of the Graustein Memorial Fund; and Ed Zigler, Director of the Bush Center for Children and Social Policy at Yale, made *The Social State of Connecticut* a reality because they believed so strongly in the idea. Christel Truglia and Brian Mattiello, members of the Connecticut State Legislature, helped to establish mandated social reporting in the State.

More recently, Lance Lindblom of the Ford Foundation provided the vision and support that enabled the work to move to a new level. We will always be grateful to him for his ability to think in creative and innovative ways. Joan Shigekawa of the Rockefeller Foundation helped us with her unique insights and assistance; her impact on the work continues to reveal itself.

Many other individuals have given us extensive comments on the manuscript. Each has contributed a special perspective. These include Jeffrey Madrick, Leo Goldstone, Frances Stewart, Harold Richman, Al Tarlov, Heidi Hartmann, Ruth Wooden, Alex Kroll, and Ken Prewitt. We are profoundly grateful to each. Thanks, also, to Kelli Peduzzi, who copy edited the entire manuscript and contributed significantly to its clarity, and to Gail Lee of CBS for her insights about media coverage of social problems.

We would also like to thank the members of the Working Group on the Arts and Humanities, supported by the Rockefeller Foundation: Carol Becker, Beverley Carlson, Amy Cheng, Charis Conn, Christine Dwyer, Patrice Flynn, Leo Goldstone, Alicia Gonzalez, Gayle Pemberton, Karen Robertson, Earl Shorris, Mark Stern, and Patricia Wallace. Together, they helped to provide a new and creative perspective on social indicators. Also special thanks to Caron Atlas, Thomas Ybarra-Frausto, and Pamela Johnson of the Rockefeller Foundation, and Michael McCarthy of the Philosophy Department at Vassar College.

At Oxford University Press, we worked with numerous people whose level of professionalism has been exemplary. Most particularly, we would like to thank Kenneth MacLeod, Senior Editor, for his advice and support.

Finally, and most importantly, our gratitude to Sandra Opdycke, who has worked with us for more than two decades, helped to shape our vision and find a way to make it real, and contributed enormously to the concepts and material of this book.

Contents

The Social Health of the Nation

Introduction

In the media and in the speeches of our national leaders, we are often presented with an official portrait of America's progress. This portrait typically includes the Gross Domestic Product, the stock market, the Index of Leading Economic Indicators, the balance of trade, the inflation rate, and other similar measures. The view created by these measures molds our perception of the state of the nation and supplies a well-defined, accessible, and timely answer to the question: "How are we doing?"

It is the central argument of this book that other elements need to be present in the portrait in order to give us a fuller and deeper view. These elements include the well-being of America's children and youth, the accessibility of health care, the quality of education, the adequacy of housing, the security and satisfaction of work, and the nation's sense of community, citizenship, and diversity. These conditions must be as sharply and clearly visible as is the rest of the picture.

A more complete view of the nation's progress would enable us to expand the public dialogue about who we are, where we are headed, and what issues we must address. A more informed public dialogue would make what is vague far more specific, what is diffuse more defined, and would enlarge our understanding of the fabric that joins us as a society.

Traditionally, when we think of strengthening the public dialogue, we envision more people voting in elections and primaries, greater attention to political events, and a more diverse range of people seeking elective office. But the public's involvement can be enhanced, not only by urging greater participation, but also by enlarging the variety of reasons that inspire it. To strengthen the public dialogue, we need to deepen our sense of connection to the public sphere by expanding the range, depth, and visibility of issues that are conducive to debate and resolution.

The path toward a fuller public discourse, more grounded in fact and information, is of course filled with obstacles. But the need is apparent. Today, it is widely acknowledged that the public is deeply discouraged about the content of public debate, particularly at the national level. There is a growing sense, dangerous to a democracy, that government and politics rarely concern our daily lives. Public opinion data show an alarming, consistent, and long-term decline in the public's trust in both government and the media. This is not surprising when so much attention is focused on the machinations of the Beltway and the power ploys of Capitol Hill rather than on the bread-and-butter health and well-being issues that involve us each day.

The presidential campaigns of recent years illustrate this point. Media analysts observe that when professional journalists interview political candidates, they tend to ask "gaming" or "strategy-oriented" questions intended to catch candidates off guard, uncover motives and character flaws, and challenge their public persona. In contrast, when the public has the opportunity to question candidates, it asks "governing" or "problem-oriented" questions that are more closely tied to issues such as jobs, wages, safety, education, and health care.

It is these everyday concerns and the ways in which the public is informed about them, that compose the focus of this book. The book rests on the premise that the more clearly the social side of the nation's portrait can be drawn and the more accessibly its contents can be communicated, the deeper the discussion and debate it can stimulate and the stronger our democracy can become.

We need this social portrait not only because it would enlarge our view of our national life, but because there is strong evidence that it would provide a very different picture from what is conveyed by traditional business and economic barometers. Each year, the Council of Economic Advisors prepares the *Economic Report of the President*, the official overview of the state of the economy. In 1995, for example, the *Economic Report* noted:

> By most standard macroeconomic indicators, the performance of the U.S. economy in 1994 was, in a word, outstanding. The economy has not enjoyed such a healthy expansion of strong growth and modest inflation in more than a generation. . . . Nineteen ninety-four was a very good year for the American economy. Indeed, robust growth, a dramatic decline in the unemployment rate, low inflation, and a much improved outlook for the Federal budget combined to yield the best overall economic performance in at least a generation.

And similarly in 1996—

> Economic performance during the past 3 years has been exceptional.

And in 1997—

> Economic growth has been strong and sustainable. The economic expansion has been marked by a healthy balance among the components of demand. . . . In-

vestment is booming: real spending on producers' durable equipment has grown a stunning 11 percent since 1993. . . . The new structures and equipment that it represents will remain part of the Nation's capital stock, promoting growth and productivity for years to come.

And in 1998—

The past year saw the nation's economy turn in its best performance in a generation.

If there were a Council of Social Advisors charged with preparing a *Social Report of the President,* and if that document were recognized as the annual official accounting of the social state of the nation, its contents might include the following:

On the whole, long-term trends in social performance may be viewed as less than encouraging. While some indicators show improvement and signify areas where we have made gains in the nation's social health, many have worsened significantly over time and are currently performing at levels far below what was achieved in previous decades. These are warning signs which require attention. A number of other key indicators have shown mixed results, rising and falling at different times. These need to be closely monitored.

Several indicators are performing poorly. Suicide rates among the young are 36 percent higher than they were in 1970 and nearly triple the rate in 1950. Income inequality is at its third worst level in fifty years. More than 41 million Americans are without health insurance, the worst performance since records have been kept. Violent crime remains almost double what it was in 1970, even with substantial improvements during the 1990s. Average wages for American workers have fallen sharply since the early 1970s, despite the strong economy. Child abuse has increased dramatically: an estimated 3.1 million children were reported abused in 1996 alone. Approximately one in every five children in America today lives in poverty, a 33 percent increase since 1970. The magnitude of the downward trend in the performance of these indicators is a matter for serious deliberation.

There are several bright spots. A range of indicators affecting different age groups in society have experienced significant improvement. One is poverty among the elderly, which has improved by more than fifty percent since the 1970s. This performance represents a significant achievement for the nation. Infant mortality is currently at its best point in the nation's history. High school dropout rates and life expectancy have improved since the 1970s as well. In these areas, the challenge is to ensure that all groups in society share in the gains that have been made.

Some indicators have risen and fallen several times over the past few decades. Teenage drug use, for example, grew worse in the 1990s after improving during the 1980s. In contrast, teenage births have improved during the past five years after a worsening trend during the 1980s. Other shifting indicators include affordable housing, unemployment, and alcohol-related traffic fatalities, all of which have made some gains during the 1990s after reversals during the 1980s. These issues require our continuing vigilance.

Despite the significance of these trends, there is no *Social Report,* no Council of Social Advisors, no presidential press conference to convey these results and answer questions about them, no congressional committee to review and assess their consequences, no programs on the media to discuss their implications; in short, there is no sustained attention to the social health of the nation. But the data are real, as are the conditions they describe. Had the important story they tell about America been conveyed as it unfolded, through a series of recognized measures and barometers, day by day, month by month, quarter by quarter, or even just annually, the nation would have been far more informed, would have understood better the changes occurring in society, and would have been more able to respond to them.

It is possible, as well, that if the American people had watched these trends as they developed it would have singled out those areas which required attention, urged concrete action from political leaders, and made electoral decisions based on visible results. Such vigilance might have helped to foster the traditional democratic belief that information—objectively collected, reported, and discussed—should be more important in shaping events than power and influence, a necessary reiteration in our distrustful age.

The social side of America's official portrait, however, does not exist in any accessible form, and the data provided above represent only a beginning step toward its creation. Part Two of this book carries the task much further. Using these indicators and other related information about the social conditions of the country, it pieces together a mosaic of America's social health. It then adds an important context, the language of performance, presenting standards by which we can judge how we are doing now and how well we might do in the future. Our intent is to develop an approach that can portray an important aspect of our national life that, like the economy, can be measured, monitored, reported, and discussed in the public forum.

But developing a social portrait to the point where it can have lasting impact on the public dialogue will need to go further still. It will require new ideas, resources, continuity of effort, and a sustained commitment. It must involve the participation of diverse sectors of society, including the academic and research communities, the news media, and key agencies of government. It will need to draw upon the contributions of the community indicators movement now emerging in localities across the country and upon advances by other nations in the systematic reporting of social conditions.

To achieve this, the following initiatives are needed:

Timely reporting by the federal government of a series of officially recognized indicators of social health that systematically monitor important areas of society, such as work, income, safety, and education, as well as the status of groups such as children, women, the aging, and minorities.

The creation of new indicators that probe some of the deeper and less frequently monitored aspects of society, such as the quality of our political discourse, our level of civic engagement, and our sense of community.

The development and wide recognition of positive and negative standards against which the performance of key indicators can be judged so that their consequences for society can be more clearly understood and communicated.

The creation of new barometers similar in their utility and clarity to those used to anticipate major changes in the economy; for example, an Index of Leading Social Indicators might be designed that could predict the coming of "social recessions."

The evolution of a more coherent system of social information that would narrate, interpret, and communicate the results of government and private surveys. These surveys currently generate the majority of the nation's social data on income, education, youth, aging, women, work, and other areas of social concern. Their key findings must be far more accessible to the media, to the makers of policy, and to the general public.

The initiation of a process outside of government that would bring together experts from different fields—drawn from both the humanities and social sciences—to make a periodic assessment of national social trends that would be regularly communicated to the government, the media, and the public.

The eventual development of an official government entity that would serve as a Council of Social Advisors to the President, providing the public and the policy-making process with an annual, official, objective social analysis, such as a *Social Report of the President* (or a national social report, as it is called in other countries) that could be reviewed and assessed by a joint committee of Congress.

The creation of social "segments" or "beats" in radio, television, and newspapers that would cover issues of social health with the same kind of context and regularity now provided by business pages, arts and leisure segments, sports sections, and weather reports. These beats would describe significant new studies, explore changes in long-term trends, report human interest stories that illuminate data, provide regular updates on "how we are doing," and offer commentaries, similar to those in politics and economics, that interpret and analyze recent developments.

The encouragement of courses of study in schools of journalism to help train future reporters to cover issues of social health at the community, state, and national level. Support is needed, as well, for multidisciplinary courses in undergraduate and graduate curricula in America's colleges and universities, to address key issues of the nation's social health.

The publication of popular periodicals that could portray the social side of American life in the way that *Fortune, Business Week,* or the *Wall Street Journal* regularly portray our economic and business life.

The search for ways to enrich and advance the community indicators movement now emerging in many localities across the country, to help increase its impact and contribution to the national dialogue.

The idea that we need to monitor our social conditions more closely in order to enrich the public dialogue is not new. These initiatives build on traditions that began in America at the turn of the twentieth century. Some of them can be achieved with resources that are currently available, others await new efforts and new ideas. Most importantly, they represent the possibility of progress in the immediate future. This book explores that possibility.

Part One

Seeking the Social Side
of the Portrait

Chapter One

How Are We Doing?

The Dominance of the "Economy."   Is the GDP rising? Is the stock market strong? Are businesses prospering? Is inflation low? Is the deficit shrinking? Are exports increasing? These are the types of questions we ask when we wish to know "how we are doing" as a nation.

What we do well in the United States, perhaps better than any other country in the world, is monitor our economy. We ask hundreds of precise questions to assess its strength. To answer these questions, we have an array of well-recognized and frequently reported business-economic indicators and indexes.

The Gross Domestic Product, for example, tracks the size and growth of the economic sector. The monthly Index of Leading Economic Indicators combines critical indicators to forecast the coming business cycle. The Index of Consumer Confidence gives a broad picture of public sentiment and people's willingness to purchase costly goods and services. The Dow Jones Industrial Average assesses the strength of blue-chip stocks and is reported to the nation on a minute-by-minute basis. The nation's economy is closely observed by such measures. They provide a timely and widely accessible portrait of our economic life. Each aspect has a gauge or meter to tell us precisely where we stand.

Movement in these many measures is assumed to affect us all. If exports are strong, dividends high, interest rates low, inflation stable, the stock market bullish, and the GDP rising, we have come to believe we are doing well. If these indicators worsen, we quickly become concerned. The various parts of the economy that we monitor are viewed as interdependent, affecting each other and affecting the whole.

The economy is about "us," and its precise measurement provides vital information. A "2.5 percent gain over the last quarter" implies vigilance and rationality. When the Federal Reserve Board increases the interest rate by a "quarter of one percent" there is a sense of surgery about it.

To interpret the continuous flow of information, economists, politicians, and business leaders convene on a regular basis to assess the economic life of the nation. The annual publication of the *Economic Report of the President,* prepared by the Council of Economic Advisors, provides a routine point of departure to gauge the overall state of the economy. In-depth analyses of the dynamics of the various sectors are presented. The previous year's events are documented in great detail, as are trends over time, some dating back as far as 1929.

Every six weeks, the nation focuses on another important set of economic indicators when the Federal Reserve Board issues its Beige Book, a systematic survey of economic activity. Network and other national news programs report economic data every night. Most newspapers have a daily section devoted to business and economic news which includes regular updates of stocks, business activity, consumption patterns, and other related activity. A range of newspapers and magazines are devoted exclusively to the economy, including the *Wall Street Journal, Business Week*, and *Fortune*.

In contrast to the tools, structures, and mechanisms of the economic sphere, the richness and variety of its indicators, and the regularity with which they are reported, our vision of the social sphere is far more obscure. Social data are collected once a year at best, rather than daily, weekly, monthly, or quarterly, as in economics. Moreover, they are often two to three years out of date by the time they are released, making the information they convey far less compelling and our ability to deliberate or to respond far less likely. Even the occasional front-page story on a social problem, such as teenage suicide, may present data that are more than two years old, and the common caveat, "the last year for which data are available," is an all too familiar aside. In fact, there may be as many as twelve or more regular monthly reports to the nation about the availability of durable goods or the size of factory inventories for each single, out-of-date, accounting of how many teenagers were sufficiently depressed to take their own lives (see Chart 1.1).

Most significantly, social data are not generally thought of, collected, or released as *indicators* that chart the performance of a larger condition like the "social state of the nation," nor are they combined into accessible indexes or barometers designed to keep track on a regular basis of what is considered important. Furthermore, there are no official bodies to review the processes of data conception, collection, and release, to issue statements of interpretation and analysis, to relate the various results to each other, or to provide a perspective on their implications for the condition of society as a whole.

The child abuse rate, for example, may be issued once a year, but not in the context

1.1 Reporting frequency of social data and business-economic indicators

Numbers in parentheses indicate publication lag time

	Daily	Weekly	Monthly	Quarterly	Annually
Business-economic indicators	CRB Futures Price Index (15 sec.) Dow Jones Industrial Avg. (60 sec.) New York Stock Exchange Composite Index (60 sec.) Standard & Poor's 500 Composite Price Index (60 sec.) Wilshire 5000 Equity Index (1 day)	Bank Loans: Com. & Industrial (9 days) Business Failures (5 days) Business Starts (5 days) Money Supply (10 days)	Average Hourly Earnings Index (1-2 wks.) Average Weekly Earnings (1-2 wks.) Average Weekly Hours (1-2 wks.) Balance of Trade (45 days) Capacity Utilization (2.5 wks.) Consumer Confidence Index (5-10 days) Consumer Installment Credit (6 wks.) Consumer Price Index (3-4 wks.) Consumer Sentiment Index (5-10 days) Employment (1-2 wks.) Government Budgets and Debt (3-4 wks.) Housing Starts (3 wks.) Import and Export Prices Indexes (1 mo.) Industrial Production Index (2.5 wks.) Inventory-Sales Ratios (45 days) Leading, Coincident, & Lagging Indexes (1 mo.) Manufacturers' Orders (1 mo.) Personal Income and Saving (3-4 wks.) Producer Price Index (2.5 wks.) Unemployment (1-2 wks.)	Balance of Payments (75 days) Capital Appropriations (70 days) Employment Cost Index (1 mo.) Farm Parity Ratio (1 mo.) Flow of Funds (2 mo.) GNP Price Measures (3-4 wks.) Gross National Product (3-4 wks.) Plant and Equipment Expenditures (2 wks.) Productivity (2 mo.) Unit Labor Costs (2 mo.)	Distribution of Income (8 mo.) Intl. Investment Position of the U.S. (6 mo.) Poverty (8 mo.)
Social data					Amer. Housing Survey (biennial) (1 yr.) Child Abuse (4 mo.) Drug Abuse (6 mo.) Food Stamp Enrollment (3 mo.) Health Insurance Enrollment (8 mo.) High School Dropouts (1 yr.) Highway Deaths Due to Alcohol (10 mo.) Infant Mortality (2 yr.) National Crime Survey (2 yr.) Teen Suicide (2-3 yr.) Uniform Crime Reports (8-9 mo.)

Sources: Economic indicators adapted from Norman Frumkin, *Guide to Economic Indicators* (New York: M.E. Sharpe, 1990).
Social indicators from authors' telephone survey; analysis of data sources. Lag times are approximate.

of other related data such as poverty, suicide, drugs, or crime, that would give it context and enlarge our understanding of the total picture. Health insurance coverage is another critical issue, but it is typically released apart from related issues such as infant mortality or life expectancy. Some important issues have no reliable data at all. Problems such as hunger, homelessness, and illiteracy are still not reliably measured or tracked.

Although much social data exists on many important aspects of daily life, it is usually not made available in a form that is accessible to the public, to the makers of policy, or to the media. Studies with numerous tables of raw statistics are often distributed with little interpretation or text. The results of whole surveys are sometimes published with few references to past trends or larger meanings. Some data are published under several auspices, each using a different definition of the same problem, each released at a different time of year. Reports are often technical documents meant for experts, and contribute little to the public dialogue unless a special effort is made by a journalist or scholar to make them accessible.

In effect, the data available from the literally thousands of studies and surveys conducted by the government are not narrated, as are traditional business and economic indicators. This lack of coherence frames the way in which social conditions are covered in the national news media and shapes the public's view. Social data, when they are covered, are presented as unrelated pieces of information rather than as part of a larger system that tracks and updates important on-going conditions. A subject may be presented once, but there is often little or no follow-up.

More typically, social data appear in the media as incidental information in the context of sensational events. If a particularly brutal case of child abuse occurs, coverage may include the latest data. The O. J. Simpson trial, for example, produced a smattering of statistics on domestic violence. The Los Angeles riots of 1992 evoked some discussion of poverty and inter-racial conflict. The high school killings of 1998 and 1999 brought a brief reflection on the nature of juvenile crime. In each case, news coverage was intense for a short period, but as such crises petered out and as the nation moved on, the sense of the seriousness and pervasiveness of these problems quickly faded from public view.

This approach applies even to our major print media. In the *New York Times*, for example, there were 52 stories in 1996 on the problem of infant mortality. Of these, 74 percent dealt with the death of individual infants. Two particularly sensational cases accounted for more than half the stories. Seven stories dealt with new medical interventions. None dealt with infant mortality as a social indicator. An analysis of the same year found similar results for issues of child abuse, drunk driving, and suicide.

Episodic reporting of this kind obscures the daily impact of conditions such as child and domestic abuse, poverty, low wages, the lack of health insurance, inadequate housing, and substance abuse. Instead of being acknowledged as being a part of everyday society, these problems often appear as if they were random occurrences that defy understanding or solution. Yet, as Part Two of this book clearly shows, these conditions are not idiosyncratic as the coverage often conveys; they are a pervasive part of our national life.

Other aspects of our society are far better narrated. The nation's politics are measured nearly as precisely as is the economy, and probably receive even more on-going coverage. Highly sophisticated polls keep track of the ups and downs of our responses to major politicians. Countless commentaries and reports in the print and electronic media keep us well informed of the moves and countermoves of politicians; many are devoted exclusively to the most recent poll data. Our political life is monitored, regularly and precisely.

But few newspapers have a daily or weekly section devoted exclusively to social issues or conditions. It is rare for a reporter to be assigned to cover social issues as a whole. There is no accepted social "beat" similar to those for politics or economics. Even major newspapers, such as *The New York Times, The Washington Post,* or *The Los Angeles Times*, have no section devoted solely to social issues and conditions, that routinely combines the statistical and the human to provide a continuous flow of information on what is happening to the nation in this area. There are sections which are regularly devoted to art, style, science, dining, home, and, most recently, computers; there are weather reports, business and economic reports, sports reports, and movie reports, but nowhere are there established social reports.

The lack of context and regularity in the reporting of social issues, and the absence of the kind of familiarity that an on-going narrative, grounded in fact and interpretation, could provide, have made public deliberation about social issues more vulnerable to the politics of the moment. The recent national debate about health insurance illustrates the point. It has been widely acknowledged that the fate of national health care reform turned on the effectiveness of partisan political advertising, which easily filled a void in public knowledge. The welfare reform debate was similarly intertwined with the struggle for political advantage in a presidential election year. Even the current discussion about changing the Social Security system has focused almost exclusively on fiscal and political matters, while generally ignoring the impact that the various proposals might have on the future well-being of the elderly population.

There are many problems that need to be overcome if we are to develop a fuller answer to the question, "How are we doing?" As we have argued, our ability to understand and to accurately monitor the health of our society is limited by the absence of a well-conceived and organized system of social reporting and by the lack of coherent and consistent vehicles in the print and electronic media to bring a social health perspective to the public with context, consistency, and meaning. We are limited, as well, by the sheer magnitude and impact of economic and business reporting, which provides so consistent an assessment of our progress that there may seem to be no need to look any further.

But the power of economic and business indicators suggests a framework for developing and advancing the social health perspective. The traditional economic barometers, instruments, and indicators do not furnish a complete picture of the performance of the nation. Nevertheless, their form, method, and impact provide guide posts by which to proceed.

Changing the Picture.   The effort to create and communicate the social side of American life requires innovation on many fronts. The foundation for these advances rests on the ideas and tools of the field itself.

Fields of analysis advance at different rates. Sometimes they leap ahead when a new vision is discerned. At other times, disciplines move forward in increments, creating building blocks which serve as "tools in readiness" for the time when that larger vision emerges. The building blocks for social health are social indicators. They are the basis upon which a broader vision can be built; they represent a different approach to thinking about the issues. The concept of indicators is a key to viewing social conditions in a new way—in terms of performance.

An indicator is a metaphor, a sounding, a hint of something greater. A good indicator is not "a thing in itself," to be examined and understood in isolation, but a glimpse of a broader context. It *"indicates."* Economic indicators clearly function in this manner. Business starts, business failures, interest rates, durable goods, or the money supply are aspects of that greater entity we call the "economy." Each tells us something about the larger picture.

As we have noted, social data are generally neither conceived nor recognized as indicators. To become true indicators and to have significant value to the national discourse, they cannot continue to stand alone as isolated and unrelated statistics. There must be a series of related indicators, recognized as representing key aspects of society, that are frequently and consistently monitored, indicators that can be easily charted, communicated, and discussed by policy makers and the public. Furthermore, we need to develop agreed-upon benchmarks and standards by which the performance of these indicators can be assessed. Rational judgments can then be made as to whether or not the nation has attained a desirable state. Most importantly, each indicator must be viewed as part of a system that monitors something larger that is of importance to the society and its population. At present, that "something larger" in the social sphere has a much more diffuse identity than the "economy" and no precise name other than "society," a term whose meaning is far less grounded. Because of the current vagueness of this larger frame, its significance for "us" is far less evident.

Yet if housing starts and factory inventories can be viewed as parts of a larger picture that affects us all, if the personal approval ratings of our governors, senators, and presidents are deemed vital information, then the proportion of students who drop out of school, the suicide rates of our youth, the percentage of children who are abused, the availability of low-cost housing, or the quality of our civic engagement must also be considered crucial aspects or indicators of our nation's condition, a part of the official social portrait of the nation's progress.

Such issues have great consequences for the social fabric because they go far beyond the specific population or group that is initially affected. Those who drop out of school, for example, shape not only their own lives, but the lives of many others as well, through their lower earning power, their constrained civic participation, and the effects of these on the next generation. Youth suicides are tragedies not only for the immediate families involved, but often for the children's schools, their communities, and sometimes the nation. Such events ripple outward, affecting the future. Children who are abused may never recover, suffering lifetimes of anxiety and pain, affecting those with whom they build relationships. Alternatively, a significant increase in the number of meaningful and satisfying jobs that provide means for advancement and that pay good wages has lasting significance, as well, both for those directly involved and for the society as a whole.

To gauge such effects, to connect them to one another and to a broader picture, sharper and more focused tools must be developed. One important concept that is rarely applied to the social sphere is the idea of thresholds of performance. Most economic assessments are based on such concepts. Economists routinely assess whether the economy is performing well or performing poorly. When the economy is performing particularly poorly, we have a name for the phenomenon: we declare a recession. Recessions have a working definition—two or more quarters of declining GDP—and there is an official oversight body, the National Bureau of Economic Research, which assesses the depth and longevity of each episode. Recessions usually embody many problems at once: employment drops, housing sales decline, consumer spending falls, businesses fail, profits decline. The engines of the economy begin to sputter and a critical period is identified.

As will be shown in Part Two, the nation has experienced comparable conditions in the social sphere, and we need comparable concepts to define and communicate these developments when they occur. Rising inequality, the poverty of children, the lack of health insurance, the increase in youth suicide, the escalation of child abuse and drug use, the erosion of our schools, the weakening of our infrastructure, all suggest something akin to a recession—a social recession. Yet, even where problems have worsened consistently for a decade or more, we have no concept—and no words—to declare the episode special. When problems improve, we have little sense of their significance. We have no widely recognized indexes or indicators that "lead" or "lag" critical periods, telling us if upheavals are imminent or past. Are we in recession or recovery? The inner workings of the social sphere have yet to be defined.

When the economy as a whole is not in recession but instead has specific weaknesses—perhaps in housing sales or the bond market—these "soft spots " often can be clearly identified. The social sphere, too, has its soft spots. But there is no Alan Greenspan for the social health of the nation, no one in an official capacity to "sound the alarm," take stock, and recommend action. If we had a true system of social indicators, with agreed-upon benchmarks of performance which were easily communicated, we could begin to establish a firm basis on which to determine whether or not to be concerned.

The medical field, too, offers insights. In medicine, the careful monitoring of soundings, samples, or indicators is done on a routine basis. The indicators here are symptoms, and like economic indicators, they are connected to a whole. A rising temperature is usually not so much a problem in itself, but is considered a cause for concern because it may reveal an infection or a deeper underlying condition; the same is true for cell counts, antibody counts, heart rates, or other similar measures. We need the same broad framework or context in the social sphere so that we can read an indicator, like a symptom, as a reflection of something larger, which needs to be diagnosed, interpreted, and rationally discussed in order for it to be corrected.

In medicine, certain symptoms have relative urgency or priority. Some are more critical than others; they affect vital organs or the fundamental well-being or integrity of the body. In the social sphere, we need indicators that, like medical symptoms, carry similar priority. Clearly, some problems are more crucial than others. Which? A precise answer may be a while in coming, but it is a vital question to consider.

In both the medical sphere and the economic sphere, there are thresholds beyond which a critical point is reached: temperatures above or below a certain point, economic growth above or below a certain level. These lines, obviously arbitrary to some degree, are nevertheless instructive, in that they alert us to potential crises and conditions. As in physics, they point to a "critical mass."

In the social sphere, there are more than forty million people in this nation without health insurance. Is there an agreed-upon line which, when crossed, tells us that we have reached the point of urgency? How do we know when we have passed it? The child poverty rate has remained at or around twenty percent for more than a decade. When does this become significant?

By the same token, how do we know we are doing well? How many years of improvement are required to declare an issue a "non-problem" because agreed-upon and significant progress has been achieved? Violent crime has improved for six consecutive years. Is it no longer a matter of serious import? The rate of teenage births has returned to the downward trend it demonstrated in the 1970s. Should we cease to be concerned? Alcohol-related traffic fatalities have declined sharply in recent years. Is that significant? Is it likely to hold?

In summary, the creation and communication of the social side of the nation's official portrait will require new ideas and new resources. There need to be vast improvements in the way current information about our social health is conceived, analyzed, interpreted, made accessible, and presented to the media and to the public. These advances will help us to envision the nation's most pressing concerns more clearly, defining the limits of our tolerance for adverse conditions, and identifying national successes when they are achieved. They will help to move into the arena of public concern issues that too often are seen solely as examples of private misfortune.

Economic indicators took time to achieve their current power and significance, and the same will hold true for social indicators. But their advancement represents an opportunity to improve democracy by helping to stimulate a more informed involvement on the part of the public. This is particularly important at a time when there is a general concern over the ebbing quality of our public deliberations. As the next chapter will show, there is a context for this work, drawn from our own history and from current efforts both here and in other nations.

Chapter Two

Part of a Tradition

> *In a democracy, social reporting has a very special*
> *function; it is to inform the citizens about the*
> *prevailing living conditions in the society and give them*
> *a perspective on the national development.*
> — *Joachim Vogel, "Social Indicators: A Swedish Perspective," 1989*

The need to find new ways of thinking about, collecting, and reporting social information, described in the last chapter, has been recognized in other times and in other
nations. This tradition has undergone a recent renewal. The effort to create the social
side of America's official portrait is therefore part of something larger.

American Initiatives in Social Reporting. Periodically, throughout this century, individuals have taken it upon themselves to inform the nation by investigating a particular subject or condition. Upton Sinclair did this in writing *The Jungle,* exposing
the dangerous and often deadly conditions of the meat-packing industry. John
Steinbeck, in *The Grapes of Wrath*, conveyed the desperation and destitution of mi-
grant laborers during the 1930s. Michael Harrington, during the 1960s, similarly
jarred the country with his descriptions of poverty and hunger in his book, *The Other
America.*

But a nation cannot rely soley upon the motivations of individual authors. Rational
social policy and sustained public awareness can be attained only when there is a
regular and predictable basis for our understanding of social conditions. At various

times in our history there have been efforts to provide this broader picture in a more consistent fashion. Like the novelists and muckrakers, these have clustered during the periodic crises of our nation: the rapid changes of the Progressive era, the poverty of the Depression, and the social movements of the 1960s and early 70s. Each of these endeavors has helped shape the developments and new thinking that are underway today.

At the turn of this century, during the Progressive era, America faced what might be considered the first of the nation's modern social crises. Problems of increasing crime, poverty, child labor, and the rapid spread of infectious diseases led many to believe that the nation needed to chart its social state. Of particular concern was the situation of children. In 1913, Julia Lathrop, the first director of the newly created U.S. Children's Bureau, became concerned at the absence of a consistent monitoring system for the conditions of children and youth. The information, she observed, was "scattered through numerous volumes of official reports and has never been brought together and correlated."

To address this problem, Lathrop directed the Bureau to compile a *Handbook of Federal Statistics on Children,* a compendium of data on infant mortality, birth rates, poverty, and other child indicators. This publication represented the first effort by the federal government to bring together social information from a variety of agencies and other sources throughout the country. The *Handbook*, an official public document of children's well-being, became an early model for social reporting in America.

As the 1920s drew to a close, the need emerged once again for a systematic and sustained assessment of the state of the nation. This time, an ad hoc committee was established by President Herbert Hoover to consider the critical social changes beginning to occur. Economist Wesley Mitchell was appointed chair, sociologist William Ogburn served as director of research. The 1,500 page report of the committee, entitled *Recent Social Trends in the United States,* addressed a wide range of social issues, including the environment, health, recreation, religion, urban and rural life, the family, labor, crime, and the arts.

Recent Social Trends sought to weave together the various threads of American life. In the preamble, the authors wrote: "The meaning of the present study of social change is to be found not merely in the analysis of the separate trends . . . but in their interrelation—in the effort to look at America as a whole, as a national union, the parts of which are too often isolated." Only by looking at diverse conditions in relation to each other, the authors argued, could one understand the status and future prospects of American society. Though never reissued, the document still stands as America's first and only comprehensive national social report.

During the 1930s, as the Depression deepened, federal mechanisms were established to improve the gathering of social data and the monitoring of social conditions. New Deal agencies began to coordinate data which had previously been collected by the states. These agencies initiated and refined comprehensive national surveys in areas such as labor and health and developed photographic documentation of the nation's social problems.

Most forms of social monitoring lapsed during the 1940s and the early 1950s, when the nation was concerned with the war effort and recovery. During the 1960s, however, the idea once again emerged. Intriguingly, the impetus this time was the U.S. space program. NASA, the nation's newly created space agency, commissioned the American Academy of Arts and Sciences in 1962 to explore the potential side effects of space exploration on American society. Would the space program threaten or disturb the social fabric? Would new social problems occur?

The commission discovered that little of the critical information needed to assess American life was available. Raymond Bauer, the project director, wrote that "for many of the important topics on which social critics blithely pass judgment, and on which policies are made, there are no yardsticks to know if things are getting better or worse." Bauer proposed the term "social indicators" to serve as an analog to the widely used concept of economic indicators. A central focus of his work soon became the need for social indicators as a basis for rational policy-making.

In 1966, building on Bauer's work, the federal government took a first step in the direction of systematic reporting of social conditions. President Lyndon Johnson directed the Department of Health, Education, and Welfare to explore "ways to improve the nation's ability to chart its social progress." The resulting study, *Toward a Social Report*, was viewed as a "preliminary step toward the evolution of a regular system of social reporting." The study considered the types of issues and indicators necessary for regular reporting, including health and illness, social mobility, the environment, income and poverty, public order and safety, learning, science, and art. The report became an important milestone and stimulated both political and academic initiatives in the field.

In 1967, the *Annals of the American Academy of Political and Social Science* published two volumes of essays on social indicators. In the same year, then Senator Walter Mondale proposed *The Full Opportunity and Social Accounting Act,* calling for a Council of Social Advisors, a national system of social accounting, and an Annual Social Report, all parallel to the existing federal apparatus for economic reporting. The proposal was based on the 1946 Employment Act, which had helped to structure the system of economic reporting.

Extensive hearings were held on the bill. Senator Fred Harris brought together a wide range of experts testifying to the urgent need for regular social reporting and portraying the complexities of the task. Despite strong support, the bill failed to pass. A less ambitious statistical report, entitled *Social Indicators,* was subsequently published by the Bureau of the Census. *Social Indicators* reports were issued in 1973, 1976, and 1980 but were discontinued by the Reagan Administration.

In the intervening years, there have been no other efforts at comprehensive, regular social reporting by the federal government on the scale of *Recent Social Trends* or as envisioned in *Toward a Social Report*. However, studies on specific issue areas are published regularly, including such vital references as the *Uniform Crime Reports*, *Health United States*, and *The Condition of Education*. At the same time, however, federal cutbacks over the past two decades have limited the access and availability of social data by sharply reducing the staff and funding of many agencies and bureaus.

During the 1990s, recognition of the need for a system of social reporting has emerged once again, focused, as in the Progressive era, on the worsening situation of children. The federal government has made available several new on-going studies, including *Trends in the Well-Being of America's Children and Youth* by the Department of Health and Human Services and *American Children: Key National Indicators of Well-Being,* produced by the Federal Interagency Forum on Child and Family Statistics. It is yet to be seen whether these studies will serve as the foundation for new public-policy initiatives and whether they will be continued on a regular basis in the future.

Because of the troubling status of children in America, numerous reports on youth also have been generated outside of government. Among the most widely known are *Kids Count*, developed by the Annie E. Casey Foundation and the annual *State of the Nation's Children*, published by the Children's Defense Fund. These studies, like the government reports, have sought to draw attention to the social problems of children and families and highlight urgent social issues such as poverty, suicide, child abuse, and drug use.

The past decade has seen other advances as well. There has been an attempt to fashion new tools that reach beyond the state or condition of individual sectors or groups and provide a sense of the nation's overall condition. Two such efforts, aimed at different objectives, are the Genuine Progress Indicator, which seeks to expand and redefine the GDP itself, and the Index of Social Health, an effort to create a tool like the GDP that monitors a different aspect of society.

In 1993, the Genuine Progress Indicator (GPI) was issued by Redefining Progress, Inc., an independent research organization. It has been reissued once since that time. The central dilemma of economic measurement, its authors argue, is that the Gross Domestic Product counts as "growth" many costly social and environmental problems, thus failing to portray "the economy that people experience." In the calculation of the Gross Domestic Product everything produced and sold counts as a "good." Therefore, many aspects of American life that people experience as costs or burdens actually raise the GDP. "Car wrecks, divorces, disease, crime—social and environmental breakdown of all kinds—get tallied in as economic growth simply because they cost money."

Environmental problems play particular havoc with the interpretation of growth in the standard GDP, according to co-author Jonathan Rowe. "The factory pollutes the water: the GDP goes up. People buy bottled water to replace the questionable stuff from the tap: the GDP goes up some more. People contract cancers or other diseases from the toxic chemicals that are emitted: medical bills make the GDP go up again."

To correct this form of accounting, the GPI seeks to count as costs what its authors believe the public perceives as costs, and to count as gains those aspects of social life that we genuinely think of as progress. This approach includes subtracting crime costs, environmental degradation, and the burdens of ill health, while adding as growth those aspects of social life that the current GDP does not measure, such as the value of housework and volunteer work, and adjusting for other issues, such as income distribution.

A second measure is the Index of Social Health, developed by the Fordham Institute for Innovation in Social Policy. The Index, the first composite measure of its kind, has been published each year since 1987. It is an effort to portray the social dimension of American life. Like economic indexes, the Index of Social Health focuses on the concept of national performance, utilizing pivotal social indicators that assess the quality of life, such as child abuse, suicide, drug use, and health care, and key socioeconomic indicators that measure well-being, including average earnings, poverty, and inequality. It combines these indicators into a single number for each year going back to 1970.

2.1
The Index of Social Health, United States, 1970-1996

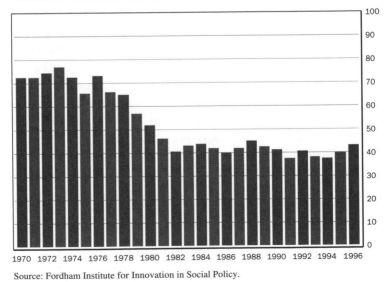

Source: Fordham Institute for Innovation in Social Policy.

The perspective of the Index is that the quality of life in a nation is shaped not by any single problem but by the combined effect of many different problems acting on each other. The central focus of the analysis is how the several problems, cumulatively, forge a national climate that is improving or worsening.

The Index has been used to track change over time, illustrating the shifting quality of life in America. The Index of Social Health portrays a very different story from traditional economic indicators, showing stagnation during the 1980s and 1990s instead of the dramatic improvement portrayed by measures like the GDP or Dow Jones Average (see Chart 2.1).

In 1996, the Index stood at 43 out of a possible 100, down from its peak performance of 76.9 in 1973. The picture of decline followed by stagnation presents a troubling and revealing perspective on the state of the nation. Also highlighted are the worsening of several key indicators since the 1970s, including average weekly earnings, inequality, child abuse, and health care coverage.

The Index approach has been applied to subgroups within populations, such as children and women, to geographic areas such as states, and to the children of industrial nations. In 1997, the State of Connecticut passed a law mandating a yearly Index of Social Health of the State. Most recently, an Index of the Social Health of Canada and its provinces, based on the Fordham Index, has been developed by the Canadian government to serve as an instrument for public policy analysis. In each of these examples, the Index serves as an alternative way to assess progress.

These two approaches—the Genuine Progress Indicator, and the Index of Social Health—are efforts to frame a broader picture of well-being. They are attempting to monitor in a comprehensive, systematic, and repeatable manner the conditions that affect a nation's citizens.

The various social reporting endeavors in the United States, from the Progressive era with its emphasis on children, to the more comprehensive efforts in the thirties and sixties, to the many contemporary undertakings that once again document the status of children and youth, along with the recent attempt to create measures that regularly monitor the conditions of the nation, have served to better inform the public and the makers of policy. Each has contributed much, but much remains to be done to establish official, widely recognized systems of collecting and reporting data about social conditions. In industrial and developing nations around the world, new ideas have been recently set into motion that are making progress toward that end.

Social reporting performs an important function. . . . All actions bearing upon our living conditions—the formation of political opinion, voting, decision making, etc.,— should be based on objective information . . . and that information should be available to everyone. Social indicators and social reporting, at both the national and international level, lluminate trends, comparative dissimilarities, and patterns of inequality.
—Living Conditions and Inequality in the European Union, *1997*

Advances in Other Nations.   Virtually all European nations, Canada, Australia, and many industrial and developing countries in Asia, Africa, and Latin America now issue periodic national social reports which map their social state. The idea was first proposed, as previously noted, in the 1966 American publication, *Toward a Social Report*. It failed to take hold in the United States, but found more fertile ground elsewhere (see Chart 2.2).

The first comprehensive national social report was developed in England. Entitled *Social Trends*, it has been issued every year since 1970. Three years later, France published *Données Sociales*. The following year, the Netherlands issued *Sociaal en Cultureel Rapport*. Since then, many other countries, both industrial and developing, have issued similar documents. Australia's, one of the most recent, began in 1993.

The various national social reports are diverse in their range and intent. Some are statistical summaries of national trends; others include analysis, public policy discussions, and targeted goals for social change. All address major social problem areas, such as housing, health, crime, employment, poverty, and inequality. Many are published annually, others every two or three years.

In most countries, the publication of these reports provides a defining moment for a nation to take stock of its social conditions and to assess its social state in a detailed and considered manner. "How well are we doing?" "Have we made progress?" "Have we fallen behind?" "What areas need investment?" "Where should we concentrate our efforts?" "Have specific groups become newly vulnerable?" "Who is at risk in our nation?"

The reports serve many specific purposes. They are widely used as reference tools by students, teachers, public officials, and the general public. They receive broad coverage in the media when released and serve as the focal point for the coverage of social problems throughout the year. In many nations, the reports provide an agreed-upon starting point for debates over social policy: "This is where we stand"; "This is how far we've come." Discussion can then follow on a more rational basis. The inclusion of many social problems in a single document gives an overview of the nation's social fabric, a sense of how problems fare in relation to each other; it profiles the state of nations in an official, reportable, and consistent form.

Despite the importance of these documents, social issues are still not reported with the regularity, precision, and impact of each country's economic and business indica-

2.2 Selected national social reports

Nation	Title	Year Begun
Great Britain	*Social Trends*	1970
France	*Données Sociales*	1973
Netherlands	*Sociaal en Cultureel Rapport*	1974
Norway	*Sosialt Utsyn*	1974
Spain	*Panorámica Social*	1974
	Indicadores Sociales	1991
Sweden	*Inequality in Sweden*	1975
	Living Conditions	1976
Denmark	*Levevilkår i Danmark*	1976
Austria	*Sozialstatistische Daten*	1977
Switzerland	*Sozialindikatoren für die Schweiz*	1982
Germany	*Datenreport*	1983
Canada	*Canadian Social Trends*	1986
	Canada Yearbook	
Hungary	*Social Report*	1990
Turkey	*Social Indicators*	1990
Italy	*Sintesi della Vita Sociale Italiana*	1990
	Statistiche e Indicatori Sociali	1991
Portugal	*Portugal Social*	1992
Cyprus	*Social Indicators*	1992
Australia	*Australian Social Trends*	1993

Sources include: Tom Griffen, "Social Indicator Publications in EC Member States: An Overview," Working Party on Social Indicators, Meeting on March 23, Eurostat, 1992; Franz Rothenbacher, "National and International Approaches to Social Reporting," *Social Indicators Research*, 29 (1993): 1-62; Heinz-Herbert Noll and Wolfgang Zapf, "Social Indicator Research: Societal Monitoring and Social Reporting," in *Trends and Perspectives in Empirical Social Research*, ed. Ingwer Borg and Peter Mohler (New York: Walter de Gruyter, 1994).

tors. Nor have these nations created a sophisticated network of barometers and indexes to monitor and communicate changes in social performance. Nonetheless, the development and widespread use of national social reports in the past thirty years have advanced the idea and application of the regular reporting of social conditions. Moreover, these documents represent a contribution to the public dialogue of their respective countries that is not present in the United States.

In addition to the establishment of national social reports, one of the most important recent advances has been the development of social surveys that are used in many countries to probe and assess social well-being. The first of these was the Swedish Level of Living survey. Begun in 1974, the annual survey focuses on the range of social resources available to the country's population. The variety of resources and social experiences addressed is unique, including everything from health, housing, education, safety, and employment issues, to more subtle social resources—the presence of a gathering place in the community for people to meet for recreation or for discussing mutual problems, privacy and quiet in one's home, a greenway to explore nature. In seeking to examine citizens' access to these resources, the survey stresses behavior and concrete experience rather than opinions and attitudes. For example, instead of asking what respondents think about the level of crime, it asks how often they have refrained from going out at night because they were afraid.

Because of the success of the Level of Living survey in probing the national temper, versions were adopted throughout the Nordic nations during the late 1980s. Finland and Norway conducted surveys identical to the Swedish. An Icelandic version was done in 1988 and Danish data were added from several special surveys. The combined result was an important multinational study entitled *Social Report for the Nordic Countries: Living Conditions and Inequality in the Late 1980s.*

More recently, the Level of Living approach has been adopted throughout the European Union, the multinational organization that is seeking to merge the broader national interests of Europe. Eurostat, the statistical office for the European Union, conducted 14,200 interviews in fifteen member nations. The recent report, entitled *Living Conditions and Inequality in the European Union, 1997,* is a path-breaking effort to provide a view of social conditions and developments throughout Europe. It is the first comparative report of its type, based on "harmonized" social survey data from all fifteen countries.

The effort to create a multinational social report of this kind was spurred by the social problems that have become as endemic to the European nations as they are to the United States: inequality by income, race, ethnicity, and gender, and the depletion of the resources needed to support the welfare state. According to its authors, "the primary use of European social indicators and social reporting is *general enlightenment* on living conditions, needed for public debate and monitoring of the social dimension of Europe."

Other social reports, based on available data rather than survey data, have been developed by multinational organizations such as UNICEF, the World Health Organization, the World Bank, and the Organization for Economic Cooperation and Development (OECD). All bring together in single documents information on the social conditions of nations. Like the Level of Living surveys, they are assessments, mostly annual, of progress achieved and lost. Like economic studies, they seek to monitor social performance objectively, providing clear yardsticks for analysis and public policy debates.

One important advance was made by the United Nations Development Programme, which used its annual *Human Development Report* in 1990 to introduce the Human Development Index (HDI). Like the Genuine Progress Indicator and the Index of Social Health in America, the HDI represents an attempt to reach beyond the standard economic measures and assess the quality of life for each country's citizens. It is, according to the authors, "a new yardstick of human progress," applicable to both developing and industrial nations.

Three core indicators are included in the Human Development Index. The first, real purchasing power, is measured by real GDP per capita. It seeks to assess average income. The second, education, combines adult literacy with average years of schooling, assessing the typical level of educational attainment in each country. The third indicator is life expectancy at birth, perhaps the most revealing measure of the state of health and health care in a nation. By combining these several measures, the authors argue, the Human Development Index offers "a measure of development much more comprehensive than GNP alone."

One of the most important findings of the Human Development Index is its contrast to traditional economic measures. The *Report* notes that from the perspective of a nation as a whole, "there is no automatic link between income and human development." While there is similarity in some countries, other nations such as "Algeria, Angola, Gabon, Guinea, Namibia, Saudi Arabia, Senegal, South Africa, and United Arab Emirates—have income ranks far above their human development rank." These international findings illustrate the disparity between social progress and economic progress as it is traditionally defined.

The Human Development Index also has been used to compare the well-being of men and women, tracking progress in eliminating gender discrimination. For the thirty-three nations where information is available, the findings are striking: "No country treats its women as well as it treats its men, a disappointing result after so many years of debate on gender equality, so many struggles by women, and so many changes in national laws."

The Human Development Index has had considerable international impact. With the assistance of the United Nations Development Programme, many nations are currently preparing comprehensive human development initiatives. These efforts include refining their social data, creating more precise national profiles, constructing human development goals, and planning their implementation.

The ability of the Human Development Index to crystallize the social progress of each nation in a single number, providing a snapshot of social well-being, has served a vital function, allowing the achievements of nations to be compared, gaps to be identified, and priorities to be framed. The Human Development Index advances the task of thinking more holistically about social health.

Together, the various national and multinational reports represent an emerging and significant enterprise, attempting to report social conditions and make more rational the discussion and formation of public policy. Though many of these projects are still in a beginning phase, they cumulatively represent the leading edge of an international movement.

At the same time as these national and multinational reports have emerged, parallel reporting systems have begun to develop at the local level. With increasing energy and vision, a large number of localities have begun to establish projects to monitor and report on the quality of community life. The United States, which has been relatively inactive at the national level since the early 1970s, is among the most active participants in the new community indicators movement.

We've been playing the football game without a scoreboard
telling us whether the team is winning or losing. . . .
How are we doing? What is the score?
As taxpayers and Floridians, citizens have a right to know.
—Florida Benchmarks Report

New Stirrings at the Local Level.   In many localities, both in America and around the world, there have been significant developments in the collection and reporting of social data. Like the efforts at the national and multinational levels, many of these projects represent a different view from the traditional business-economic approach to the understanding and assessment of progress. Most are concerned with enhancing public understanding and deliberation about the state and condition of their communities. Viewed as a whole, they may be considered a social movement, not yet fully realized, but certainly the beginnings of a "bottom-up" approach to improved social reporting.

In the United States there are now more than one hundred and fifty local indicators projects underway in the communities, cities, counties, and states of the nation. A number of these local initiatives have gone further than the nation as a whole in developing agreed-upon indicators to monitor social performance. Local indicators projects approach the tasks of reporting in several different ways. Some work toward the development and recognition of regular "benchmarks," or "milestones," to communicate major achievements and goals. Others, focused on the environment, use the yardstick of "sustainability" to report on development and growth. Still others attempt to generate a public dialogue about the "quality of life." (See Chart 2.3)

Some indicator projects are linked to the international Healthy Cities initiative, sponsored by the World Health Organization. Healthy Cities began in Europe in 1987 as a response to the fact that, as a WHO report explained, "some of the most intractable public health problems—accidents, AIDS, drug abuse, respiratory disease, and violence—are particularly associated with the interaction between social conditions and the urban environment." At present, about 1,100 cities around the world are part of the Healthy Cities network, ranging from Barcelona, Dublin, and Stockholm to Jerusalem and Turku. A number of American cities, especially in California and Colorado, are affiliated with Healthy Cities or with its American offshoot, Healthy Communities.

Viewed as a whole, the major significance of these community efforts to date lies not in their technical or conceptual advances, but in their great diversity, the degree of participation they have stimulated, and the fact that so many similar endeavors designed to achieve similar ends have emerged in so brief a time.

Most of the projects have come about through a desire on the part of citizens and local officials to get a clearer picture of the problems, strengths, resources, and gaps within their communities and states. In the Roaring Fork-Grand Valley region of Colorado, for example, the authors of their report ask, "What does a healthy community look like? How can we tell if our communities are moving in that direction? The Indicators Project aims to answer these questions by raising awareness of the trends facing our region."

Floridians set a comparable goal: "The Commission wants to answer the question, 'How are we doing?'... Where we are doing well, we can feel good. Where the results are are not good, we can start by asking 'Why?' and 'What can we do about it?' We can use the *Benchmarks Report* to track our progress, or lack of it, and prioritize issues that need our attention."

These new approaches are being created by citizen groups involving hundreds, sometimes thousands, of participants. Groups meet, debate, decide on critical indicators, then plan a document which will inform the broader community. The projects evoke the town meetings of past eras. Alexis de Tocqueville, traveling through America during the 1830s, wrote of the United States as a participatory nation; he would find familiar ground in the community indicators projects occurring today. For example, in St. Paul, Minnesota, they relate how "a variety of citizen groups and public officials in the East Metro area," got together and posed the question, "Are there 'ingredients' that are critical to the well being of our community? Could a 'thermometer' be developed?"

In the view of local participants, there appear to be two major purposes for identifying such "ingredients" and "thermometers." One is pragmatic accountability, the idea that a community must know, in hard numbers, whether its vital investments are having the desired effects. As the report from Alberta, Canada, explains, citizens "want proof that our strategies are working and producing the results we want . . . . Albertans expect that government resources will be directed to programs that work, that achieve the results we set out to achieve."

The second purpose for developing community indicators is more visionary, a sense that all aspects of community life must be looked at together, because the community is an interconnected entity, the different parts affecting and interacting with each other, losses on one side ultimately undermining gains on the other. In many ways, this view of the "whole" community is more advanced than what has thus far been developed for the nation as a whole.

Participation in the indicators process appears to strengthen this sense of connectedness. The report from Portland/Multnomah County, Oregon, explains: "Citizens no longer identify one issue in their community as dominating their concerns . . . . In citizen forums, participants often expressed an understanding of the interrelationships of different issues and of the need to work on all fronts to address issues, all of which would contribute to the prosperity of their neighborhoods." In Hawaii, too, spokespersons stress the appeal of a common vision. "Our aim," says one, "is not to show that everyone in the state has the same vision of the future, but that we can find a vision that includes enough of what everyone believes in that it can be endorsed by a broad consensus."

Citizens of Oakland, California, too, appear willing to see increasing interconnections. "We are ready to expand our notion of needy children beyond adorable infants and preschoolers, to include the teenagers we see on the street corner, who may perplex or even frighten us, but who need our help to grow up to be strong, proud adults . . . . We are also ready to acknowledge that helping children requires helping their parents . . . . We know that children are not raised in a social vacuum, and that we must build strong communities with vital local institutions that support parents and guide children."

Despite their innovative approach and the high level of participation the projects have attained, there are many obstacles to progress. As is true at the national level, local economic data are more widely available than social data and richer in specifics. Participants in Greater Rochester, New York, note: "Indicators of economic activities were far more numerous, have been collected for much longer periods, and were available with significantly greater detail, than information in other areas." In addition, much of the data at the local level lacks coordination in the way it is collected and issued, thereby making regular assessments of performance difficult to determine and to convey. The project coordinator in Hamilton County, Tennessee, observes: "It's almost as if you have one department that keeps score to the left of the decimal

2.3 Selected local indicator projects

Community Projects

San Francisco	California	*Sustainable San Francisco*
Pasadena	California	*Quality of Life Index*
Oakland	California	*Chance 2*
Silicon Valley	California	*Joint Venture's Index*
Roaring Fork-Grand Valley	Colorado	*Healthy Community Indicators*
Jacksonville & Duval Counties	Florida	*Life in Jacksonville*
Atlanta	Georgia	*Community Scorecards*
Noblesville	Indiana	*Noblesville Benchmarking Report*
St. Joseph County	Indiana	*Community Health Profile*
Manhattan	Kansas	*Sustainable Manhattan*
Boston	Massachusetts	*Sustainable Boston*
Cambridge	Massachusetts	*Sustainable Community Indicators*
St. Paul	Minnesota	*Social Outcomes*
Missoula County	Montana	*Missoula Measures*
Flathead	Montana	*Flathead Gauges*
Truckee Meadows	Nevada	*Quality of Life in Truckee Meadows*
Greater Rochester	New York	*State of Greater Rochester*
Greater Cleveland	Ohio	*Rating the Region*
Franklin County	Ohio	*Together 2000*
Portland, Multnomah County	Oregon	*Community Benchmarks*
Greenville County	South Carolina	*Community Indicators*
Spartanburg County	South Carolina	*Critical Indicators*
Hamilton County	Tennessee	*Life in Hamilton County*
Upper Valley	Vermont	*Valley Vital Signs*
Pierce County	Washington	*Quality of Life Benchmarks Project*
Seattle	Washington	*Indicators of Sustainable Community*
South Puget Sound	Washington	*State of the Community*
Alberta	Canada	*Measuring Up*

State Projects

Colorado	*Choices for Colorado's Future*
Florida	*Florida Benchmarks*
Connecticut	*The Social State of Connecticut*
Hawaii	*Ke Ala Hoku*
Maine	*Sustainable Maine*
Maryland	*Maryland Profiles*
Minnesota	*Minnesota Milestones*
Mississippi	*Monitor Mississippi*
New Jersey	*Sustainable State*
North Carolina	*Measuring Up To The Challenge*
Oregon	*Oregon Benchmarks*

We appreciate the assistance of the following organizations in gathering these data: Redefining Progress, Inc.; The National Civic League; The World Health Organization Healthy Cities Program.

point and another that keeps score to the right of the decimal point, and they're not talking to each other."

The data, when found, are often out of date; some no more recent than the last census, a far different situation from the economic data that is available. Furthermore, critical areas are often omitted because of the absence of reliable record-keeping. Often there is little rationale for what information is collected. In Pasadena, California, participants note, "We can tell you exactly how many trees are growing in the city's parks right now, but we still can only guess at the number of our citizens who cannot read and do not avail themselves of literacy resources." In Florida, "The Commissioners were shocked to find that the average class size is not measured beyond the third grade."

Indicator efforts may be both easier and more difficult to achieve at the local level than the national. The economic and business indicators and their vast reporting mechanism are not as dominant at the local level. The question, "How are we doing?" in Rochester or Seattle may not have the traditionally repeated answers. The stock market and the Index of Leading Economic Indicators may seem far removed from evaluating progress in the local community. Ways of thinking about and discussing progress at the local level may therefore be more flexible. It also may be the case that the "whole" is easier to perceive and enunciate at the local level; it may be easier to feel connected to the "community," than it is the "nation." On the other hand, local efforts tend to be idiosyncratic, dependent on local energies, resources, volunteers, and the ability to sustain interest and intent may be limited. Such efforts can therefore be fleeting and their institutionalization difficult.

That literally thousands of citizens with such similar intent are engaged in these efforts across the country tells us much about the needs of our time. But this movement is little known in the media, in the academy, and at the national reaches of government. Such invisibility may be the result of the fact that much of the effort at the state and community level has occurred in isolation; the perspectives, processes, and outcomes have developed one by one. Although information is exchanged and some approaches have been shared, no mechanism now exists to draw on these individual centers of energy and increase their impact.

It is difficult to determine whether the emergence of these many projects both in the United States and around the world will continue to gain momentum and evolve to the point of lasting significance. But the size and spontaneity of this movement and its emergence in so many diverse settings tells us something important. It reflects a deep and demonstrable need to know more about the quality of life and the forces that shape it, and a wish to strengthen the public dialogue around these issues of deep concern. These projects are evidence of, and support for, the need to develop a social side of the nation's official portrait, to complement the things about ourselves and our progress that we already know well.

Renewing the National Effort.   The United States needs to renew its tradition of working toward a better national perspective on social conditions. The many new efforts being conducted at the local level are important, but the current devolution of focus and effort in our national public life can obscure an overall vision that is needed to inspire progress. Ironically, there is far more and richer data at the national level, but less has been done to narrate it, give it meaning, and make it accessible.

All of these efforts, in the past and present, in the United States and in different parts of the world, point to the conviction on the part of many people, from many different perspectives, that there is "something else out there" which requires constant attention. Ultimately, these efforts, the processes they have initiated, and the visibility they have sought, are about democracy. They seek to strengthen the public dialogue around issues of deep concern, to increase the engagement and participation of the public, and ultimately to make policy more rational and responsive.

But despite these advances, our society continues to be taken aback at the exposure of conditions in America that we should have been regularly and consistently monitoring. We continue to be alarmed each time a social problem that has been developing for months or years suddenly bursts on the scene as a newly discovered crisis. While we follow on a week by week basis the approval ratings of our politicians or the dips in our money supply, we are still shocked at the lack of safety in our schools, the depth of hunger in the nation, the deterioration of our infrastructure, or the decline in real wages.

In Part Two, we will attempt to present a more coherent view of "what is out there" in America. Using data and information that is currently available, we will begin the effort to form a social health perspective for the nation.

Part Two

Framing a Social Health
Perspective
for the Nation

Chapter Three

There's Something Else Out There

It is not surprising that Americans feel uncertain about the well-being of society. While the economy has been doing relatively well, there is a sense that the nation remains off-course in many critical areas that affect the day-to-day lives of its citizens.

The insight that sustained economic growth alone does not create well-being for the broader public has long been acknowledged by those who study developing countries, but only later gained influence in developed countries. Ian Miles, for example, a development analyst, observes, "during the 1960s it had . . . become apparent that GNP growth was not necessarily benefiting the masses of the poor in Third World countries. Indeed, evidence began to be accumulated that in some instances, absolute poverty was being increased by a process of 'immiserizing' growth . . . . Over the last decade . . . it has been widely questioned whether GNP is . . . appropriate to the First World too."

Senator Robert F. Kennedy framed this idea most poetically in a speech more than thirty years ago.

> The Gross National Product does not allow for the health of our children, the quality of their education, or the joy of their play. It does not include the beauty of our poetry or the strength of our marriages; the intelligence of our public debate or the integrity of our public officials. It measures neither our wit nor our courage; neither our wisdom nor our learning; neither our compassion nor our devotion to our country; it measures everything, in short, except that which makes life worthwhile.

Since Kennedy's time, there has been an increasing sense that the GDP, the central subject of the nation's official portrait, does not assess and report many important aspects of our lives. This view is reflected in a comparison of the Fordham Institute's Index of Social Health to the GDP. Looking at the period 1959 to 1996, using nine social indicators that were measured consistently during that time, it can be seen that until the mid-1970s the Index tended to rise and fall with the GDP. From the mid-1970s through the early 1990s, however, the two trends diverged sharply (see Chart 3.1). The GDP continued its upward climb, while social health began a relatively steady fall, rising again only slightly during the past two years. Overall, the relationship between the two measures has changed dramatically in the past twenty years; they now appear to be depicting quite different phenomena, reflecting separate dynamics in society.

The disparity between GDP and social health suggests the vital role served by tracking social indicators as well as traditional business-economic indicators in assessing the nation's well-being. As Martha Nussbaum and Amartya Sen have written:

> When we inquire about the prosperity of a nation or a region of the world, and about the quality of life of its inhabitants . . . . What information do we require? . . . We need to know not only about the money they do or do not have, but a great deal about how they are able to conduct their lives. We need surely to know about their life expectancy. . . . We need to know about their health care and their medical services. We need to know about education—and not only about its availability, but its nature and quality. . . . We need to know about labour—

3.1
Index of Social Health and Gross Domestic Product, 1959-1996

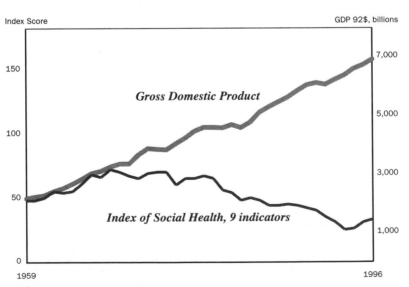

Source: Fordham Institute for Innovation in Social Policy

whether it is rewarding or grindingly monotonous, whether the workers enjoy any measure of dignity and control, whether relations between employers and 'hands' are human or debased. . . . We need, perhaps above all, to know how people are enabled by the society in question to imagine, to wonder, to feel emotions such as love and gratitude, that presuppose that life is more than a set of commercial relations. . . .

Today, perhaps more than at any other time, growth and monetary analyses alone fail to provide a true picture of American life. Social change is now occurring at a far faster pace, both in the United States and around the world. The globalization of economies has begun to alter the nature of modern society. Downsizing, outsourcing, the weakened position of large segments of the work force, and declining or stagnating wages have become pervasive phenomena, significantly altering the social contract among government, corporations, and employees. This "system shift," as Joachim Vogel writes, is occurring in Europe as well as the United States and "has inevitably led to growing social inequality, as measured by most indicators of material living conditions." This may be part of the impetus behind the community indicators movement.

These problems are reflected in public-opinion data. When asked in 1998 whether they thought that the American Dream would be easier or harder to achieve in the next generation, a full 55 percent of those surveyed said harder, while 9 percent said easier, and 34 percent felt it would be about the same. The results are even more significant in that the survey was conducted during a period considered to be a time of economic boom.

Many of the profound changes underway in our society remain hidden when we look at the traditional business-economic barometers. Much has been lost from our national dialogue that could have enriched and informed it and provided it with a sound factual basis. There is something else out there that we are not accounting for.

There is a need then for a social health perspective that delineates a whole area of our national life, an area that remains officially unacknowledged and unmonitored in a frequent and accessible way. Social performance needs to be viewed side by side with the performance of the economy so that we may know more about what is happening to the society and so that we may conduct a more rational, less vague, public dialogue. To use an economic analog, "soft spots" in social performance need to be identified and closely watched, as do areas where we are consistently doing well. To begin this process we need to define a social health perspective that illuminates these important areas of our national life. We need to begin to precisely delineate this perspective, and its key and ancillary indicators. We must more clearly locate our current standing—compared to our past, compared to the achievements of other nations, and compared to our expectations for ourselves and for the nation.

The Indicators.

In the following pages, we present a range of indicators in order to begin to explicate in detail the missing elements in the portrait of American life. Sixteen social indicators have been selected as a starting point, all meeting the following criteria:

1. They are measured reliably and consistently over time by government or recognized private research organizations. All of the indicators included have been measured on a systematic basis since the 1970s.

2. They represent a distribution over the age spectrum. The chosen indicators reflect conditions of children, youth, adults, the aged, and some that affect all age groups.

3. They reflect a balance between social and socioeconomic dimensions. The selected indicators address social concerns such as health, longevity, education, and public safety, as well as issues of socioeconomic well-being such as poverty, wages, employment, and inequality.

4. They address major issues that have long been at the center of public concern or policy debate. All of the indicators address widely recognized issues that government or research organizations consistently monitor because of their central significance to the nation. Each has been a focus of public policy concern or deliberation during the period under study.

5. They have been studied in sufficient depth, over time, to make an assessment of their performance in relation to key subgroups in the nation. Each indicator can be examined in terms of its performance by race, ethnicity, gender, age, class, or other relevant demographic category.

6. They are indicators that can be viewed in an international context. They are recognized international concerns and many can be compared directly to statistics available for other industrial nations.

7. They are indicators which have undergone significant change, reflecting an important alteration in performance over time.

Taken together, these indicators and their related social data reveal much about the nation's social performance. Other indicators—of the arts, the environment, civil society, the strength of community—ultimately should be included, but here we begin with a foundation. The following are the sixteen indicators, presented first by age group in Chart 3.2.

3.2 Social indicators by age

Children	Youth	Adults	Aging	All ages
Infant mortality	Youth suicide	Unemployment	Poverty, aged 65+	Violent crime
Child abuse	Teenage drug use	Wages	Life expectancy, aged 65	Alcohol-related traffic fatalities
Child poverty	High school dropouts	Health care coverage		Affordable housing
	Teenage births			Inequality

The Approach. In order to highlight the idea of long-term performance, the sixteen indicators are organized in the next three chapters by their dominant movement over time. They are grouped according to those that have shown relatively consistent improvement, those that have been steadily worsening, and those that have made one or more significant shifts during the period under study, as shown in Chart 3.3.

3.3 Social indicators by performance, 1970-1996

Improving Performance	Worsening Performance	Shifting Performance
Chapter Four	*Chapter Five*	*Chapter Six*
Infant mortality	Child abuse	Teenage drug use
High school dropouts	Child poverty	Teenage births
Poverty, aged 65+	Youth suicide	Alcohol-related traffic fatalities
Life expectancy, aged 65	Health care coverage	Affordable housing
	Wages	Unemployment
	Inequality	
	Violent crime	

Within this performance framework, each indicator is analyzed, not only in terms of its own long-term performance, but in the context of related social trends, to provide a fuller view of each subject area. Infant mortality, for example, is assessed in light of the nation's performance on low birthweight and prenatal care. The high school dropout rate is examined in terms of the effects on unemployment, health care coverage, and income. Each indicator also is viewed in terms of relevant subgroups such as age, race, ethnicity, gender, or class, and by the nation's standing in the international community, where such data are available.

The nation's long-term performance on the sixteen main indicators is synopsized in Chart 3.4. Each indicator is portrayed more fully in the pages that follow, but here we illustrate simply the major trend lines of performance and the degree of change over time. Each represents a complex picture, a mosaic of issues that help to characterize how well we are doing as a people. Together, these indicators begin to form a portion of the social side of the nation's official portrait.

The performance of these indicators, as well as trends that are closely related, provide a beginning view of the nation's social health. All represent events that reflect some of life's major thresholds; they shape and change its course. How long may we expect to live? How many of our children die in infancy, suffer abuse, grow up in poverty, finish high school, or become teen parents? Do adults and families have adequate health insurance, sufficient income, job security, and appropriate housing? Do our elderly live in poverty? How many of us are victims of violent crime or alcohol-related traffic accidents? All of these indicators help to answer the question, "How are we doing?" in a way that the traditional business-economic indicators cannot do.

Chapter Four: Indicators of Improving Performance

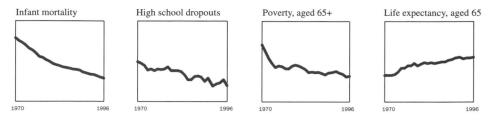

Infant mortality   High school dropouts   Poverty, aged 65+   Life expectancy, aged 65

Chapter Five: Indicators of Worsening Performance

Child abuse   Child poverty   Teenage suicide   Health care coverage- the uninsured

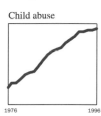
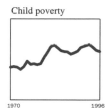

Average weekly wages   Inequality   Violent crime

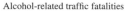

Chapter Six: Indicators of Shifting Performance

Teenage drug use   Teenage births   Alcohol-related traffic fatalities

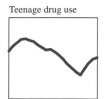

Affordable housing   Unemployment

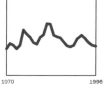

Chapter Four

Indicators of Improving Performance

Several key indicators have shown consistent improvement over time and represent important national achievements in social health. These include:

> Infant mortality
> High school dropouts
> Poverty, aged 65 and over
> Life expectancy

Improvements in infant mortality and life expectancy are due largely to advances in medical technology, drugs, treatments, nutrition, health education, and access to needed services. High school dropout rates have shown a small improvement over time as the nation's demand for greater skills has increased at all levels of employment. The reduction in poverty among the aging represents one of the great successes of American domestic policy. A combination of Social Security and Medicare payments has transformed the elderly, once the country's poorest age group, into the least poor group.

As will be seen in the following pages, the positive performance of these indicators requires some qualification. In some cases there are significant differences by race, class, gender, age, or ethnicity. In other cases, the U.S. lags behind many other nations. Nevertheless, our performance on these indicators constitutes a significant advance over the past three decades.

*The infant mortality rate has been called "the most sensitive index
of social welfare and of sanitary improvements which we possess."*
—Dennis Wrong, *Population and Society,* 1967

Infant Mortality

■ The performance of the United States in reducing the nation's
infant mortality rate has been very good. Infant mortality is now
at its lowest point in our history: 7.3 deaths per 1,000 live births.

■ Infant mortality rates vary significantly by race. Among
minorities, particularly African Americans, infant mortality is
substantially higher than for whites, and has remained so over
time.

■ Measured against the performance of other industrial nations, the U.S. compares poorly. The U.S. infant mortality rate is
worse than that of twenty other industrialized nations.

The Nation Continues to Improve.   The infant mortality rate—the number of deaths in the first year of life for each 1,000 live births—is monitored closely by international organizations as a critical marker of where nations stand in protecting their most vulnerable citizens. It represents a measure of a nation's success in applying its technical knowledge to social well-being and serves as an indicator of the effectiveness of its public policies.

Over time, infant mortality has shown itself sensitive to even small changes in technology and public policy. As sanitation, health care, medical technology, and economic well-being improve, more infants survive. In most developing countries, infant mortality rates are high, reflecting their states of economic and social development. Among industrial countries, infant mortality is far lower, and even small differences may indicate important variations in social investment.

 In the United States, the infant mortality rate has been improving steadily throughout the twentieth century, and is now at its best performance ever. In 1996, there were 28,487 infant deaths in the U.S., a rate of 7.3 per 1,000 live births. This represents a 64 percent improvement over the rate of 20 deaths per thousand recorded in 1970.

Causes of Reduction.   The four leading causes of infant deaths are congenital anomalies, prematurity/low birthweight, Sudden Infant Death Syndrome (SIDS), and Respiratory Distress Syndrome. These accounted for more than 50 percent of all infant deaths in 1996. Much of the recent success in improving infant mortality has

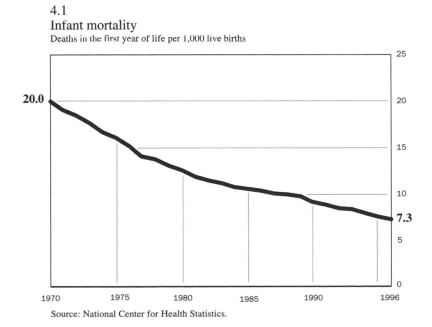

4.1
Infant mortality
Deaths in the first year of life per 1,000 live births

Source: National Center for Health Statistics.

been due to a reduction in Sudden Infant Death Syndrome, which declined by 10 percent between 1995 and 1996. Deaths attributable to congenital anomalies, prematurity, and Respiratory Distress Syndrome showed little change in this time period.

An Unequal Distribution.   All races have shown significant improvement in infant mortality, but the gap between blacks and whites remains. In 1996, the infant mortality rate for white infants was a relatively low 6.1 deaths per thousand live births, compared to 14.7 among black births. The black rate is more than twice as high as the white rate, a proportional gap that is larger than the one in 1970.

Because of the significant disparity between the races, the Department of Health and Human Services' *Healthy People 2000* project has set a goal for black infant mortality of 11 infant deaths per 1,000 live births for the year 2000, a goal not likely to be reached, given the current rate of 14.7. The goal for *all* infant mortality is 7 deaths per 1,000, a more likely achievement based on the current figure of 7.3. Thus, the nation's performance as a whole is close to the target, but for minorities it still lags far behind.

Poverty and Infant Mortality.   According to the U.S. Centers for Disease Control (CDC), the relationship between high infant mortality and poverty has been recognized since the early 1900s, but recent data on this issue have been scarce. To address this issue, the CDC conducted an analysis of the National Maternal and Infant Health Survey.

The CDC found the relationship between infant mortality and poverty to be much stronger than expected. The infant mortality rate was a full 60 percent higher for infants born to women with incomes below the poverty rate, than for women with incomes above it. This relationship held even where poor women were at low risk for other factors, such as smoking, age, and prenatal care.

4.2
Infant mortality by race
Deaths in the first year of life per 1,000 live births

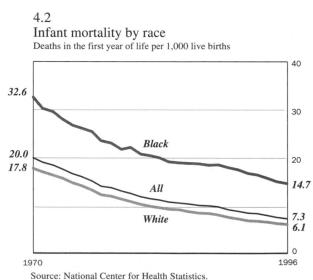

Source: National Center for Health Statistics.
Note: 1970-1979 by race of child, 1980-1996 by race of mother.

Low Birthweight—No Advance.   An important factor contributing to higher infant mortality is low birthweight—a weight of five and one-half pounds or less. Low birthweight causes multiple problems, accounting for nearly two-thirds of all deaths in the first twenty-eight days of life. Low birthweight infants are five times more likely than full-size babies to die during their first year.

The United States has made relatively little progress over time in addressing this problem. During the past several years, it has worsened. In 1996, 7.4 percent of all births were below full weight, a total of 287,230 low birthweight infants. This was the highest level recorded since 1975 and 10 percent worse than the best level recorded: 6.7 percent in 1984. Like infant mortality, low birthweight varies by race. The rate of low birthweight for white infants in 1996 was 6.3 percent, while for black infants it was more than double, at 13 percent.

Low Birthweight—Differences by State.   There are substantial state variations in low birthweight. Low birthweight is generally highest in the South and lower in the Midwest and parts of the East. The states with the greatest proportion of low birthweight infants in 1996 were Mississippi and Louisiana, followed by Alabama, South Carolina, Tennessee, Colorado, and North Carolina. The states with the lowest percentages were New Hampshire, Oregon, Alaska, Washington, North Dakota, South Dakota, Minnesota, and Idaho.

4.3
Low birthweight infants
Percent of all births 5 lb. 8oz. or less

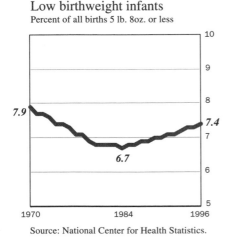

Source: National Center for Health Statistics.

4.4
Low birthweight infants
Selected states, 1996
Percent of all births 5 lb. 8 oz. or less

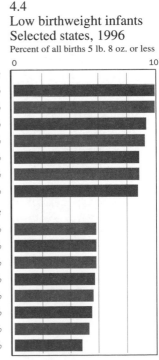

Source: National Center for Health Statistics.

Progress in Prenatal Care.   Prenatal care is a low-cost, primarily low-technology, approach to infant health. It seeks to prevent problems and detect pre-existing conditions early in pregnancy. It provides for on-going monitoring and risk assessment, and it functions as a gateway to other medical specialties. Without prenatal care, risks increase for prematurity, low birthweight, and infant mortality. Because it is viewed as an indispensable element in infant health, the CDC has declared the lack of prenatal care "a sentinel health event."

Since 1970, progress has been made in increasing the number of women who receive on-time prenatal care. In 1996, only 4 percent of all mothers failed to receive timely care, down from a high of 7.9 percent in 1970.

Both minorities and whites have benefited from improvements in access to prenatal care, although a substantial gap remains. In 1996, only 3.3 percent of white mothers received delayed or no care, compared to 7.3 percent of black mothers. The persistence of a gap between white and black mothers is a problem still to be addressed.

Maternal Mortality.   While infant mortality has improved in the last decade, maternal mortality has not. According to the Centers for Disease Control, substantial improvements in the United States were recorded during the 1940s and 1950s, with continuing improvements through 1982. Since that time, the maternal mortality rate has stagnated, remaining between 7 and 8 deaths per 100,000 live births. In 1996, the maternal mortality rate was 7.6 deaths, a worsening from 7.1 in 1995. The black rate in 1996, at 20.3, was almost four times higher than the white rate of 5.1. The World Health Organization estimates that twenty nations have maternal mortality rates lower than those of the United States.

4.5
Late or no prenatal care
Percent of all births with care beginning in the
third trimester or not at all

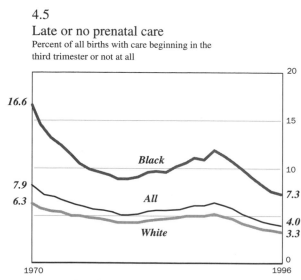

Source: National Center for Health Statistics.

Our Standing in the World.   As with maternal mortality, the United States compares poorly to other nations in its infant mortality rate, despite significant declines. The U.S. infant mortality rate of 7.3 in 1996 was more than twice that of the nation with the lowest rate, Sweden, which had a rate of 3.5. Other nations with very low infant mortality rates include Finland, Norway, Japan, Switzerland, Slovenia, and France, all with rates below 5.

This nation still has a substantial distance to go to achieve the gains accomplished by other nations. Also of concern are the high rates of infant mortality, low birthweight, inadequate prenatal care, and maternal mortality for minorities. Such continuing problems suggest that though advances have been made, many families do not benefit from the improvements in health care, medical technology, and public policy that have minimized these problems for the larger population.

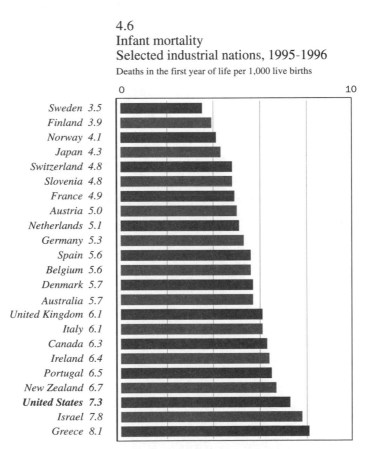

4.6
Infant mortality
Selected industrial nations, 1995-1996
Deaths in the first year of life per 1,000 live births

Sources: Industrial nations: *United Nations Demographic Yearbook*; U.S.: National Center for Health Statistics.

*Nations have increasingly turned to formal education for a number of
political and economic purposes, including the training of a competitive
work force and the reduction of social problems. Indeed, policy makers
around the world have actively embraced the notion that
a highly educated citizenry is vital to a country's economic success.*
—Education Indicators: An International Perspective
U.S. Department of Education, 1996

High School Dropouts

■ The nation's performance in reducing the high school dropout
rate has been good. Between 1970 and 1996, the percentage of students aged 18-24 who dropped out of school declined from 17.3 percent to 12.8 percent.

■ The improvement in school completion is unequally distributed
in the population. White and black youth show substantial improvement, but the gap between them and Hispanic youth has widened.

■ The United States, long a leader among industrial nations in
school completion, has begun to slip behind. The U.S. now ranks below most other industrial nations in its high school graduation rate.

Progress Made.   The nation's high school dropout rate is a key performance indicator for our educational system. This issue shows, perhaps more clearly than any other, the proportion of students receiving less than what we have come to think of in the United States as a minimum education. Among those who fail to complete high school, literacy and skill rates are likely to be low and the prospects for negotiating the modern terrain more precarious.

There are two key measures of dropouts. The first, called status dropouts, is a measure of longer-term performance. It assesses the proportion of young people aged 18-24 who are not enrolled in school and have not finished high school. This measure went from a high of 17.3 percent in 1970 to 12.8 percent in 1996, an improvement of 26 percent.

The second measure, called event dropouts, assesses short-term performance. It counts the number of tenth, eleventh, and twelfth graders who drop out of school each year. Event dropout rates began in 1970 at 5.7 percent, worsened to 6.7 percent in 1979, and have since improved to 4.7 percent. Both status dropouts and event dropouts have shown improvement over time.

Differences Between Groups.   Improvements in high school completion have been unevenly distributed in the population. White achievement levels have remained

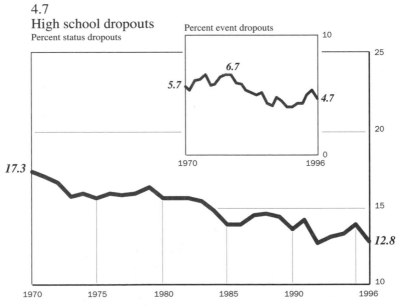

4.7
High school dropouts
Percent status dropouts

Percent event dropouts

Source: U.S. Bureau of the Census.
Note: Status dropouts—percent of persons 18-24 not enrolled in school who have not finished high school; Event dropouts—percent of 10th, 11th, and 12th graders who drop out of school each year.

relatively constant over time, blacks have improved dramatically, and Hispanic youth have made uneven progress, periodically improving and then worsening over time.

In 1996, the white dropout rate was 12.5 percent. The black dropout rate, at 16.0 percent, was less than half of what it was in 1970, though showing a slight worsening in 1996. Hispanic dropout rates, at 34.5 percent, were more than twice those of either blacks or whites.

School Infrastructure.   There are many reasons why students drop out of school, including economic pressures, personal and family problems, and academic difficulties, each of these often interacting with the others. The physical environment of the school that students attend is a contributing factor as well.

According to a 1995 study by the U.S. General Accounting Office (GAO), "Schools in unsatisfactory condition can be found in every part of the country." The GAO reports that "more than 14 million students attend schools needing significant repairs. . . ." Relatively greater repairs were needed in inner-city schools, schools in the West, schools with 50.5 percent or more minority students, and schools with 70 percent or more poor students.

The High Costs of Dropping Out.   For those who drop out of school, the costs are enormous and continue throughout one's lifetime. Unemployment rates are far higher for high school dropouts, benefits such as health insurance are more scarce, and average incomes are considerably lower than for those with a high school degree.

For example, the unemployment rate for a high school dropout, at 10.9 percent in 1996, was twice the rate of 5.5 percent for a high school graduate. Unemployment dropped even more sharply for those with a college degree and beyond.

4.8
High school dropouts by race and ethnicity
Percent status dropouts

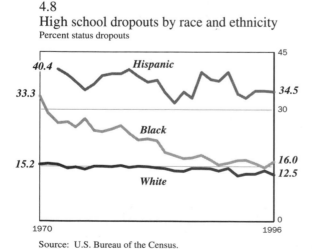

Source: U.S. Bureau of the Census.
Note: Status dropouts—percent of persons 18-24 not enrolled in school who have not finished high school.

Similarly, a full 29.3 percent of high school dropouts lacked health insurance coverage in 1996, compared to 19.5 percent of high school graduates. College graduates were more likely to be insured, and those with graduate degrees most likely of all.

The same pattern could be seen for average earnings. In 1996, average earnings for high school dropouts were $15,011, approximately seven thousand dollars lower than the $22,154 received by high school graduates. Incomes rose still more sharply for those with college or professional degrees.

These are only a few of the costs faced by high school dropouts. In addition, the typical jobs available for dropouts are far more limited, opportunities for advancement are more remote, and a secure retirement is less likely.

School Achievement.   School enrollment is only part of the issue; what one learns there is the more critical concern. On measures which assess academic performance, the nation has seen some improvement in recent years. One of the longest-running tests of achievement, the Scholastic Assessment Test (SAT), is taken by high school

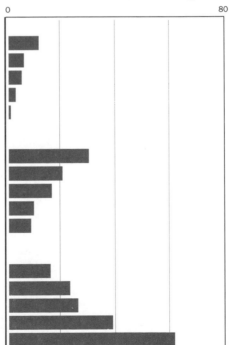

4.9
Educational attainment by employment status, health insurance status, and average earnings, 1996

Sources: Unemployment, ages 25-64: Bureau of Labor Statistics;
No health insurance: Employee Benefits Research Institute;
Average Earnings: U.S. Bureau of the Census.

students who are college-bound. While an imperfect measure, for a variety of cultural and methodological reasons, it nevertheless serves as a common standard of comparison over time.

SAT performance was highest during the late 1960s, but took a sharp drop during the 1970s. During the 1980s and 1990s, math scores improved, while verbal scores have shown improvement only in the last few years. It should be noted that the pool of people who take the exam has expanded rapidly over time. Thus, performance during the 1990s reflects the achievements of a much larger and more diverse group of young people than those who took the test in earlier years.

College Completion.   Of those young people who complete high school, only a portion go on to finish college or higher degrees. In 1996, 27.1 percent of the population aged 25-29 had completed four or more years of college, up from 16.4 percent in 1970, a substantial improvement over time.

As with high school completion, rates of college completion vary markedly by race. In 1996, white students had the highest college completion rates, at 28.1 percent. Black students showed the greatest proportional increase over time, from 7.3 percent in 1970 to 14.6 percent in 1996. Hispanic college completion rates improved during the 1970s and early 1980s, but have been relatively static since then, showing a slight improvement in the last two years.

International Standing.   Among industrial countries, the United States has traditionally ranked high in the proportion of the population which completes high school or college. In the last few years, however, the United States has begun to slip behind. According to a new study conducted by the Organization for Economic Cooperation and De-

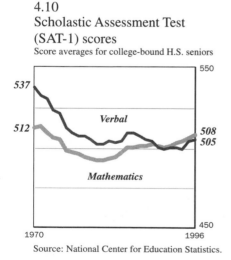

4.10
Scholastic Assessment Test
(SAT-1) scores
Score averages for college-bound H.S. seniors

Source: National Center for Education Statistics.

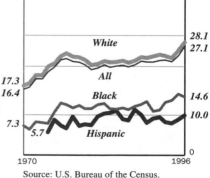

4.11
College completion
Percent of 25-29 year olds with 4 years
of college or more

Source: U.S. Bureau of the Census.

velopment (OECD), the United States ranked last in its rate of high school graduation.

According to the study, "the past decade has seen a catching-up of those countries whose rates had remained relatively low," with many reaching graduation rates above 85 percent. In contrast, "in Canada, . . . Spain, and the United States graduation rates remain below 75 percent." Though overall educational attainment remains high in the U.S., indications are that the ranks of current students are falling behind those of other nations.

Education: A Vital Necessity.   In the past, higher education provided opportunities for upward mobility and expanded choices. Intangible values gained from education, such as personal growth and knowledge offered the possibility of a richer and more cultured life. Today, in contrast, an education is a necessity.

In our present economic climate, the costs of dropping out of school are severe. As the American job market edges further and further toward advanced technologies, opportunities for those with limited education will become increasingly scarce. Even a college degree has become more difficult to translate into career choices or job security. The need for a more fully educated populace has become more urgent than ever before.

4.12
High school graduation rates
Selected industrial nations, 1996
Percent of current students graduating

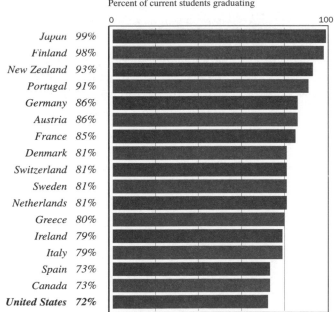

Source: OECD.

*Every qualified individual ... shall be entitled to receive, with respect to the
period beginning on the date he attains the age of sixty-five ... and ending on
the date of his death, an old-age benefit ....*
—Social Security Act of 1935

Poverty among
Those Aged 65 and Over

- The performance of the United States in reducing the poverty of the elderly has been good. From a high of 24.6 percent in 1970, the poverty rate of the elderly dropped to 10.8 percent in 1996, the second-best percentage ever recorded. Currently, there are 3.4 million poor elderly in the nation.

- Among the elderly, black and Hispanic poverty rates are more than two and one-half times those of whites. Females have double the poverty rate of males. Those over age 75 have substantially greater poverty rates than those 65-74 years of age.

- Measured by the international poverty standard of "less than one half the median income," the United States performance does not compare favorably. Among 17 industrial countries, the U.S. has the third-worst poverty rate for the elderly, exceeded only by the United Kingdom and Australia.

Far Fewer Than in the Past.   Not long ago, the poorest age group in America was the elderly. Many older people may still remember the social movements of the 1930s, when the elderly organized against their widespread poverty by seeking retirement benefits and health care. The notion that the elderly, having long worked or cared for families, should be left with little at the end of their life, seemed fundamentally un-democratic. Today, many of the goals of that period have been achieved.

In 1996, 3.4 million Americans, aged 65 and over, were poor. This is a significant number of people in poverty, but still far fewer than the 4.8 million who were poor in 1970, or the estimated 5.5 million who were poor in 1960. The poverty rate among those aged 65 and over has declined from 24.6 percent in 1970 to 10.8 percent in 1996, a 56 percent improvement.

Although the long-term pattern reflects substantial gains, the greatest declines in poverty took place during the 1960s and 1970s, with much slower improvement during the 1980s and 1990s.

Compared to Younger Adults.   With the gains that have taken place, the elderly now have the lowest poverty levels of the major age groups. In 1970, poverty rates for the elderly were almost three times those of adults under age 65. By 1996, however, the poverty rate of the elderly, at 10.8 percent, was slightly better than the poverty rate for adults 18-64, at 11.4 percent. Poverty among the elderly is now only about half the current rate for children, which is at 19.8 percent.

4.13
Poverty among persons aged 65 years and over
Percent in poverty

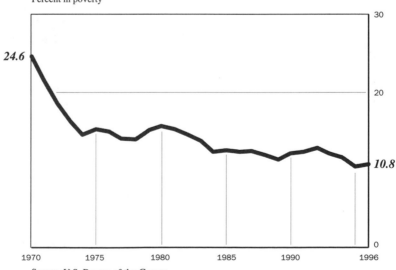

Source: U.S. Bureau of the Census.

Uneven Progress.   Despite successes in the reduction in poverty for the aging population as a whole, improvements have not affected equally all members of this age group. Rates are higher for minorities, for women, and for the very old. These patterns have been consistent over time.

In 1996, the percentage of white people over the age of 65 living in poverty was a relatively low 9.4, compared to 25.3 percent for black elderly Americans and 24.4 percent for Hispanic Americans. Poverty among elderly minorities was more than two and one half times the rate for whites.

A comparable pattern of inequality exists between males and females. Poverty among women, the largest group among the elderly, was 13.6 percent in 1996, compared to only 6.8 percent among elderly men.

Today, the elderly are often divided into the young old, aged 65-74, and the older old, aged 75 and up. Here, too, a sharp distinction exists. The oldest among us are the poorest. Among those 65-74, the poverty rate in 1996 was 8.8 percent, while for those

4.14
Poverty among persons aged 65 and over
and persons aged 18 to 64
Percent in poverty

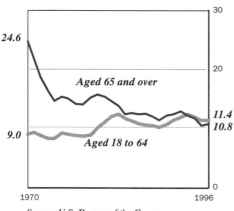

Source: U.S. Bureau of the Census.

4.15
Poverty among persons
aged 65 and over by
race/ethnicity, gender, and
age, 1996
Percent in poverty

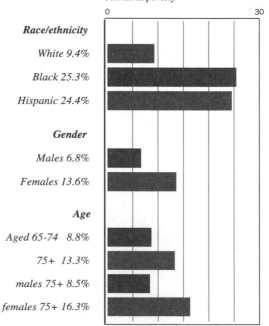

Source: U.S. Bureau of the Census.

75 and over it was a much higher 13.3 percent. Moreover, the poverty rate for women over 75 was 16.3 percent, almost double the men's rate of 8.5 percent.

Close to the Poverty Line.   In 1996, the poverty line for an individual aged 65 or over was $7,525; for a two-person household it was $9,491. While fewer people today fall under this threshold, many fall close to it and may be considered "near poor."

In 1996, 7.6 percent of the elderly were defined by the Census Bureau as near poor (with incomes between 100 and 125 percent of the poverty line), making the total poor and near poor combined a full 18.4 percent. An even larger proportion of the elderly have low incomes—measured at one and one-half times the poverty line (150 percent) or twice the poverty line (200 percent). In 1996, one-quarter of the elderly had incomes below 150 percent of the poverty threshold, and a full 40.2 percent had incomes below twice the threshold. Elderly women fall into these low-income categories far more frequently than men.

While poverty among the elderly has been decreasing, a substantial proportion

4.16
Close to the poverty line, 1996
Percent of persons aged 65 and over with incomes
less than 125%, 150%, and 200% of the poverty line

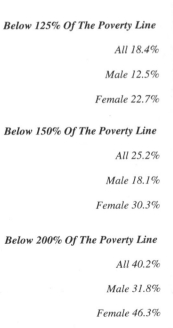
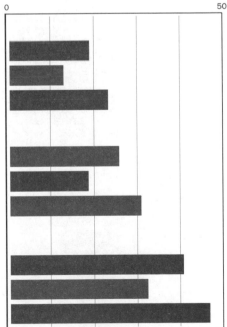

0   50

Below 125% Of The Poverty Line

All 18.4%

Male 12.5%

Female 22.7%

Below 150% Of The Poverty Line

All 25.2%

Male 18.1%

Female 30.3%

Below 200% Of The Poverty Line

All 40.2%

Male 31.8%

Female 46.3%

Source: U.S. Bureau of the Census

continue to live close to the poverty line. Their resources, even at twice the poverty line, are quite minimal.

Special Pressures—Out-of-Pocket Health Costs.   One of the most significant expenditures for the elderly, even those with adequate incomes, is out-of-pocket health-care costs. While year-by-year estimates are unavailable, a series of studies conducted by research institutes points to a considerable economic burden placed on the elderly by such costs. According to the most recent AARP/Lewin Group study, for example, average out-of-pocket costs for Medicare beneficiaries were estimated at $2,149 per elderly person in 1997, or 19 percent of average income. Those over age 75 were projected to pay even higher costs, roughly 21 percent of their income. More troubling, those below the poverty line were estimated to spend, on average, 35 percent of their income; low-income persons without Medicaid spend 50 percent of their income. Such expenditures, for many, erode the small economic gains made over the past years.

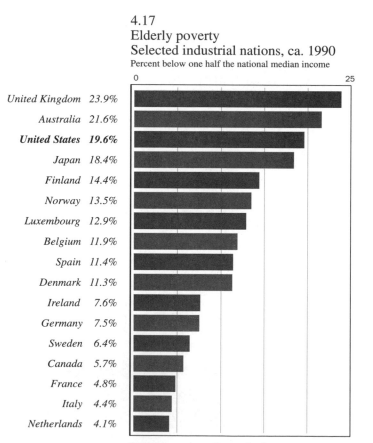

4.17
Elderly poverty
Selected industrial nations, ca. 1990
Percent below one half the national median income

United Kingdom	23.9%
Australia	21.6%
United States	19.6%
Japan	18.4%
Finland	14.4%
Norway	13.5%
Luxembourg	12.9%
Belgium	11.9%
Spain	11.4%
Denmark	11.3%
Ireland	7.6%
Germany	7.5%
Sweden	6.4%
Canada	5.7%
France	4.8%
Italy	4.4%
Netherlands	4.1%

Source: Luxembourg Income Studies.

A Different View—The International Context.   The Luxembourg Income Studies have developed a wide range of methods for comparing different countries' incomes and poverty rates. One measure which they utilize—poverty defined as "less than one-half the median income"—is a well-established international indicator that allows for comparisons across industrial countries. It has also been adopted by both the Organization for Economic Cooperation and Development (OECD) and the European Commission.

This measure takes as its point of reference the typical income within each country. By defining as poor those whose income is less than half the median, it provides for each country a standard that represents the distance from the "average."

Measured by this international standard, the United States does not fare well, even for elderly poverty. Among 17 industrial nations, American elderly had the third-highest rate of poverty, exceeded only by the United Kingdom and Australia. While the United States has improved upon its own poverty rates of the past, it has yet to attain the considerably lower levels achieved by other nations.

To Be Old and Poor.   To be old and poor is a special kind of tragedy, a harsh ending to a long-lived life. Virtually every industrial society has sought to eliminate or reduce poverty among the elderly through a mix of social policies and retirement programs.

In the United States, two social programs are credited with improving the economic situation of the elderly: Medicare and Social Security. Medicare covers important health-care costs. Social Security and its cost-of-living adjustments allow government retirement benefits to keep pace with inflation. Over the past two and one-half decades, these policies have made a significant difference in the economic position of the elderly, particularly compared to other segments of the population.

The overall reduction in poverty among the elderly suggests that public policy interventions can make a difference in improving the lives of citizens. Yet, while poverty has been reduced, we have failed to reach the lower levels attained by other nations. Moreover, the higher rates of poverty among minorities, women, and among the "old-old" highlight the need to readdress this issue. The fact that many elderly live near the poverty line—a very low standard—points to further concerns. Finally, substantial out-of-pocket health-care costs constitute a continuing burden for the elderly, encroaching on what are already low incomes for many.

The reductions in elderly poverty that have occurred over the past quarter century provide a model for what can yet be done in the future. The fact that most other industrial countries have done better also provides targets for what this nation might yet achieve. The continuing amelioration of poverty among the elderly is a commitment most industrial nations acknowledge.

The most powerful impact of biomedical change has not been confined just to the body.
It has no less left its mark on those individual perspectives and
social institutions that change the way people think about themselves and live their lives.
Biomedical changes . . . have lengthened average life expectancy and
reshaped the way we think about the life cycle . . . .
—Daniel Callahan, *Hastings Center Report,* 1994

Life Expectancy

■   The performance of the United States in extending life has been good. Today, a person 65 years old can expect to live 17.5 additional years, up from 15.2 in 1970. An infant born today also can expect to live a relatively long life: average life expectancy at birth is now 76.1 years.

■   Life expectancy varies significantly by race and gender. White females live longest, followed by black females, then white males. Black males have a substantially shorter life expectancy.

■   The United States is closing the gap with other nations in terms of life expectancy. Nevertheless, 16 industrial nations still have longer life expectancies than the U.S.

A Lifetime Indicator.　　Life expectancy is typically measured at two key points: at age 65 and at birth. The first gives us the lifetime prospects for today's elderly, the second tells us the projections for the next generation.

Since 1970, life expectancy at age 65 has improved. In 1996, older Americans could expect, on the average, an additional 17.5 years of life beyond age 65. This is an increase over the 15.2 years that could be expected in 1970. These additional years continue a trend that has been rising throughout this century. In 1900, people reaching the age of 65 averaged only 11.9 additional years of life.

Life expectancy at birth, which includes the effects of infant mortality, child mortality, and early adult death, also has been substantially extended. In 1970, the average newborn could expect to live 70.8 years. By 1996, the expectation had improved to 76.1 years. This is a significant improvement over 1900, when the average life expectancy was only 47.3 years, primarily because of the high infant mortality rates of that period.

Both life expectancy at birth and at age 65 are at record highs. Much of the gain can be attributed to improvements in lifestyle and disease prevention, with significant declines in heart disease, cancer, homicide, perinatal conditions, and chronic liver diseases.

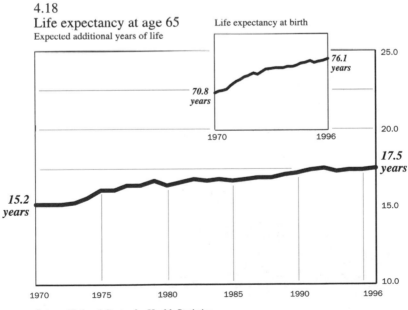

4.18
Life expectancy at age 65
Expected additional years of life

Life expectancy at birth

76.1
years

70.8
years

25.0

1970　　　　　　1996

20.0

17.5
years

15.2
years

15.0

10.0

1970　　1975　　1980　　1985　　1990　　1996

Source: National Center for Health Statistics.

The Nation Grows Older.   The effect of extending life, both for current and future populations, is an aging society. The proportion of the population which is aged 65 and over has risen from only 4.1 percent at the turn of the century to 12.5 percent in 1990, and is projected to grow to more than 20 percent by the year 2030.

The shift from a society that was primarily young to a society that is older will mean a change in societal patterns. Major institutions and policies that will need to be addressed include the health-care system, the Social Security system, housing, recreation, education, and transportation, to name but a few.

A revised view of the life cycle and its critical moments also will be needed, as a vital and active older age becomes a reality for many. Potential conflicts of interest between the generations may emerge and will need to be considered, particularly as they affect the allocation of resources.

Differences in Life Expectations.   Groups within the elderly population have significantly different life expectancies. White females have the longest life expectancy, followed by black females, and then white males. Black males can expect the fewest years after age 65.

Today, white females at the age of 65 can expect, on the average, 19.1 additional years of life. For black females, it is 17.2 years, and for white males 15.8 years. Black males' average life expectancy is only 13.9 years beyond age 65.

White males at age 65 have made the greatest improvement since 1970, a full 21 percent. White females have made a 12 percent improvement over time, black males 11 percent, and black females 10 percent.

4.19
Population aged 65 and over
Percent of population

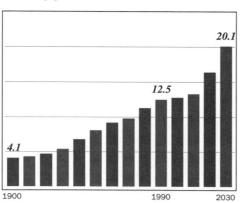

Source: U.S. Bureau of the Census.
Note: Middle series projections are presented.

Life expectancy at birth, a projection for the next generation, mirrors that for the last. White females can expect to live longest, followed by black females, white males, and black males.

White females reached a life expectancy at birth of 70 years as early as the 1950s; their life expectancy is now almost 80. Black females reached this threshold in 1974, and white males in 1977. Black males have not reached this point since records have been kept.

In Different Parts of the Nation.　In 1998, Harvard University scientist, Christopher Murray, released the first portion of an on-going study which indicates that life expectancy in the United States varies significantly by geographic locale. Men in some counties of the United Sates were found to live only as long as those in developing countries such as India and Bolivia.

Counties with the longest male life expectancies were found in Utah, Colorado, Iowa, Virginia, Wisconsin, and Minnesota. The shortest life expectancies were found in S. Dakota, Washington, D.C., Baltimore, and St. Louis.

The worst counties in South Dakota were those where Native American males on reservations had a life expectancy of only 56.5 years. In some central cities, black men averaged a life expectancy of 57.9 years, "as low as parts of Africa." In contrast, on average, Asian males in affluent counties in New York and Massachusetts live to 89.5 years and Asian women live into their mid 90s.

According to the researchers, the differences found within the United States are

4.20
Life expectancy at age 65 by race and gender
Expected additional years of life

Life expectancy at birth
by race and gender

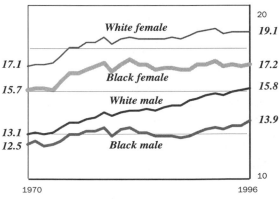

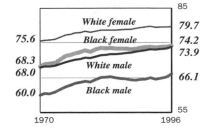

Source: National Center for Health Statistics.

comparable to disparities between developing and industrialized countries. Murray notes that "even if you look at all of Europe you would not find this variation." These findings are part of a long-term study of health and disease being conducted by Harvard University School of Public Health and the Centers for Disease Control.

Closing the Gap Internationally.   Internationally, the highest life expectancy at birth is 80 years in Japan; close behind are Canada and France at 79 years. The United States, averaging 76 years, remains behind 16 industrialized nations, a performance still in need of improvement. Overall, the higher life expectancies mean that all industrial nations are aging and will need to reexamine their life styles and priorities.

Human Capital.   Like infant mortality, high school completion, and the poverty of the elderly, life expectancy is a key indicator of the nation's investment in its human capital. The extension of life since 1970 has been substantial. Progress in medical

4.21
Life expectancy
Selected U.S. counties, males, ca. 1990
Years

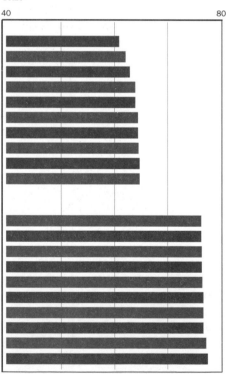

Worst Counties	
South Dakota*	61.0
Washington, D.C.	62.2
Baltimore, Md.	63.0
St. Louis, Mo.	64.0
Orleans, La.	64.0
McDowell, W. Va.	64.5
Dillon, S.C.	64.5
The Bronx, N.Y.	64.6
Phillips, Ark.	64.8
Richmond, Va.	64.8
Best Counties	
Gallatin, Mont.	76.3
Olmstead, Minn.	76.3
Steele, Minn.	76.4
Sioux, Lyon, Iowa	76.4
Davis, Utah	76.5
Ozaukee, Wis.	76.7
Fairfax, Va.	76.7
Story, Iowa	76.7
Douglas, Elbert, Colo.	77.2
Cache, Rich, Utah	77.5

Source: Harvard Center for Population and Development Studies;
Centers for Disease Control.
*Bennet, Jackson, Mellette, Shannon, Todd, and Washabaugh Counties.

technology and living conditions have contributed greatly to these advances. But the benefits have not yet been evenly distributed. The lower life expectancies among minorities and in selected geographic areas are issues of continuing concern. The higher life expectancies attained by the other industrial nations of the world remain to be reached for all groups in this nation.

The aging of the baby boomers and their longer life expectancies also can be expected to create significant pressures to reshape America's fundamental institutions. What has been called a "demographic revolution" is occurring—the "graying of America." To address these changes, the elderly population will need new opportunities. The challenge will be to live long and live well.

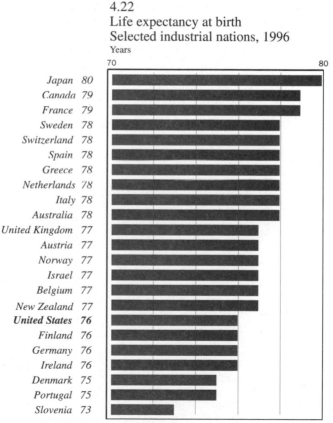

4.22
Life expectancy at birth
Selected industrial nations, 1996
Years

| | 70 | | 80 |

Japan	80
Canada	79
France	79
Sweden	78
Switzerland	78
Spain	78
Greece	78
Netherlands	78
Italy	78
Australia	78
United Kingdom	77
Austria	77
Norway	77
Israel	77
Belgium	77
New Zealand	77
United States	**76**
Finland	76
Germany	76
Ireland	76
Denmark	75
Portugal	75
Slovenia	73

Source: UNICEF.

Chapter Five

Indicators of Worsening Performance

A number of indicators in critical areas of society have worsened steadily and significantly over the past quarter century, but the magnitude and consistency of their deterioration has attracted relatively little public attention. If such changes were to occur in the economic or business sphere, the news would quickly resonate throughout our society. Yet, these worsening social trends have remained largely invisible. The indicators showing worsening performance are:

>Child abuse
>Child poverty
>Youth suicide
>Health care coverage
>Wages
>Inequality
>Violent crime

The performance of America with regard to its children is a cause for particular concern. Trends presented in this chapter on child abuse, child poverty, and youth suicide show significant deterioration. There are also growing problems with wage stagnation, inequality, and the loss of health insurance coverage, all reflections of a changing economy. Finally, the violent crime rate, while diminishing for the past six years, remains higher than it was in 1970, exceeding that of virtually all other industrial nations. The recent improvement is significant, but the current level of crime is still substantially higher than what this nation previously achieved.

What is significant is that we have done better on each of these indicators in the past than we are doing today. These important areas of social health provide useful insights into the nation's social conditions; each merits close analysis and serious public attention.

Public Law 104-235, section 111 . . . defines child abuse and neglect as . . . any recent act
or failure to act resulting in imminent risk of serious harm, death, serious physical or
emotional harm, sexual abuse, or exploitation of a child . . . by a parent or caretaker . . . .
—Child Abuse Prevention and Treatment Act, *as amended, October 1996*

Child Abuse

■ The performance of the United States in preventing child abuse
has grown steadily worse for more than twenty years. In 1996, an
estimated 3.1 million children were reported to have been abused, a
rate of 47 cases for every 1,000 children.

■ The greatest proportion of child abuse victims are the very young.
Among recent victims, 39 percent were under the age of five; 69 percent were under the age of ten.

■ Between 1,000 and 2,000 child abuse fatalities occur each year.
More than 80 percent involve children under the age of five; more
than 40 percent of the victims are under the age of one.

A Public Issue.   Historically, child abuse was an ugly family secret, unreported, un-counted, and undocumented. Since the passage of the 1974 *Child Abuse Prevention and Treatment Act*, it has become a recognized social problem. We now require that suspected cases be reported by physicians, emergency room personnel, teachers, and other care providers.

During the first years after official reporting began, rising rates were attributed to enhanced public awareness and improved reporting. Over time, however, as the in-creases continued, the causes have come to be viewed as more complex, due not only to awareness and reporting, but as real increases brought on by economic stress, sub-stance abuse, and violence in the home and the larger society.

Since 1976, child abuse has worsened by more than 300 percent, from 10.1 reported cases for every 1,000 children in 1976, the best performance we have recorded, to 47 per 1,000 in 1996. Over 3.1 million children were reported as abused in 1996 alone.

A recent study by the Department of Health and Human Services examined the problem of child abuse from 1986 to 1993. They reported that total rates of abuse nearly doubled in that time period, and serious injury and endangerment quadrupled. These increases were so dramatic the researchers judged them to be a "true rise" in the severity of the problem.

Types of Abuse.   Neglect consistently has been the most frequently reported form of abuse. In 1996, 46 percent of all cases were classified in this category. Neglect may

5.1
Child abuse

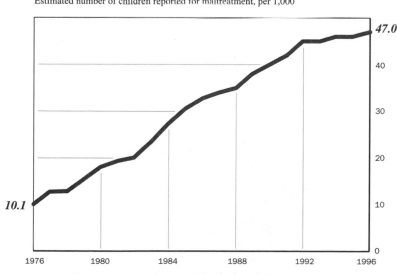

Sources: 1976-1986 American Association for Protecting Children;
1987-1996 National Committee to Prevent Child Abuse.

be so severe that it becomes the cause of serious injury, either through malnutrition, failure to provide appropriate medical care, or a lack of supervision which allows the child to smother, have an accident, or otherwise come to harm.

Physical abuse has been the second most frequently reported problem, accounting for a full 21 percent in 1996. Serious forms of physical abuse include severe head trauma, Shaken Baby Syndrome, injury to abdomen or thorax, scalding, drowning, intentional suffocation, and poisoning.

Sexual abuse constituted 11 percent of the cases reported in 1996. This type of abuse, which includes various forms of rape and sexual contact, affects significantly more female than male children. There has been some decline in sexual abuse over time.

Other less common forms of abuse include emotional maltreatment, and what are grouped as other, which includes medical neglect, abandonment, congenital drug addiction, and threats to harm a child. Children may experience multiple forms of abuse.

Abuse Fatalities.   Some child abuse is serious enough to end in death. The National Committee to Prevent Child Abuse reports that in each of the past eleven years, from 1986 through 1996, approximately 1,000 children died from injuries caused by abuse. This amounts to approximately three children in America dying each day from abuse or neglect.

The Committee's figure of 1,000 deaths may actually fall on the conservative side. The National U.S. Advisory Commission on Child Abuse and Neglect estimates the number of deaths attributable to abuse and neglect at approximately 2,000 per year. Even these higher numbers may be an undercount. Studies indicate that many deaths attributable to neglect are officially recorded as home or traffic accidents.

5.2
Child abuse by maltreatment type, 1996
Percent of cases

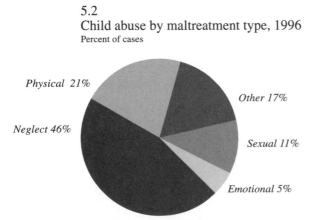

Physical 21%

Other 17%

Neglect 46%

Sexual 11%

Emotional 5%

Source: U.S. Department of Health and Human Services, Children's Bureau.
Note: Categories include both indicated and substantiated cases,
unknown category not included in percentages, calculations by the Fordham
Institute for Innovation in Social Policy.

Who Are the Victims and Perpetrators?   One of the most serious aspects of abuse is its concentration at the youngest ages, when children have so few defenses. According to the National Center on Child Abuse and Neglect, 39 percent of all child abuse cases in 1996 involved victims under the age of five, and 69 percent involved victims under the age of ten. Most fatalities also occur among the youngest children. According to the National Committee to Prevent Child Abuse, 82 percent of the deaths recorded involved children under the age of five, while almost 43 percent involved children under the age of one.

Both male and female children are victims of abuse. Over time, the gender distribution has remained relatively constant, at around 50 percent. In 1996, 52 percent of cases were female, 48 percent were male. White children accounted for 55 percent of the reported cases in 1996, compared to 28 percent who were black, and 12 percent who were Hispanic.

The overwhelming majority of those who commit child abuse, including neglect and physical and sexual harm, are family members. Parents are the perpetrators in 80

5.3
Child abuse victims by age, gender,
race, and ethnicity, 1996
Percent of cases

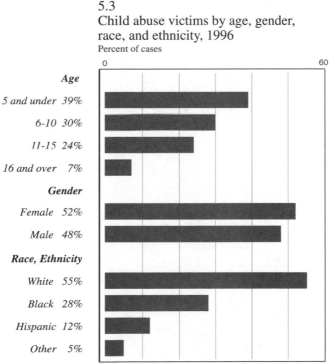

Source: U.S. Department of Health and Human Services, Children's Bureau.
Note: Categories include both indicated and substantiated cases,
unknown category not included in percentages, calculations by the Fordham
Institute for Innovation in Social Policy.

percent of the cases and relatives constitute another 12 percent. Only 8 percent of child abuse is committed by persons outside the family.

Because child abuse typically occurs within the family unit, aspects of domestic violence may become intimately connected to the problem; this relationship needs further examination. Recent state investigations indicate that domestic abuse has been reported in more than 40 percent of the homes where serious child abuse had occurred and in almost 50 percent of the homes where children died from abuse.

Reporting and Substantiation.   Reporting a suspected case of abuse to child protective services or the police is often a difficult and painful process for those involved. Currently more than 50 percent of reports come from professionals who work with children, particularly educators. Legal authorities or lawyers, social-service providers, and medical professionals also provide a significant number of reports. Family members are another source of reports, relatives in particular. Anonymous reports and those from friends and neighbors account for approximately 20 percent of reports.

5.4
Sources of child abuse reports, 1996
Percent of reports

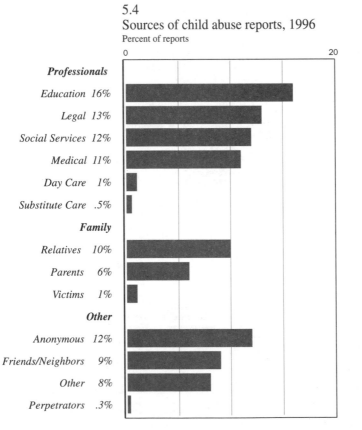

Source: Department of Health and Human Services, Children's Bureau.
Note: Calculations by the Forham Institute for Innovation in Social Policy.

After a report is made, substantiation or confirmation is the next step in the process. In 1996, approximately one-third of all reports, or about one million, were substantiated. Substantiation rates, however, are not considered reliable indicators of the actual frequency of abuse because they are affected as much by the investigative capacity, staff size, and policies of local child protective services as by the merits of the case.

For example, according to a recent Health and Human Services study, between 1986 and 1993 the number of reported abuse cases rose while the number investigated stayed the same. Thus, the proportion of all cases investigated declined, from 44 percent in 1986 to 28 percent in 1993, bringing substantiation rates down, not because of changing prevalence, but because of a change in investigative practice.

Funding cutbacks also have forced child protective agencies to adopt new "triage policies" in which priority is given to those cases that appear most urgent. This change has caused additional problems in substantiation; a Child Welfare League study indicates that almost half of all state administrators confirmed that "triage policies" have caused some "abuse and neglect reports to go uninvestigated that would have been investigated five years ago."

Investigation and substantiation rates are not solely a matter of record-keeping. Many children are placed at risk because they fall through the cracks of child-protective systems. Harm may occur that investigation or substantiation might have prevented.

Understanding the Problem.   Comparative rates of child abuse across nations are not currently available. Definitions of abuse are too variable and different nations focus on different concerns. As in the United States, child abuse in other nations is just beginning to be publicly addressed, and what were once only private concerns are now just beginning to be public matters.

In developing nations, child abuse cases may concentrate on such issues as prostitution, child labor, genital mutilation, and ritual murder, as well as neglect and physical abuse. Some of these concerns involve international law; others are matters of national consideration.

In industrial countries, the concerns are more similar to those in the United States and tend more frequently to involve sexual and physical abuse and neglect. Internationally, we have not yet arrived at standardized methods for recording and reporting such cases, nor is there yet cross-national agreement on appropriate interventions.

Even within our own country, we need to arrive at a clearer approach to the problem of child abuse. With more than three million cases reported annually, the United States needs to acknowledge the pervasiveness and searing impact of the problem. It affects people of all social backgrounds and constitutes an assault on the most vulnerable among us. Child abuse has become one of the leading social problems of American families. The rising number of reports and the continuing fatalities are cause for serious alarm and a warning sign for the future.

All other industrialized nations do more
to lift their children out of poverty than the United States,
according to a recent survey by the Luxembourg Income Study
—UNICEF, The Progress of Nations, *1996*

Child Poverty

■ Child poverty has seriously worsened in the United States over time. Currently there are 13.8 million American children in poverty. Among those under 18, poverty has increased from 14.9 percent in 1970 to 19.8 percent in 1996, a 33 percent increase.

■ Child poverty is most prevalent among the very young—those under the age of six—and among minorities, particularly black and Hispanic youth.

■ The United States has the worst record among industrialized nations in reducing the poverty of children. Government programs reduce the poverty rates of children far more effectively in other countries than in the United States.

A Special Problem.   In many parts of the industrial world, a range of social policies serve to prevent widespread poverty and ensure that very few children live in extreme need. In the U.S. the picture is quite different. The U.S. has a child poverty rate among the highest in the industrial world.

In 1996, 13.8 million young people under the age of 18, or 19.8 percent of all American children, lived in poverty. This is 39 percent higher than in 1973, when the poverty rate was at its lowest point during this period, 14.2 percent. Moreover, the 1996 rate is only slightly better than the levels recorded during the worst years of the early 1980s and 1990s recessions.

The problem of child poverty is one of progress lost. During the 1950s and 1960s, a strong economy and a range of public policy interventions began to reduce child poverty rates to new lows. From the early 1970s on, however, poverty rates once again began to rise and have either continued to worsen or remain at high levels since that time. Only in the past three years, with the economy again growing, has there been a small improvement, but even these rates remain higher than in any single year between 1966 and 1981.

The Two Ends of the Life Cycle.   Child poverty rates are even higher for the nation's youngest children—those under the age of six—than for all children under the age of 18, and they have remained so over time. Currently, 22.7 percent of children under six are living in poverty, an increase of 37 percent since 1970.

5.5
Child poverty
Percent, related children in families under age 18, in poverty

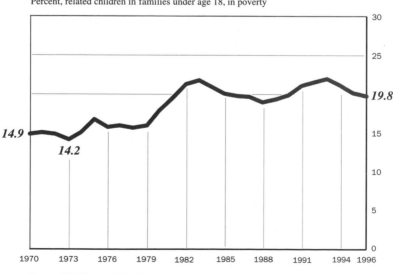

Source: U.S. Bureau of the Census.

Poverty can have its most harmful effects at these youngest ages, when a lack of proper nutrition during a child's early years can cause a lifetime of physical and developmental problems. Mental retardation may be caused by lead poisoning from poor housing conditions, and the inadequate early schooling available in many low-income areas can deprive children of opportunities that may affect them for a lifetime.

The worsening situation for the nation's youngest children over time stands in sharp contrast to the improving situation for the elderly. While the poverty rate for those over age 65 has been improving, the rate for those under the age of six has been worsening. Since 1970, the two groups have virtually changed places. In 1996, the poverty of young children, at 22.7 percent, was more than twice that of the elderly at 10.8 percent.

The nation's ability to improve the economic circumstances of at least one age group, the elderly, clearly suggests the capacity of the society to address this type of problem. Moreover, the fact that child poverty was lower in the recent past, averaging about 15 percent between 1970 and 1974, also indicates that the nation can ameliorate this problem.

Profiling the Nation's Poor Children.   In absolute numbers, white youth constitute the majority of poor children under the age of 18. In the U.S. today, 8.5 million white children live in poverty, compared to 4.4 million black children and 4.1 million Hispanic children.

Proportionately, however, poverty occurs more frequently among minorities than among whites. Among white youth, 15.5 percent were in poverty; among blacks, it

5.6
Poverty among children under 6 and
persons aged 65 and over
Percent in poverty

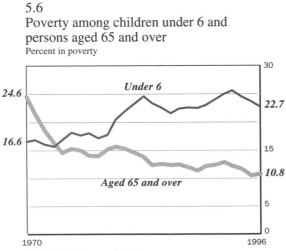

Source: U.S. Bureau of the Census.

was a high 39.5 percent; and among Hispanic youth, a slightly higher 39.9 percent. In 1996, the child poverty rate of Hispanics exceeded the black rate for the first time.

Among children under the age of six, disparities were even greater. In this age group 18.2 percent of white children were in poverty, compared to 44.6 percent of black children and 42.2 percent of Hispanic children.

Poverty among the nation's minority children is an issue of serious concern. These continuing conditions point to constrained opportunities and limited prospects for a substantial segment of the nation's young people.

Extreme Poverty.   According to a new report, *Trends in the Well-being of America's Children and Youth,* prepared by the Department of Health and Human Services, "there has been a striking increase in the percentage of children raised in extreme poverty, that is, with family incomes less than one half the official poverty line." Between 1975 and 1993, the proportion of children in extreme poverty doubled, from 5 percent to 10 percent of all children. Such extreme poverty may severely injure a child's life chances, causing serious problems of malnutrition, poor shelter, and lack of safety.

Internationally, the U.S. Compares Poorly.   Several studies have begun the process

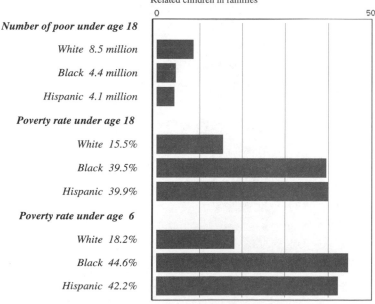

5.7
Child poverty by race/ethnicity and age, 1996
Related children in families

Number of poor under age 18
White 8.5 million
Black 4.4 million
Hispanic 4.1 million

Poverty rate under age 18
White 15.5%
Black 39.5%
Hispanic 39.9%

Poverty rate under age 6
White 18.2%
Black 44.6%
Hispanic 42.2%

Source: U.S. Bureau of the Census.

of creating cross-national measures of poverty for the industrial nations in order to compare their relative performance. Each has documented the lagging status of the United States compared to other nations.

The Luxembourg Income Studies, for example, use a measure defining the poverty line for each nation as less than one half its median income. By this measure, the United States, with more than 24 percent of its children in poverty, performs the worst among industrial nations. The United Kingdom, where child poverty has increased sharply during the last decade, ranks second, while most of the lowest rates were found in the Scandinavian nations.

Tax and Transfer Programs.   According to UNICEF's *Progress of Nations* report, among industrialized nations, "safety nets for children are weakest in U.S." Virtually all industrial countries have relatively high child poverty rates before the application

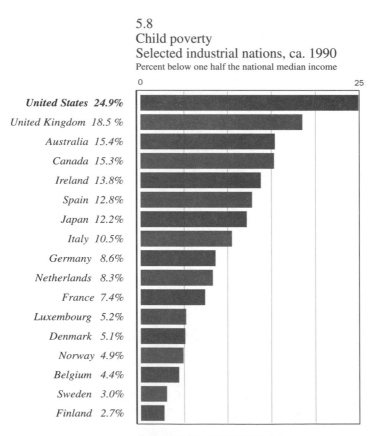

5.8
Child poverty
Selected industrial nations, ca. 1990
Percent below one half the national median income

Source: Luxembourg Income Studies.
Note: U.S. figure here is different from U.S. poverty rates presented elsewhere because of a different definition of the threshold.

of tax and transfer programs designed to improve the status of children. For example, according to the Luxembourg Income Studies, France and the United States both had approximately 25 percent of their children in poverty prior to tax and transfer payments. But in France, government programs reduced the child poverty rate to approximately 7 percent, while in the U.S. child poverty remained over 20 percent. In eight of sixteen countries surveyed, child poverty was at least halved by government programs, and in nine nations, child poverty was brought below 10 percent.

A Different Kind of Deficit. Despite the nation's booming economy, poverty among American children is commonplace. Nearly one in every five children under 18 lives in poverty. In our major cities, child poverty rates are far higher, and in the suburbs, the percentage of poor children has risen over time.

Some have argued that there are several deficits in the nation. One, the budget deficit, has been squarely and forthrightly addressed. The gap has closed and a surplus has emerged. But another deficit lies in the condition of children in America, particularly in their economic state. This deficit has not significantly closed. The potential benefit to the quality of the workforce alone makes an effort to close this deficit worthwhile.

America's failure to curb child poverty stands in sharp contrast to this nation's more successful reduction of poverty among the elderly and to the more effective efforts by other nations. Serious problems for poor children include inadequate nutrition, poor health, minimal education, higher crime, and limited employment prospects. The effects of child poverty deprive the nation a whole. The continuing high rates of child poverty constitute what should be a significant indicator, or a warning sign, that the strength and stability of the American future is at risk.

At each moment of its history . . . each
society has a definite aptitude for suicide.
—*Emile Durkheim,* Suicide, *1897*

Youth Suicide

■ The performance of the United States in addressing youth suicide
has been generally poor. Suicides among young people have risen
over the past twenty-five years. The 1996 suicide rate among youth,
aged 15-24, was 12.0 deaths per 100,000, up from 8.8 in 1970.

■ Over time, suicides have been highest for young white males; but
in recent years, black males have been rapidly catching up. Women,
both white and black, have comparatively low rates.

■ The United States ranks relatively poorly compared to other industrial nations. The U.S. suicide rate for 15-24 year olds is higher
than 14 other countries for males, 6 other countries for females. For
children under 15, the U.S. suicide rate was two times higher than that
in the other 25 industrialized countries combined.

Deaths among the Young.   The systematic study of suicide has one of the longest histories in the social sciences, dating back to Emile Durkheim's classic 1897 work, *Suicide.* According to Durkheim, suicides are a reflection of the underlying problems of a society, which may reveal themselves in individual acts of self-destruction.

For America, such an analysis bodes poorly, for among the young, suicide has been increasing for more than four decades. In 1950, the suicide rate among youth aged 15-24 was a relatively low 4.5 per 100,000. By 1970, suicides had almost doubled, to 8.8, and by 1996 the suicide rate was 12.0. The problem has worsened by 36 percent since 1970 and by more than 150 percent since 1950. It is today the third leading cause of death among all young people, and the second leading cause of death among young white males.

Suicides, particularly among the young, are significant because of their profound impact on the larger society. Each suicide resonates far beyond an individual's family. Copycat or cluster suicides have become a new syndrome. Serious depression among the victim's friends, schoolmates, and community members is common.

Male and Female, Black and White.   One of the most important factors in the continuing problem of youth suicide is the high rate among males. Females attempt suicide more often, but males are more likely to complete it. For the past twenty-five years, white male youth have had the highest rates. During the past decade, however, black male suicides have soared upwards.

5.9
Youth suicide
Deaths per 100,000, aged 15-24

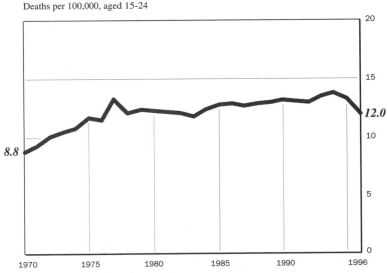

Source: National Center for Health Statistics.

Between 1984 and 1994, suicides among black males aged 15-24 rose by 84 percent, from a rate of 11.2 to 20.6, nearly closing the gap with white males. In 1995 and 1996 there was some improvement. The problem has been particularly acute among the youngest of the group, those aged 15-19, where the increase from 1984 to 1996 was approximately 95 percent.

Both white and black females have much lower rates of suicide, and both, in fact, have declined slightly since 1970. White females dropped from an already low rate of 4.2 deaths per 100,000 to 3.8. Black females, who have the lowest rates of all, declined from 3.8 to 2.3.

These differences suggest important areas for study. We need to know more about why males commit suicide more often than females, why females attempt suicide more often, and specifically, why black male youth have increased their suicide rates so dramatically during the past decade.

Suicidal Thoughts and Attempts.   Suicidal thoughts and attempts are disturbingly frequent among American youth, according to a nationwide school-based survey conducted by the Centers for Disease Control (CDC). The study, entitled "Youth Risk Behavior Surveillance," examined self-reported youth behaviors in high school and college in 1995.

This survey found that nearly one-fourth of high school students, 24.1 percent, had thought seriously about committing suicide during the past 12 months. Even more troubling, 17.7 percent of high school students reported they had made a specific plan to attempt suicide.

Among the high school students surveyed, 8.7 percent had attempted suicide

5.10
Youth suicide by race and gender
Deaths per 100,000, aged 15-24

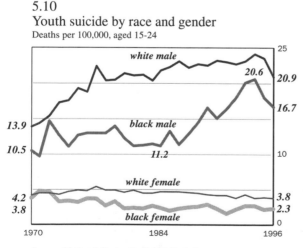

Source: National Center for Health Statistics.

within the past year. Most dangerously, 2.8 percent of high school youth had harmed themselves seriously enough through injury, poison, or drug overdose to require medical treatment. Among the students surveyed, females were higher in all categories of thoughts and attempts.

Among college-age students, the proportion who thought seriously about suicide, while still high, was substantially lower than in high school. Among those surveyed, 11.4 percent of those aged 18-24 had thought seriously about suicide, far fewer than the 24.1 percent of high school students. Gender differences also diminished as students reached college age.

International Standing.   The performance of the United States compared to the other industrialized nations of the world on youth suicide may be considered fair. Among twenty-two industrial nations, during the mid-1990s, fourteen nations had lower rates among males, six had lower rates among females. The comparable U.S.

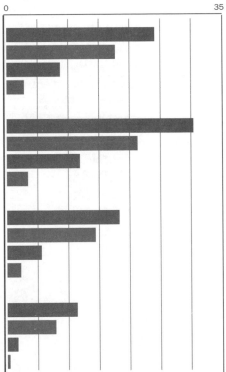

5.11
Suicidal thoughts and attempts
within the past 12 months, 1995
Percent

Source: Centers for Disease Control.

rate in 1995 was 22.5 suicides per 100,000 among males, more than five times that of the lowest nation, Greece, at 4.4. The comparable suicide rate among U.S. females in 1995, at 3.7 per 100,000, was close to that of the other industrial nations.

Among younger children, the situation appears to be far worse. In 1995, the Centers for Disease Control undertook a study of violent death among youth under the age of 15 in the United States and twenty-five other industrialized countries. The report showed that since 1950, death rates among American youth have been declining overall due to advances in the treatment of diseases such as influenza, pneumonia, cancer, and congenital anomalies. During the same period, however, death rates among youth under 15 tripled for homicide and quadrupled for suicide.

5.12
Youth suicide
Selected industrial nations, 1992-1995
Deaths per 100,000, aged 15-24

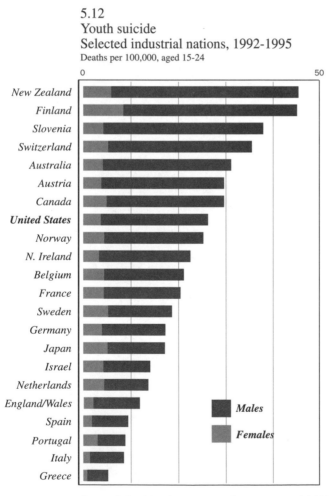

Sources: Industrial nations: *World Health Statistics Annual*, 1995,1996;
U.S.: National Center for Health Statistics.
Note: 1995 U.S. date presented here for comparability purposes.

Of all the suicides that occurred in the twenty-six countries among children under age 15, 54 percent were among American children. "The suicide rate for children in the United States was two times higher than that in the other 25 countries combined."

Year 2000 Goal.   To begin to address the problem of teenage suicide, the Department of Health and Human Services, beginning in 1992, set target goals for the year 2000 for the nation's teenage population, those aged 15-19. The goal set for this group was 8.2 deaths per 100,000. The current rate, now at 9.7 deaths, represents an improvement from a high of 11.1, but the country may not meet this goal in time.

A Need to Consider.   That suicides have increased for so long, especially among the very young, is a deeply disturbing facet of life in American society. The United States has yet to formulate a clear or consistent policy toward ameliorating the problem, although a range of alternatives exist, including hotlines, crisis centers, school training programs, screening programs, peer support groups, and the restriction of access to lethal means. At this time, there are still insufficient data to recommend one strategy over another, but each type of program can play a role. Each can serve to strengthen community ties and provide support for adolescents.

Suicide among youth remains a difficult problem to understand, even to experts in the field. What is clear, however, is that the problem is not limited to particular classes, ethnic groups, or geographic areas. It is often "contagious" and periodically affects clusters of adolescents, sometimes across the nation. Beyond the ameliorative programs, the country still needs to look to the root causes of disaffection among youth if the long-term trends are to be reversed.

5.13
Year 2000 goal for
youth suicide, aged 15-19
Deaths per 100,000

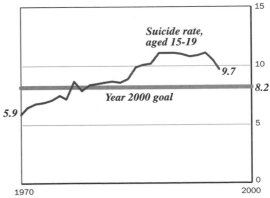

Source: National Center for Health Statistics.

The number of people without health insurance is an important indicator of the adequacy of our health care system. Between the 1930s and the late 1970s, the number of uninsured Americans declined steadily. Over the past 15 years, the rates of the uninsured have been increasing.
—The Center for National Health Program Studies, Harvard University
The Vanishing Health Care Safety Net, *1991*

Health Care Coverage

■ The proportion of the U.S. population lacking health insurance has increased over time. A total of 41.7 million Americans, or 15.6 percent, had no health insurance in 1996, up from an estimated 10.9 percent in 1976.

■ Children experience serious health insurance problems as well. In 1996, 10.6 million children, or 14.8 percent, were not covered by either Medicaid or private insurance.

■ Enrollment in employer-financed health insurance programs has declined. Among full-time workers in medium and large-size firms, the percentage of those covered fell from 97 percent in 1980 to 77 percent in 1995.

Declining Benefits.   The changing nature of the economy is producing jobs that reduce benefits for many Americans. Among these, the most significant is health insurance. The increasing number of Americans without health insurance endangers the
well-being of both adults and children.

When people lack health insurance, they often receive substantially poorer health
care. The uninsured are more likely to delay health care, receive less preventive and
primary care, have illnesses in more advanced stages, and have higher mortality rates.
The overall health and well-being of the population suffers from the absence of adequate health care coverage.

Over the past two decades, the number and proportion of Americans with no health
insurance has climbed steadily. The problem has worsened by an estimated 43 percent since 1976. In 1996, according to the Census Bureau, there were 41.7 million
people without insurance at any time during the previous year, a total of 15.6 percent
of the population.

Who are the Uninsured?   Some groups have much higher rates of non-insurance.
These include young adults between the ages of 18 and 34, Hispanics, the poor, and
those with incomes under $25,000.

More than a quarter of young adults lacked health insurance in 1996, as did more
than a third of the Hispanic population. Among the poor, the proportion without insur-

5.14
Health care coverage — the uninsured
Percent of population

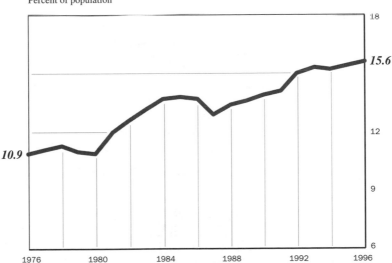

Sources: 1976-1986 Estimated percentages based on the number of uninsured from the
Center for National Health Program Studies, Harvard University/Cambridge Hospital,
published and unpublished data, as a proportion of All Persons, U.S., U.S. Bureau of the Census,
calculations by the Fordham Institute for Innovation in Social Policy; 1987-1996 U.S.
Bureau of the Census.

ance in 1996 was 30.8 percent, double the rate for the population as a whole. This is the case despite Medicaid, the program designed to provide health insurance for the poor. Almost one-quarter of those with incomes under $25,000 lacked insurance as well.

The Census Bureau conducts periodic longer-term analyses of health insurance coverage over 28-month periods. Between 1992 and 1994, 66.6 million Americans went without health insurance for at least one month. This represents 27 percent of the population, or more than one in every four Americans.

Underinsurance.   In addition to those who are uninsured, a substantial number of Americans are underinsured, having less-than-full coverage and facing problems in obtaining and paying for care. According to a recent survey published in the *Journal of the American Medical Association,* the underinsured, when added to the uninsured, may amount to as many as 50 million Americans. Of these, 34 million reported "severe health problems." According to the study, "Problems in getting needed medical care affect about 17 million uninsured adults and 17 million insured adults in America, and problems in paying medical bills are reported by 13 million uninsured and 17 million insured Americans."

The Effect on Children.   In most industrial nations, virtually all children have guar-

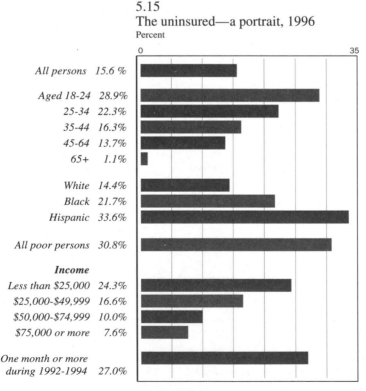

5.15
The uninsured—a portrait, 1996
Percent

Source: U.S. Bureau of the Census.

anteed health insurance. This is not the situation in the United States today. In 1996, according to the Census Bureau, 10.6 million children under the age of 18, or 14.8 percent of all American children, lacked health insurance for the entire year. This is an increase of 15 percent since 1987, when child insurance figures first became available. Poor children averaged a high 23.3 percent without health insurance in 1996, and Hispanic children were higher still, at 28.9 percent.

The Census Bureau's long-term analyses show that between 1992 and 1994, a much higher 30 percent of children went without health insurance for at least one month. In an analysis of more recent 1995-96 Census data, Families USA found totals even larger. They estimate that 33 percent, or one in every three children in the nation, went without health insurance for at least one month in 1995-1996.

Employee Coverage.   A contributing factor to the decline in health insurance coverage for both children and adults is the shift away from employer-provided health insurance. In the past, most people obtained their insurance through their jobs, and for most, it was fully funded. This situation has changed.

According to the Bureau of Labor Statistics survey of medium and large-size firms, employee participation in job-related health insurance programs has declined from 97 percent in 1980 to 77 percent in 1995. One reason is increased cost-sharing. Among the programs made available to employees, those that are fully financed by employers have declined sharply, from 74 percent in 1980 to 37 percent in 1995,

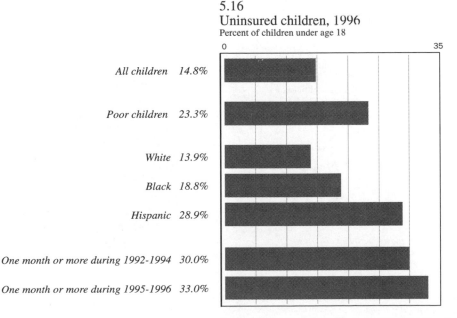

5.16
Uninsured children, 1996
Percent of children under age 18

Sources: U.S. Bureau of the Census; 1995-1996 Families U.S.A.

while partly-financed programs have increased. This change has made employer-provided insurance too expensive for many, even when it is available.

Because of the decline in employer-provided health insurance, most of the uninsured now live in families where the head of the household is employed. This, too, represents a change from the past.

In 1996, 85 percent of the uninsured lived in families where the head of the household held a job. A full 59.5 percent of the uninsured were in families where the head of household worked full-time year-round. Another 25.5 percent held jobs either part-time or part-year, and 15 percent were nonworkers.

The weakening of the ties between employment and health insurance constitutes a potential crisis for the U.S. population. The greater volatility of the job market, the need to change jobs more frequently, the increase in contingent and part-time employment, have all created fewer situations where health insurance coverage is provided on the job or at reasonable cost.

States Vary.   The proportion of people without health insurance varies markedly by state. In 1996, only eight states averaged under 10 percent uninsured. Eight states were over 18 percent.

Those states with the highest proportion of uninsured were all in the West and South. In the two states with the highest rates, Texas and Arizona, almost one in every four state residents lacked coverage. New Mexico, Arkansas, Louisiana, California, Florida, and Mississippi also had high rates of non-insurance, averaging at or close to one in every five residents.

5.17
Health insurance employee coverage
Percent of participation by full-time employees
in medium and large private establishments

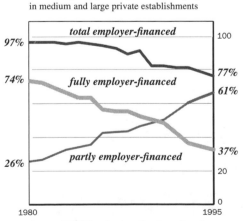

Source: *EBRI Databook on Employee Benefits.*
Note: 1980-1987 narrow BLS survey scope; 1988-1995
expanded BLS survey scope.

5.18
Work status of the uninsured, 1996
Percent of nonelderly uninsured, head of household

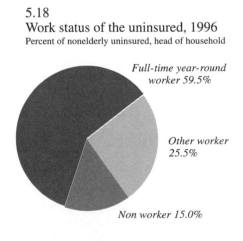

Source: Employee Benefit Research Institute.

Wisconsin registered the lowest number of uninsured, at 8.4 percent, but this was still a worsening from 7.3 percent the year before. Other states with relatively low rates were Hawaii, Michigan, New Hampshire, Pennsylvania, South Dakota, North Dakota, and Rhode Island.

A Problem Yet To Be Addressed.   The provision of health insurance, for children and adults, is not a problem in most other industrial nations, since national health insurance programs of various types exist in virtually all of those countries. This is essentially a U.S. problem.

Although recent legislation will provide health insurance for many additional children, the absence of health insurance for the larger population will continue. With structural changes in the economy, it is likely that employer-financed coverage will remain less available and more expensive than it was in the past, and substantial numbers of adults will lack insurance. Their illnesses, made both more severe and more costly by delayed treatment, constitute a condition the society needs to address.

5.19
Persons without health insurance
Selected states, 1996
Percent of state population

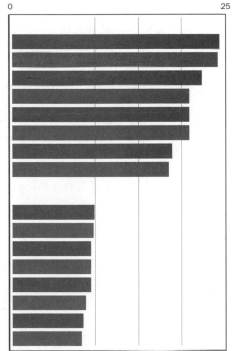

Highest States
Texas 24.3%
Arizona 24.1%
New Mexico 22.3%
Arkansas 20.9%
Louisiana 20.9%
California 20.9%
Florida 18.9%
Mississippi 18.5%

Lowest States
Rhode Island 9.9%
N. Dakota 9.8%
S. Dakota 9.5%
Pennsylvania 9.5%
New Hampshire 9.5%
Michigan 8.9%
Hawaii 8.6%
Wisconsin 8.4%

Source: U.S. Bureau of the Census.

Real wages, when adjusted for inflation by consumer prices,
have failed to keep pace with worker productivity since about 1983—
a clear departure from the pattern of preceding years.
—Economic Report of the President, *1997*

Wages

■   Average weekly earnings have fallen sharply since the early 1970s. In constant dollars, earnings went from $315 in 1973 to $256 in 1996, a decline of 19 percent.

■   The male-female earnings gap has been reduced over time, but improvement slowed during the 1990s. The earnings of both male and female year-round full-time workers declined during the 1990s.

■   The proportion of year-round, full-time workers with low earnings has increased over time. Young workers and those with less than a high school degree are most likely to have low earnings.

How We Live.   Wages, for most Americans, are the pathway to a decent home, education for their children, a reasonable retirement income, and a comfortable standard of living. Wages and salaries make up approximately three-fourths of total family income, and that proportion is even higher among the middle class.

From the end of World War II to 1973, average weekly earnings, for production or nonsupervisory workers, increased virtually every year, but from 1973 to the present, they have either declined or stagnated. This phenomenon has affected much of American life. Today, the two-earner family is commonplace in order to maintain family income. Some individuals must work two or more jobs. The erosion in earnings over time has meant a harder existence for many.

In constant dollars, average weekly earnings went from a high of $315 in 1973 down to $256 in 1996. This decline has been relatively steady and, unlike indicators such as unemployment, which rise and fall with business cycles, average weekly earnings failed to improve significantly even during the recoveries of the 1980s and mid-1990s. This stagnation stands in sharp contrast to the steady improvement achieved between 1947 and 1973. Hourly earnings show a comparable trend, rising through 1973, then declining and stagnating thereafter. In 1973, average hourly earnings, in constant dollars, were $8.55; by 1996, they had fallen to $7.43.

5.20
Average weekly earnings
Total private, nonagricultural industries, for production or nonsupervisory
workers, seasonally adjusted, 1982$

Source: *Economic Report of the President.*

The Gender Wage Gap.   The difference between male and female earnings illustrates several aspects of the wage gap facing the nation. Men continue to have substantially higher earnings than women, although the distance has closed over time.
The gap has closed, however, not only through an improvement in women's earnings,
but by a worsening in male earnings as well.

Women in 1970 earned 59.4 cents for every dollar earned by men; today they earn
73.8 cents for every dollar earned by men. This advance has brought women's earnings much closer to men's. But some of the closing of the gap has come about because
of a decline in male earnings; measured in constant dollars, these fell from $34,062 in
1970 to $32,144 in 1996. Only a part of the change was due to an improvement in
women's earnings, which rose in constant dollars from $20,222 in 1970 to $23,710 in
1996.

Finally, the 1990s have seen a slight decline in the average earnings of both males
and females. This has made the income situation still more difficult for both groups.

Low Earnings of Full-Time Workers.   One of the most troubling aspects of declining
wages is the large number of Americans who work year-round full-time and still remain poor or near poor. The expansion of the service sector of the economy, which
frequently pays low wages, has left substantial numbers of workers with incomes at
or near the poverty line.

The Census Bureau defines low-earnings workers as those making $14,640 per
year, in constant dollars. Although the last several years have seen a slight improvement, the proportion of workers with low earnings has still worsened from 12.1 per-

5.21
The gender wage gap
Median earnings, year-round full-time workers, 1996$

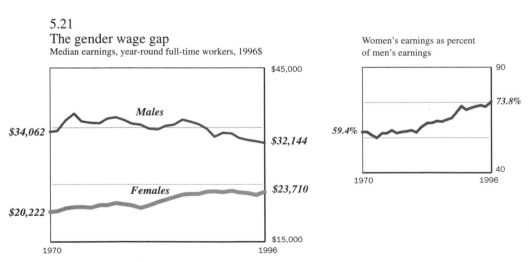

Women's earnings as percent
of men's earnings

Source: U.S. Bureau of the Census.
Note: 1970-1980 persons 14 and older, 1980-1996 persons 15 and older; prior to 1989, for civilian workers only.

cent in 1979 to 15.3 percent in 1996, a worsening of 26 percent. Since 1979, low-earnings work increased in virtually every segment of society. Only females, whose rate of low-earnings work was high to begin with, showed no change over time.

The most significant increases in low-earnings work since 1979 have been found among the young and those with less education. The proportion of those with low earnings among young workers aged 18-24 has grown particularly high, rising from 22.9 percent in 1979 to 43.1 percent in 1996, almost doubling in this time period.

Family Incomes Increase With Two Earners. The American family has responded to the decline in wages by creating the two-earner family. Women entering the work force comprise the majority of additional workers.

Multiple earners within families helped increase median family income from $37,485 in 1970 to $42,300 in 1996. The significance of having a spouse in the labor force can be seen in the striking contrast between the incomes of families with a wife working, averaging $58,381, and families without a wife working, earning only $33,748.

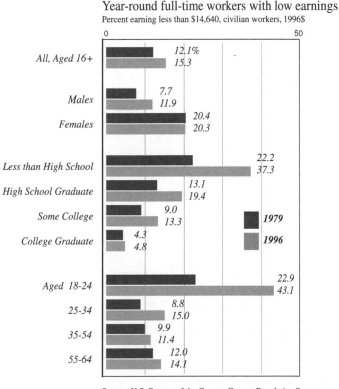

5.22
Year-round full-time workers with low earnings
Percent earning less than $14,640, civilian workers, 1996$

	1979	1996
All, Aged 16+	12.1%	15.3
Males	7.7	11.9
Females	20.4	20.3
Less than High School	22.2	37.3
High School Graduate	13.1	19.4
Some College	9.0	13.3
College Graduate	4.3	4.8
Aged 18-24	22.9	43.1
25-34	8.8	15.0
35-54	9.9	11.4
55-64	12.0	14.1

Source: U.S. Bureau of the Census, Current Population Survey, published and unpublished data.

While the two-earner family has added to household income, it also has added new pressures on the American family. These include the need for affordable day care and child care, the creation of more work stress within families, and the decline in time that can be allocated to children and the home.

The Minimum Wage.   A contributing factor to the decline in average earnings has been the diminishing value of the minimum wage. The minimum wage was increased regularly between 1974 and 1981, but was not increased again until 1989. This resulted in an erosion in the real value of the minimum wage. By 1989, the minimum wage had fallen well below the poverty threshold for a family of four.

The minimum wage was increased again in 1991 to $4.25 per hour, to $4.75 in 1996, and then again to $5.15 in 1997. Despite these increases, it remains substantially below the poverty threshold for a family of four, which in 1997 was $16,400. Even the poverty threshold for families of only two people exceeds the annual earnings of a minimum wage worker.

International Compensation Costs.   In 1985, the United States stood first among industrial nations in hourly compensation costs—wages plus benefits—for its workers. Since that time, compensation costs in the United States have dropped below those of many other nations.

Using the index of hourly compensation costs, which sets the U.S. at 100, twelve industrial nations had compensation costs higher than the U.S in 1996, while ten in-

5.23
Median family income
1996$

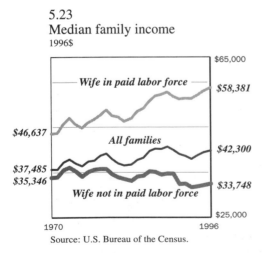

Source: U.S. Bureau of the Census.

5.24
Minimum wage and poverty threshold
Annual minimum wage $

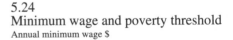
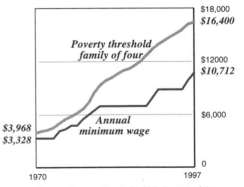

Source: Poverty threshold: U.S. Bureau of the Census; Hourly minimum wage: U.S. House of Representatives, *Green Book*; Annual minimum wage: Calculations by the Fordham Institute for Innovation in Social Policy.

dustrial countries fell below the U.S. From the perspective of competitiveness, low compensation costs contribute to a greater edge for American business. From the perspective of those who work for wages, diminishing compensation is a matter of serious concern.

Expectations for the Future.　The decline in earnings remains a continuing problem for American workers. It affects all Americans, but especially the young, single-earner families, the less educated, and people earning at or near the minimum wage. The decline in wages reverses the post-World-War-II wage boom that built the American middle class and created a sense of optimism about the future. While jobs are now available, the wages they pay and the standard of living they provide often fall short of what Americans have come to expect as compensation for their efforts.

5.25
Index of hourly compensation costs
Selected industrial nations, 1996
Production workers in manufacturing, U.S.=100

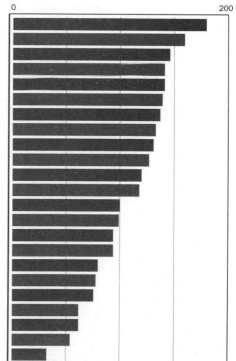

Germany	180
Switzerland	160
Belgium	146
Austria	141
Norway	141
Sweden	139
Denmark	137
Finland	133
Netherlands	131
Luxembourg	127
France	120
Japan	118
United States	**100**
Italy	99
Canada	94
Australia	94
United Kingdom	80
Ireland	78
Spain	76
Israel	62
New Zealand	62
Greece	54
Portugal	32

Source: U.S. Department of Labor.

Families have been affected unevenly by recent income trends. Real incomes at the top
have increased smartly, real incomes at the middle have essentially stagnated,
and real incomes at the bottom have fallen.
—Economic Report of the President, *1994*

Inequality

■   In the United States, inequality has increased over time. The proportion of the nation's income received by the poorest fifth of American families has declined; the proportion held by the richest fifth has
increased. The Gini Index, one measure of this form of inequality, has
worsened by 20 percent since 1970.

■   Reflecting the widening gap between the rich and the poor, the
mean income of the poorest fifth has declined, while the mean income of both the top fifth and top 5 percent have risen significantly.
The mean income of the poorest fifth in 1996 was $11,388, the mean
income of the top fifth was $125,627, and that of the top 5 percent was
$217, 355.

■   The United States has the largest gap between rich and poor
among industrialized nations.

Sharp Contrasts.   Inequality, or the gap between the rich and the poor, addresses the distribution of a society's financial resources among its citizens. The rich-poor gap has widened sharply in America in recent years, increasing the risk of raising barriers of social class.

There are several methods for measuring income inequality. One, reported annually by the Census Bureau, is the Gini Index of inequality, which assesses a nation's distance from total equality. If everyone had a completely equal share of income, there would be perfect equality, and the Gini Index would be 0. In contrast, if there was total inequality the Index would be 1. All nations fall somewhere in between.

In the United States, the Gini Index has worsened by 20 percent since 1970, going from .353 in 1970 to .425 in 1996, in an almost uninterrupted rise. Inequality in the United States began to worsen sharply after 1968, and has continued to do so fairly steadily since that time. From 1947 to 1988, the Index never reached .400; since 1992, while stabilizing, it has not once fallen below .400.

Different Shares.   Another way of visualizing inequality is to divide the U.S. population into fifths, ranking them from the poorest fifth to the richest fifth. We can then look at the share of the national income held by the poorest fifth and richest fifth over time. Since 1970, the richest fifth has increased its share of the national income, while the poorest fifth has seen its share shrink.

5.26
Inequality in family income
Gini Index, range from 0 to 1

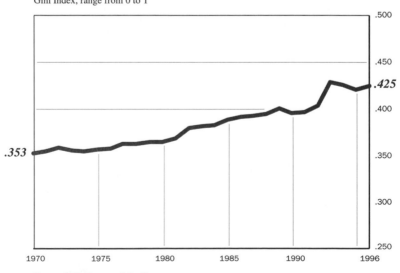

Source: U.S. Bureau of the Census.

In 1996, the income share of the richest fifth was 46.8 percent, up from 40.9 percent in 1970. Meanwhile, the income share of the poorest fifth had fallen to 4.2 percent, down from 5.4 percent in 1970. Today, the richest fifth of American families receives 11 times the income share of the poorest fifth, an increase since 1970, when the richest received only 7.6 times the income share of the poorest.

Growing disparities also can be analyzed by looking at the average annual income of each group. In constant dollars, the mean annual income of the poorest fifth of the nation has actually declined since 1970, going from $11,640 to $11,388 in 1996. The mean income of the top fifth of the nation has risen since 1970 from $86,325 to $125,627, a 45 percent increase. The top 5 percent of the nation went from $131,450 to $217,355, a startling 65 percent rise.

What's Happening in the Middle?   In newspapers and magazines, we often read about "the shrinking middle class" or the "middle-class squeeze." These reports have a basis in fact. The income share of the middle three-fifths of the nation has shrunk over time, while the income share of the top 20 percent has increased.

The income share of the middle three-fifths of the U.S. population, like the poorest fifth, has declined slightly since 1970, from 53.6 percent to 48.9 percent. Illustrating the growing inequality in the nation, the top 20 percent of the population now receives only 2.1 percent less income than the entire middle 60 percent of the population.

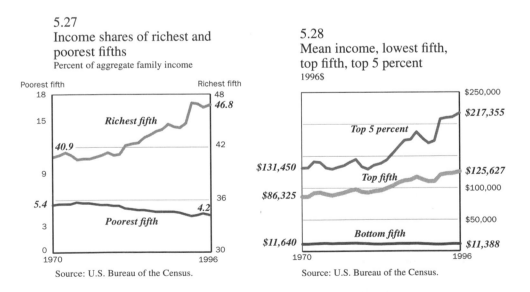

5.27
Income shares of richest and
poorest fifths
Percent of aggregate family income

Source: U.S. Bureau of the Census.

5.28
Mean income, lowest fifth,
top fifth, top 5 percent
1996$

Source: U.S. Bureau of the Census.

   The stability of the middle class is becoming precarious. While jobs are plentiful and unemployment is low, many of the positions that people obtain today have lower salaries than jobs available in the past. Manufacturing jobs, for example, traditionally well-paying, have dwindled. Among white-collar employees, downsizing has led to new jobs which are often lower-paying and have fewer benefits. Adequate health insurance and retirement plans are becoming more difficult to obtain than they were in the past, since they are less tied to jobs, and may add additional economic pressures to middle-class incomes.

   International Comparisons.   According to the Luxembourg Income Studies, the United States had the highest level of inequality of the industrial nations studied. Measured by disposable income, the U.S. had a score of .343, far higher than the low of Finland at .233. The study also shows that several nations, especially the United Kingdom, are rapidly increasing in inequality, similar to the pattern of the United States.

   The Luxembourg data also show that of ten industrial nations studied, the poor in the United states had the least disposable income. The rich in the U.S. had the most disposable income, between almost one-quarter to almost one-half more than any other nation. The U.S. also had the highest disposable income in the middle among the ten industrial nations. The differences suggest a national pattern, in which the rich

5.29
Income shares of middle three-fifths and top fifth
Percent of aggregate family income

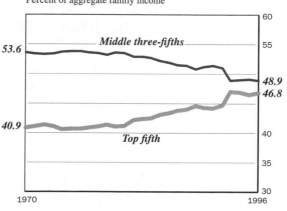

Source: U.S. Bureau of the Census.

are very rich, the middle have been doing relatively well compared to other nations, although their position is now beginning to decline, and the poor are among the poorest in the industrial world.

Does Inequality Matter?   There are serious debates about the meaning of inequality. Some argue that disparities provide incentive to achieve. Others argue that they create a loss of social cohesion and civic trust. Because inequality has widened sharply during the past several years in a number of the advanced industrial nations, it has become a focus for new research. A series of studies in England, for example, published by the *British Medical Journal* and *The Lancet*, suggest that growing inequality is having a worsening impact on the health and well-being of the British nation.

Several of these studies have been conducted by Richard Wilkinson of Sussex University. According to *The Lancet,* "The speed with which inequality has widened

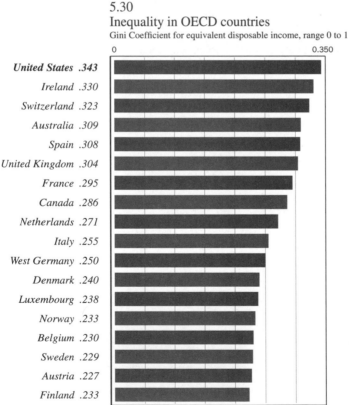

5.30
Inequality in OECD countries
Gini Coefficient for equivalent disposable income, range 0 to 1

United States	.343
Ireland	.330
Switzerland	.323
Australia	.309
Spain	.308
United Kingdom	.304
France	.295
Canada	.286
Netherlands	.271
Italy	.255
West Germany	.250
Denmark	.240
Luxembourg	.238
Norway	.233
Belgium	.230
Sweden	.229
Austria	.227
Finland	.233

Source: Luxembourg Income Studies.
Note: Years are variable, ranging from the oldest, 1982 in
Switzerland, to 1992 in Sweden, Belgium, and Denmark.

in the UK has given researchers a chance to study its effects. What Wilkinson is able to show is that the slow down in declining mortality and morbidity rates for infants, children, and young adults in Britain coincided with the stark widening of income differentials. He goes on to show that the countries with the longest life-expectancy are not the richest, but the states with the smallest spread of incomes. These differences are not due to better public services in more egalitarian societies, but attributable in large part to differences in income distribution alone." Other studies also have shown a "widening health gap" between Britain's poor and the rest of the population. Higher rates of illness and infant mortality have been found in the poorest 10 percent of census wards, where death rates among men aged 45-54 have climbed back to the rates of the 1950s.

Like Britain, the United States has a widening gap between rich and poor. The combination of declining incomes for the poorest fifth of the nation, stagnating incomes for the middle three-fifths, and rising incomes for the top 20 percent and top 5 percent of the country, have increased the level of inequality for the nation. Such inequality may deprive substantial sectors of the population from sharing in the potential benefits of the American economy and may weaken the overall quality of life. Inequality may pose a particularly serious problem where severe destitution exists in the midst of luxury. Many American communities reveal such contrasts. In the coming years we will need to consider the impact of these divisions on those at the bottom of the pyramid, and on society as a whole.

*From midyear 1996 through midyear 1997 the total population incarcerated
in the country's jails and prisons increased by 96,100 men and women—
or 1,849 inmates per week on average. Since 1990 the number of people in custody has
risen more than 577,100 inmates—or 1,708 inmates per week on average. By midyear
1997 one in every 155 U.S. residents was behind bars.*
— *U.S. Department of Justice
Press Release, January 18, 1998*

Violent Crime

■ The violent crime rate in America has improved for the past six years, but is still higher than it was in 1970. The crime rate was a relatively low 363.5 per 100,000 in 1970; in 1996 it was 634.1.

■ Although violent crime has declined, the incarceration rate has risen. Since 1972, the state and federal prison population has increased from 93 per 100,000 to 427 in 1996, a 359 percent increase.

■ The United States still leads the industrial world in its youth homicide rate. Rates in two age groups—under 15 and 15-24—are significantly higher than in any other industrial nation.

Distrust in the Nation.   The threat of crime weakens the fabric of trust among Americans and contributes to an atmosphere of fear. When personal safety is at issue, people take steps to ward off harm. Although the crime rate has declined significantly for the past six years, the American landscape is still littered with locks, alarms, fences, guards, gates, guns, and prisons. The energies and resources devoted to crime prevention and prosecution are immense.

The lives lost from crime are a national tragedy. Despite sharp declines in the homicide rate, in 1996 it was the second leading cause of death among youth aged 15-24, preceded only by accidents. Among black youth aged 15-24, homicide was the leading cause of death. The United States is first in the industrial world in youth homicides and firearm deaths. While sharply improving, violent crime still remains a part of American life.

The violent crime rate, published in the Uniform Crime Reports by the Federal Bureau of Investigation, combines four types of crime: murder/non-negligent manslaughter; forcible rape; robbery; and aggravated assault. It has worsened over time. In 1970 there were 738,000 violent crimes; in 1996, 1.68 million. The rate of violent crime increased from 363.5 crimes per 100,000 in 1970 to 634.1 in 1996, a 74 percent increase.

Since 1991, violent crime declined by 16 percent. In that time period, all four types of crime have gone down—murder by 24 percent, rape by 15 percent, robbery by 26 percent, and assault by 10 percent. Preliminary data for 1997 and 1998 show a continuation of these steeply declining trends.

5.31
Violent crime
Crimes per 100,000 population

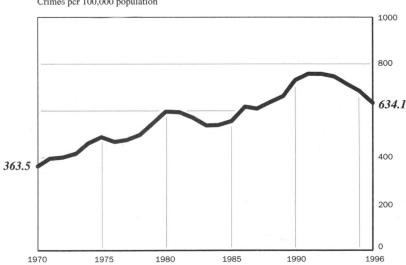

Source: Federal Bureau of Investigation, *Uniform Crime Reports.*
Note: Includes murder/non-negligent manslaughter, forcible rape, robbery, and aggravated assault.

Crime Patterns.   According to the Uniform Crime Reports, each of the four types of violent crimes shows a distinct pattern since 1970. The murder rate, surprising even the experts, is now lower than it was in 1970, an improvement of 6 percent. Rapes have almost doubled, rising by 93 percent. Robberies increased by 18 percent, and aggravated assaults by a very high 136 percent. Murders and rapes constitute the smallest proportion of violent crime, 1 percent and 6 percent respectively. Robberies and aggravated assaults are the most common, and together make up 93 percent of all violent crime.

The Bureau of Justice Statistics publishes a second measure of violent crime, obtained through its National Crime Victimization Survey, a telephone survey of 45,000 households. This survey shows all forms of violent crime dropping, even more sharply than the Uniform Crime Reports, with murder, rape, robbery, and aggravated assault lower than they were in 1973, and simple assaults only fractionally higher.

Among the Young.   Although crime has been diminishing, the young remain its victims. Young people, aged 12-24, are victimized at a rate higher than any other age group. The most vulnerable age group is 16-18. They are the victims of crime twice as often as those aged 25-34, and three times more often than those between the ages of 35 and 49. Young people also constitute a disproportionate share of arrests in the United States; more than 45 percent of all arrests are of people 24 and under.

Imprisonment.   Although violent crime in America has declined, imprisonment continues to rise. For males and females, blacks and whites, imprisonment rates have increased sharply.

In state and federal prisons, the shift over time has been striking. Taking the long

5.32
Violent crime by type
Crimes per 100,000 population

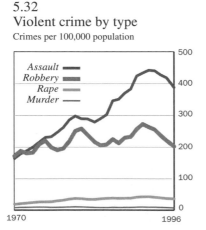

Source: Federal Bureau of Investigation,
Uniform Crime Reports.

5.33
Violent crime victimization
by age, 1996
Victimization per 1,000 population,
persons 12 and over, all crimes of violence

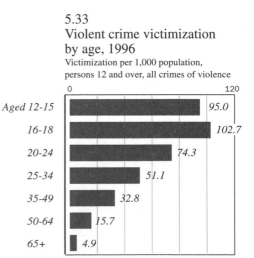

Source: Bureau of Justice Statistics, National
Crime Victimization Survey.

view, from 1926 to 1972, rates of incarceration remained relatively stable, hovering between 75 and 100 sentenced prisoners per 100,000 population. Since 1972 there has been a steep rise, from 93 per 100,000 to 427 in 1996, a remarkable 359 percent increase.

Jail populations also show a sharp increase in recent years. In 1985, the rate of imprisonment in jails was 108 persons per 100,000. By 1996 it had risen to 196 persons, almost double, in slightly more than a decade. Total inmate rates, combining jails and state and federal prisons, increased from 313 per 100,000 in 1985 to 618 per 100,000 in 1996.

Preliminary data from 1997 show that both prison and jail populations are continuing to increase in the United States. These sharp increases constitute a substantial change in American life.

The Cost of Imprisonment.   With the rise in incarcerations has come a corresponding rise in the cost of building and maintaining prisons and jails and in the prosecution of offenses. These increases have been substantial.

Between 1982 and 1993, the most recent years for which data are available, total justice-system expenditures nearly tripled, from 35.8 billion to 97.5 billion dollars. Federal monies quadrupled, from 4.4 billion to 18.6 billion; state monies nearly tripled, from 11.6 billion to 34.2 billion; local monies rose from 20.9 billion to 52.6 billion.

A recent study conducted by the State University of New York's Center for the Study of the States found that in six states, California, Connecticut, Florida, Massachusetts, Michigan, and Minnesota, spending for higher education was declining while spending for corrections was increasing. In 1996, for the first time, California's

5.34
Sentenced prisoners in state and federal
institutions, December 31, each year
Prisoners per 100,000 resident population

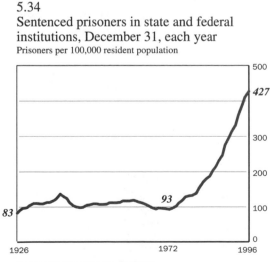

Source: Bureau of Justice Statistics.

expenditures on corrections were projected to exceed those for higher education, excluding community colleges.

Imprisonment in the States.   Imprisonment patterns vary markedly by state. The states with the highest incarceration rates in the nation are in the West and South. Texas had the highest rate in 1996, with 686 prisoners per 100,000. Close behind was Louisiana, with 615, Oklahoma with 591, and South Carolina with 532. Only eight states in the nation had rates below 200. The lowest was North Dakota at 101, Minnesota at 110, and Maine at 112. Other states with relatively low rates were Vermont, West Virginia, New Hampshire, Nebraska, and Utah.

Leading the World.   The United States has one of the highest incarceration rates among industrialized nations and one of the highest rates of violent crime among youth. World Health Organization data show that among youth aged 15-24, the United States homicide rate is double that of Northern Ireland and more than ten times those of the remaining industrial nations.

5.35
Sentenced prisoners
Selected states, 1996
Prisoners per 100,000 resident population

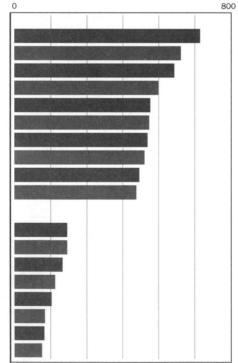

Source: Bureau of Justice Statistics.

The Centers for Disease Control reports that among twenty-six industrialized countries, the U.S. leads the industrial world in homicides of youth under the age of 15, accounting for 73 percent of all such homicides. They note that "the homicide rate for children in the United States was five times higher than that for children in the other 25 countries combined."

Good News Tempered.   The recent decline in the most violent forms of crime brings a sense of relief to the nation, long accustomed to steady increases. From a comparative perspective, however, these improvements are only a beginning. Hopefully, the recent declines will continue, and problems such as youth crime and youth victimization will be addressed.

The high rates of incarceration also need to be considered. With "one in every 155 Americans behind bars," and with those numbers increasing every year, we need to reflect upon the direction in which the nation is headed, and the long-term implications of such high levels of imprisonment.

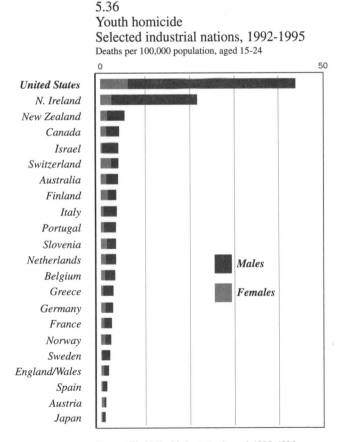

5.36
Youth homicide
Selected industrial nations, 1992-1995
Deaths per 100,000 population, aged 15-24

Source: *World Health Statistics Annual*, 1995, 1996.

Chapter Six

Indicators of Shifting Performance

Much can be learned about the nation's social health from indicators whose performance has shifted significantly over time. For some indicators this has occurred at one critical point; for others there have been periodic shifts. These course changes have been brought about by a number of factors, including social policy interventions, attitudinal changes in the society, and the cyclical nature of the economy. The indicators showing shifting performance are:

> Teenage drug use
> Teenage births
> Alcohol-related traffic fatalities
> Affordable housing
> Unemployment

Both teenage drug use and teenage births have experienced several shifts caused by social policy and changes in attitude. Teenage drug use, at its peak during the late 1970s, was addressed by a variety of interventions, and improved during the 1980s. With fewer interventions during the 1990s, it has begun to worsen once again. In contrast, the rate of teenage births rose during the 1980s but has fallen during each of the past six years.

Drunk driving and its consequent dangers have been the object of large public information campaigns, increased sanctions, and changing social attitudes. Rates of alcohol-related traffic fatalities, high during the 1970s, dropped sharply during the 1980s and 1990s.

Both housing costs and unemployment reflect the cycles of the economy. Unemployment peaked during the past two recessions, but has dropped to new lows in recent years. Housing costs, which rose sharply during the 1980s, have once again become more affordable.

The indicators charted in the following pages suggest how issues may change course when influenced by public policy, social attitudes, and macroeconomic factors. They illustrate the sensitivity of social indicators to outside forces and offer insight into the way in which they change over time.

By their late twenties, 70% of ... American young adults today have tried an illicit drug ....
Three out of ten young Americans have tried cocaine ... by the age of 30 .... Despite the
improvements between 1979 and 1991, it is still true that this nation's secondary school
students and young adults show a level of involvement with illicit drugs which is greater
than has been documented in any other industrialized nation in the world.
—Monitoring the Future Study, National Survey Results on Drug Use, *1997*

Teenage Drug Use

■ The U.S. performance in addressing teenage drug use has been
mixed. After improving during the 1980s, drug use has once again
worsened during the 1990s. In 1996, more than 40 percent of all high
school seniors reported having used some form of illicit drug during
the past twelve months.

■ Drug use has been increasing among junior high and early high
school students. In 1996, almost a quarter of all eighth graders and
more than a third of tenth graders said they had used illicit drugs in the
past year, almost double the percentage five years earlier.

■ Drug use has increased among college-age youth. In 1995, more
than one-third of all college students had used some form of illicit
drug in the past year.

Reemergence in the Nineties. Drug use among youth first emerged as a national and international issue in the late 1960s, during the Vietnam War. The problem reached record levels in the late 1970s, tapered off during the 1980s, but rose once again during the mid-1990s.

Drug use creates a distinctive set of problems for young people. Serious abuse can create a climate of alienation, making it difficult to navigate successfully through adolescence. Heavy drug use, particularly when begun at young ages, may cause a lifetime of problems, including suicide, crime, failure to complete school, impairment of health, and the disruption and endangerment of future careers and families.

Teenage drug use is measured by two major federal surveys. One, the *Monitoring the Future Study*, surveys young people from eighth grade through post-college. The other, the *National Household Survey*, studies the whole population and reports its findings by age-group.

Both surveys found a decline in drug use during the 1980s and a rise during the 1990s. *Monitoring the Future* reported that 40.2 percent of twelfth graders had used drugs during 1996, an increase from a low of 27.1 percent in 1992. The *National Household Survey* found declines in drug use among 12-17 year-olds between 1979

6.1
Drug use among twelfth graders
Percent using any illicit drug in past 12 months

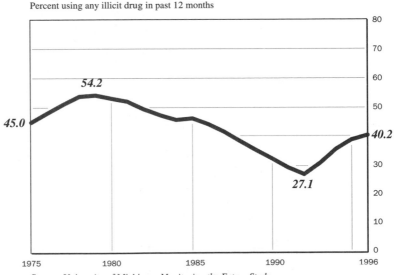

Source: University of Michigan, *Monitoring the Future Study.*

and 1992 and increases thereafter, with only a slight improvement in 1996.

Increases Among the Very Young.   Drug use today can begin quite early. In junior high as well as early high school, students face serious choices about the use of drugs. In some parts of the country, communities have responded by trying to create drug-free schools or drug-free zones. These programs include serious penalties for any use of drugs, but peer pressure at these younger ages still can be intense.

Because drug use has trickled down to these younger ages, *Monitoring the Future* began measuring drug use among eighth and tenth graders in 1991. Since that time, they have found significant increases. Between 1991 and 1996, annual use of illicit drugs more than doubled among eighth graders, going from 11.3 percent to 23.6 percent. Among tenth graders, more than one-third were found to have used illicit drugs, an increase of 75 percent since 1991.

For some, the use of drugs at these younger ages may be experimentation that will taper off. For others, however, it may create a pattern of abuse which can lead to seriously debilitating consequences for their health and education.

College Age and Beyond.   Similar to eighth, tenth, and twelfth graders, college students and youth between the ages of 18-25 were found to reduce their drug use during the 1980s. These groups also showed increases during the 1990s, though these were smaller than among the lower grades.

Monitoring the Future reports that drug use among college students declined by 48

6.2
Drug use among eighth and tenth graders
Percent using any illicit drug in past 12 months

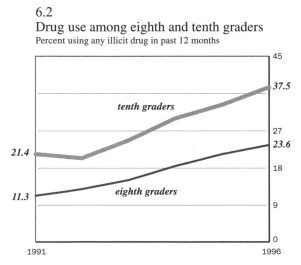

Source: University of Michigan, *Monitoring the Future Study.*

percent between 1980 and 1991, then rose by 17 percent through 1996. In 1991, 29.2 percent reported using illicit drugs. By 1996, the proportion had risen to 34.2.

Like their counterparts at younger ages, college students report that many drugs are easily accessible. Because of recent increases, college campuses may now be getting tougher on drug issues. A 1997 study by the *Chronicle of Higher Education* surveyed 489 campuses on drug issues, and reported that campus drug arrests had increased by 18 percent over the previous year.

The *National Household Survey's* study of a similar age group, but including young people not in college, finds that overall, 18-25 year-olds decreased their use of drugs during the past 18 years. In 1979, 45.5 percent reported using drugs; by 1996, it was only slightly more than 25 percent. This survey shows only a slight increase during the 1990s.

Marijuana Use and Attitude Changes.   While the use of most drugs grew during the 1990s, the drug that accounted for the sharpest recent increases was marijuana. Most other drugs are used more sparingly, but marijuana use increased at all grade levels between 1991 and 1996. Among eighth graders, annual use tripled, from 6 percent to 18 percent; among tenth graders it doubled, from 17 percent to 34 percent; and among twelfth graders, use increased by almost two-thirds, from 24 percent to 39 percent.

Monitoring the Future assesses not only the use of drugs but also attitudes toward them. They have found a consistent relationship between the perception of potential

6.3
Drug use among college students and 18-25 year-olds
Percent using any illicit drug in past 12 months

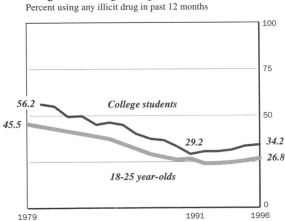

Sources: College students: University of Michigan, *Monitoring the Future Study;*
18-25 year-olds: U.S.Department of Health and Human Services,
National Household Survey on Drug Abuse.

harm from drugs and the tendency to use them. In the case of marijuana, a perception of greater risk preceded its declining use among twelfth graders during the 1980s; a perception of less risk preceded its wider use during the 1990s. The change served, in effect, as a warning sign or leading indicator, showing that reservations were either "hardening" or "softening," and that behaviors were shifting.

Among factors that *Monitoring the Future* considers influential in creating these attitudes are the national campaign opposing drug use and media influences favoring use, particularly messages communicated by favorite youth figures in film and music.

International Concerns.   Standardized comparative data on drug use are unavailable, but international concerns over teenage drug use are widespread. In 1998, a fifty-three member commission on drugs established by the United Nations met for eight days to begin to design strategies to address rising drug problems. The group considered most "at risk" was youth, and data indicate that there are youth drug problems in virtually every nation of the world, concentrated particularly, but not exclusively, in urban centers. Severe drug problems among youth have been reported in countries as diverse as Great Britain, Cuba, China, Russia, Indonesia, Australia, and Kuwait. In the worst cases, drugs are contributing to rising AIDS rates among youth because of shared needles or prostitution. In countries with weak economies, youth drug abuse has become particularly rampant. In Russia, for example, studies report

6.4
Marijuana use and perceived harm
Percent using marijuana/hashish in past 12 months
and perceived harm in smoking regularly, twelfth graders

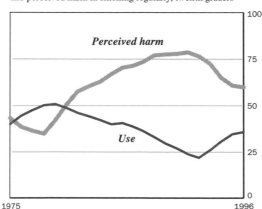

Source: The University of Michigan, *Monitoring the Future Study.*

that as many as one of every three schoolchildren between the ages of 7-9 may already be using drugs.

Drug Use Implications   The youth drug problem demonstrates the effects that a concerted national effort can have. Public information campaigns and educational programs appear to have made some difference during the 1980s in reducing the prevalence of drug use among young people. With the diminution of those efforts, substance abuse began to resume.

As *Monitoring the Future* notes, "The nation does have the capacity to deal quite effectively with the drug problem. It has done it before." The principal investigator warns: "I hope that we have learned from the relapse in the drug epidemic in the 1990s that drug use among kids is a persistent and recurring problem—one which needs consistent and unremitting attention." He observes that with the substantial declines in drug use during the late 1970s and 1980s, young people had fewer opportunities to observe firsthand the adverse consequences of drug use. Such "generational forgetting," combined with fewer national public policy efforts, may precipitate an increase in use.

Moreover, studies indicate that it is not the supply side of the equation which appears to have changed. Young people's perceptions of the availability of drugs have remained fairly stable. What has shifted over time is demand, or the desire for drugs, based on changing perceptions about the attractiveness of drugs.

It would appear that the several turn-abouts in youth drug use reflect, at least in part, changing societal efforts toward drug use. They illustrate as well that the problem is not insoluble or intractable, but is instead responsive to major efforts and investments.

The children of adolescent parents are more likely to suffer poor health,
to lag in school, and to become teenage parents themselves.
—Starting Points: Meeting the Needs of our Youngest Children,
Carnegie Task Force, 1994

Teenage Births

■ Teenage births in the United States are now improving after worsening for several years. The teenage birth rate was on a steady downward course during the 1960s and early 1970s, remained stable from the mid-1970s through the mid-1980s, then rose during the late 1980s, but has been improving once again since 1992.

■ Teenage births are associated with multiple problems for the offspring. One of the most significant concerns is the high rate of preterm and low-weight births, which increase the likelihood of physical disability, sensory disorders, mental retardation, and chronic illness.

■ Teenage births are associated with multiple problems for the parents. Significant problems include failure to complete school and low earnings.

Family Redefined.   During the Baby Boom era of the 1950s, large families were
commonplace, two-parent households were the norm, and many people married and
started their families very young. Since that time, family life has changed dramatically. The average number of children per family has dropped from a record high of
3.7 in 1957 to approximately 2 today. Both women and men are older when they
marry. Single-parent households are commonplace.

For many adults, these changes have created new choices, including the freedom
to delay marriage or to have a child on their own. For teenagers, however, the choice
of parenthood may become a complex of physical, social, and economic difficulties
for themselves and their children.

The proportion of teenagers who become parents has shifted sharply over time.
From 1960 through the mid-1970s, birth rates among teenagers dropped steadily,
then remained relatively stable between the mid-1970s and the mid-1980s. Between
1986 and 1991, birth rates increased sharply. Since 1992 they have once again begun
to drop.

Despite increases in the last decade, the rate of childbearing among adolescents is
lower today than it was in 1960 or 1970, although it remains slightly higher than 1980.
In 1996, adolescent birth rates were 54.4 per 1,000 women aged 15-19, for a total of
491,577 births. This represents a 39 percent decrease since 1960, a 20 percent decrease since 1970, and a 3 percent increase since 1980.

6.5
Teenage births

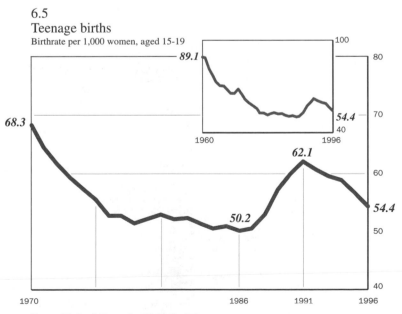

Source: National Center for Health Statistics.

Lingering Issues.   Although the rate of teenage births has been improving significantly, two important issues remain: continuing high birth rates for minority teenagers and continuing high rates of unwed births.

Among all births to teenagers, white births account for the largest proportion, almost half. Black and Hispanic births each make up approximately one quarter. In contrast to the numbers, however, the rate of teenage births among minorities is substantially higher, more than twice as high as that of white teenagers. These rates may cause undue problems in educational completion and job retention for minority youth. All racial and ethnic groups have shown declining teenage birth rates in recent years, but the greatest decline has been among blacks. This has begun to narrow the difference.

A second concern has been the rate of unwed parenthood, which continues to be high in America for both older and younger women. The rate of births to unmarried teenagers aged 15 to 19 was 42.9 per 1,000 women in 1996, almost double the rate of 22.4 births in 1970.

The high rate of unwed parenthood among teenagers precisely mirrors the rate among women in the population as a whole. The 1996 teenage rate was approximately two percentage points below the rate for all women in their childbearing years. Unwed parenthood is not limited to teenagers; teenagers represent less than one-third of all unwed births.

Although rates of teenage unwed births continue to be high, like the teenage birth-

6.6
Teenage births by race/ethnicity
and marital status, 1996

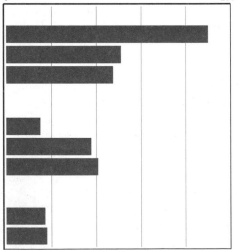

Number of births to women aged 15-19	
White Non-Hispanic	225,197
Black Non-Hispanic	127,616
Hispanic	118,878
Rate of births to women aged 15-19/per 1,000	
White Non-Hispanic	37.6
Black Non-Hispanic	94.2
Hispanic	101.8
Rate of unwed parenthood/per 1,000	
Aged 15-19	42.9
Aged 14-44	44.8

Source: National Center for Health Statistics.
Note: White and black rates differ from those in Appendix
because of the additional breakdown here by Hispanic origin.

rate as a whole, there have been declines during the 1990s. The largest declines have been among black women, both teenagers and adults.

Associated Problems.   Teenage parenthood carries with it several important risks. Among them, for the infant, is the danger of being born preterm and low birthweight. The risk of bearing a low birthweight infant is higher for young mothers than for any other age except for women in their late forties. Low birthweight infants have far higher rates of disability, sensory disorders, mental retardation, chronic illness, and death. The birth of a low weight infant may severely complicate the lives of young parents and increase their financial and medical burdens.

For the parents, there are also other problems. Individuals who begin families in their teenage years often face serious educational and economic hurdles. Failure to complete school is one common result; low income and poverty are others. According to the National Educational Longitudinal Studies, 62 percent of all high school age females who had babies dropped out of school at some point in their high school careers, 25 percent prior to their pregnancy, and 37 percent after their pregnancy. Only 38 percent did not drop out at all.

Young parents also face serious financial problems, more so than in the past. In 1970, the median income of families with household head aged 15-24 was just under $27,000.

6.7
Low birthweight by age, 1996
Percent

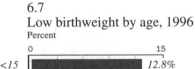
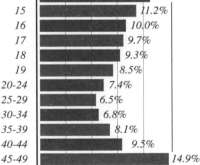

Source: National Center for Health
Statistics.

6.8
Dropout rates, median income, and poverty rates by teenage birth or family type, 1994-1996

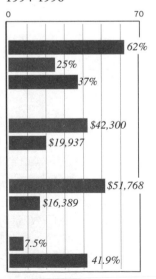

Sources: Dropout rates: Child Trends,
Inc.; Median income and poverty
rates: U.S. Bureau of the Census.
Note: With children—under 18
years of age.

Today, in constant dollars, those same families have a median income of only $19,937. This is less than half the median income for all families, which was $42,300. For young women who become single parents, the prospects for economic well-being are even more difficult. In 1996, female single-parent households had a median income of $16,389 per year, compared to $51,768 for married couples with children. More than 40 percent of all female-headed families with children had incomes below the poverty line.

State Differences.   The various states have very different teenage birth rates. Cultural and historical patterns may account for some of the variation. The highest teenage birth rate in 1996 was in Mississippi at 75.5 per 1,000 women. Other states with high rates were Arkansas, Arizona, Texas, New Mexico, and Nevada, all in the West or South. The lowest rate was New Hampshire's 28.6 per 1,000 women. Other states with low rates were Vermont, Maine, Minnesota, Massachusetts, and North Dakota, most in the East or Midwest.

International Differences.   Parenthood at a young age is a common phenomenon in developing countries. While the percentage of young or very young women bearing a child before the age of 18 is dropping, it remains high, causing serious hurdles to educational and economic advancement. The proportion of women having babies before age 18 was 53 percent in Niger, 47 percent in Bangladesh, and 46 percent in Cameroon.

In industrial countries, teenage parenthood is far rarer, but the United States is on the high end of the scale. According to the Alan Guttmacher Institute's analysis of the inter-

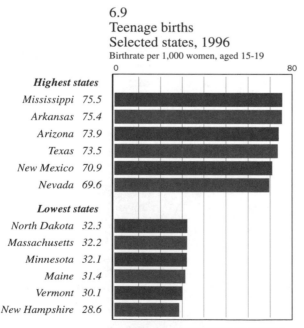

6.9
Teenage births
Selected states, 1996
Birthrate per 1,000 women, aged 15-19

Highest states	
Mississippi	75.5
Arkansas	75.4
Arizona	73.9
Texas	73.5
New Mexico	70.9
Nevada	69.6
Lowest states	
North Dakota	32.3
Massachusetts	32.2
Minnesota	32.1
Maine	31.4
Vermont	30.1
New Hampshire	28.6

Source: National Center for Health Statistics.

national Demographic and Health Survey (DHS), which studied six industrial nations, the U.S. ranked highest with 9 percent, Great Britain second with 6 percent, France with 2 percent, and Germany, Japan, and Poland with 1 percent. Among the factors in the higher U.S. rate are early sexual activity and unwed parenthood.

Causes or Consequences?   One of the most serious concerns about teenage child-bearing is its relationship to poverty. Analysts differ, however, in their assessment of the relationship. Some argue that teenage births cause later-life poverty. Others believe the reverse, that poverty and its associated problems cause early births.

The Alan Guttmacher Institute, for example, reports that "there is little difference in levels of sexual activity among adolescents of different income levels," but notes that lower-income youth have many more births. Poor teenagers' more limited use and access to contraception and abortion may lead to higher birthrates. Teenage childbearing, they argue, is a product of "early disadvantage."

The need for greater clarity on this issue is critical, for if childbearing is the cause of poverty, then changes in sexual practices become more significant. However, if poverty is the more fundamental cause, then a very different set of approaches are needed, ones which are social and economic.

What we do know, is that teenage parenthood is in many ways like teenage drug use. It has responded to external social pressures. Recently, as social disapproval has heightened and new programs have been implemented, the proportion of teenagers engaging in sexual activity at early ages has diminished and the use of contraception has increased. There is good evidence to show, as with teen drug use, that prevention and education programs do make some difference in the choices teenagers make.

6.10
Teenage births
Selected industrial nations, 1991-1995
Percent of women, aged 20-24, who gave birth by age 18

Source: Alan Guttmacher Institute.

About three in every ten Americans will be involved
in an alcohol-related crash at sometime in their lives.
—National Highway Traffic Safety Administration
Traffic Safety Facts, *1996*

Alcohol-Related Traffic Fatalities

■   The rate of alcohol-related traffic fatalities has shown a marked
shift over time, with improving performance during the last decade.
Alcohol-related traffic fatalities fell during the late 1980s and 1990s
by 24 percent, after rising by 19 percent during the 1970s through the
mid 1980s.

■   Motor vehicle crashes are the leading cause of death among
young people between the ages of 1 and 24. More than 30 percent of
these crashes are alcohol-related.

■   The National Highway Traffic Safety Administration ranks minimum drinking age laws as a major factor in lowering alcohol-related
traffic fatalities. They estimate that since 1975, 16,513 lives have
been saved by such laws.

Nearly a Decade of Improvement.   Traffic accidents are the leading cause of death among people aged 1-24 and the fourth leading cause of death among adults aged 25-44. Alcohol plays a role in more than 30 percent of these accidents. Because of the seriousness of this issue, the United States has made a concerted effort to reduce the number of traffic crashes and alcohol-related fatalities. This effort has met with considerable success.

Policies such as raising the minimum drinking age, lowering maximum speed limits, criminal charges for serving liquor to the intoxicated, license suspensions for drunk driving, mandatory breathalyzer tests, designated-driver practices, enforced safety-belt use, and increased public awareness, have reduced both the number and seriousness of drunk-driving accidents. These policies have saved thousands of lives.

The Alcohol Epidemiologic Data System (AEDS) is a branch of the National Institute on Alcohol Abuse and Alcoholism. It is the only monitoring system which provides data going back to the 1970s. AEDS reports that alcohol-related fatalities are now at their lowest point, 33.2 percent, approximately the same as in 1977, and down from a high of 43.5 in 1986.

Fatal Accident Reporting System.   The Fatal Accident Reporting System is a component of the National Highway Traffic Safety Administration. It provides an additional monitoring system for alcohol-related traffic accidents dating back to 1986.

6.11
Alcohol-related traffic fatalities
Percent alcohol-related, Alcohol Epidemiological Data System (AEDS)

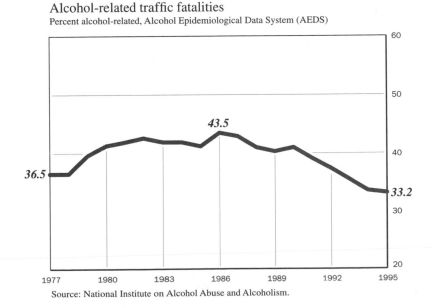

Source: National Institute on Alcohol Abuse and Alcoholism.

This system counts nondriver as well as driver alcoholism and therefore reports slightly higher figures than AEDS. It shows a parallel decline between 1986 and 1996, from 52.2 percent to 40.9 percent.

During the past three years the rate of decline has tapered off. The National Safety Council has warned that new higher speed limits are a concern, and cautions that traffic crashes and alcohol-related fatalities may rise in the future, if additional speeding limits are eliminated.

Deaths Are Still High, Injuries Severe.   Despite substantial improvements in reducing the proportion of alcohol-related traffic fatalities, the actual number of deaths which occur each year is still high. In 1995, 13,881 traffic deaths were recorded by the Alcohol Epidemiologic Data System as alcohol-related. The Fatal Accident Reporting System recorded 17,126 deaths in 1996, including pedestrians, approximately one alcohol-related traffic fatality in America every thirty-one minutes.

Even when people do not die from traffic crashes, they may sustain serious and permanent injuries, including head wounds, spinal cord injuries, multiple fractures, and impairment of sight or hearing. The National Highway Traffic Safety Administration estimates that in 1996, more than 321,000 persons were injured in traffic crashes where police reported that alcohol was present. This was an average of one person injured in America every two minutes.

6.12
Alcohol-related traffic fatalities, AEDS and FARS
Percent alcohol-related

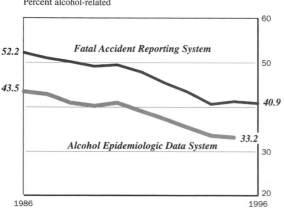

Sources: National Institute on Alcohol Abuse and Alcoholism;
National Highway Traffic Safety Administration.

Who and When?   Among those who die in traffic accidents, the toll is greatest among young adults. People between the ages of 21 and 34 have the highest rate of alcohol-related fatalities, although the proportion is dropping for all ages. In 1996, among 21-24 year olds, 27 percent of all traffic crashes were alcohol-related, down from 36 percent in 1986. Among 25-34 years olds, 26 percent were alcohol-related in 1996, down from 33 percent in 1986.

Males continue to have higher rates of alcohol-related fatalities than females, although rates for both males have females have declined. In 1996, the proportion of alcohol-related fatalities for males was 21 percent, down from 29 percent in 1986. For females, 11 percent of fatal accidents were alcohol-related, a drop from 15 percent in 1986.

Fatal car crashes involving alcohol occur most often on weekends and at night. The most dangerous time of the week is midnight to 3 A.M., Saturday night. During the nighttime, 50 percent of all crashes are alcohol-related, compared to 12 percent

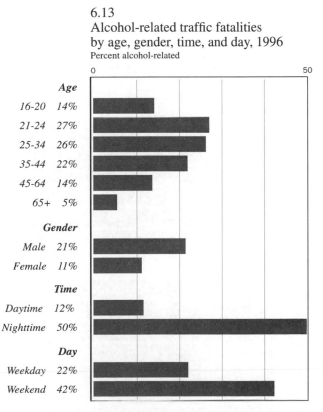

6.13
Alcohol-related traffic fatalities
by age, gender, time, and day, 1996
Percent alcohol-related

Source: National Highway Traffic Safety Administration.

during the day. On weekends, 42 percent of all crashes are alcohol-related, compared to 22 percent during the week. These findings clearly indicate that the times when the greatest vigilance is needed are nights and weekends.

State Differences.   There are significant differences in alcohol-related traffic fatalities by state. Estimates are provided by the Fatal Accident Reporting System. Some of these differences may be due to such factors as population demographics, urbanization, and the types of vehicles driven. The highest rates are found North Dakota, Texas, Louisiana, Alaska, New Mexico, and Washington. States with the lowest rates include Utah, Ohio, Maryland, New York, Nebraska, and Idaho.

Saving Lives.   Each of the many policies devoted to curbing drunk driving has contributed to lowering alcohol-related fatalities, but the minimum drinking age laws may have contributed the most. The National Highway Traffic Safety Administration estimates that minimum drinking age laws have saved 16,513 lives since 1975, many of them young lives. All states and the District of Columbia now use age 21 as the minimum drinking age.

Despite the effectiveness of minimum drinking laws as well as the several other mea-

6.14
Alcohol-related traffic fatalities
Selected states, 1996
Percent alcohol-related

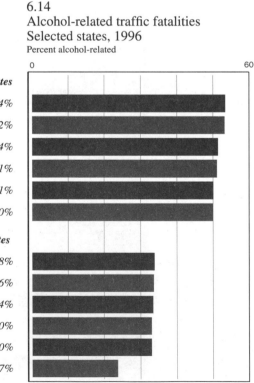

Source: National Highway Traffic Safety Administration.

sures taken, advocates for safe driving believe that their message is no longer being heard as it has been in the recent past. The current slowdown in the rate of improvement suggests that fewer people are listening and the message may be getting "old."

Like the concerns over rising teenage drug use, it is suspected that the very successes of the movement have led to a dulling of concern, as fewer people see firsthand the devastation that drunk driving can create. Also similar to concerns over drugs, those who have been involved suggest that only through continued vigilance and strong media attention can lower rates of alcohol-related fatalities be maintained.

Future Gains? Thus far, the decline in alcohol-related traffic fatalities represents a remarkable achievement in public policy and public awareness. It demonstrates that with a strong public-information campaign and the cooperation of state governments, behavior can be altered and lives saved. Alcohol-related traffic fatalities are a danger to the entire society and no one is immune. That motor vehicle deaths remain the leading cause of death among young people, outranking all diseases, suggests that a serious public health concern is at issue here. Hopefully, signs pointing to a slowdown will not continue, the safety messages will still be heard, and the gains made and lives saved will be furthered.

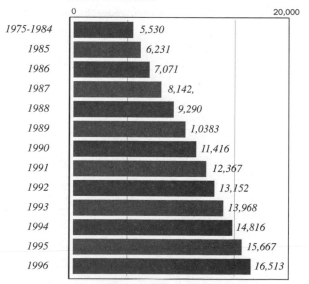

6.15
Cumulative estimated lives saved
by minimum drinking age laws
Number of lives saved

1975-1984	5,530
1985	6,231
1986	7,071
1987	8,142,
1988	9,290
1989	1,0383
1990	11,416
1991	12,367
1992	13,152
1993	13,968
1994	14,816
1995	15,667
1996	16,513

Source: National Highway Traffic Safety Administration.

The Congress hereby declares that the general welfare and security of the Nation and the health and living standards of its people require . . . the realization . . . of the goal of a decent home and a suitable living environment for every American family, thus contributing to the development and redevelopment of communities and to the advancement of the growth, wealth, and security of the Nation.
—Housing Act of 1949

Affordable Housing

■ In the United States, housing prices today are just slightly less affordable than they were in 1970. Home buying, relatively inexpensive during the early 1970s, became significantly more costly by the early 1980s. During the mid- 1980s and 1990s, the cost of housing gradually returned to more affordable levels.

■ Home ownership remains more difficult today for young families than it was during the early 1970s. A smaller proportion of young families, 33.9 percent in 1995 compared to 43.6 percent in 1973, were able to buy a home.

■ Rental costs remain high and the stock of low-cost housing is declining. A record 5.3 million low-income households have "worst case needs"—either spending 50 percent or more of their income on rental housing or living in severely substandard housing.

The American Dream.   Home ownership has deep symbolic meaning for Americans. Beyond the practical provision of private space and the investment value of property, home ownership signifies membership in the on-going life of a community.

The purchase of a first home is often viewed as a milestone in one's life, measured in the number of years taken to accomplish the feat. One of the more significant achievements of the post-World-War-II economy was to make home ownership possible for millions of Americans who would have been unable to buy a home in the past.

Since 1970, housing affordability has taken several turns. All measures show that during the early 1970s, housing was relatively affordable. Homes became more expensive by the 1980s, but once again become more accessible during the 1990s.

One measure demonstrating this pattern is the National Association of Realtor's Housing Affordability Index. This Index estimates the likelihood that a typical American family, measured by median income, could afford the national median-priced home with a 20 percent down payment. A score of 100 means a typical family would have just enough, a score above 100 means they should have more than enough, and a score below 100 means they would have less than enough. In 1970, the Index was a relatively good 147.3. The Index then declined to a poor 68.9 during the early 1980s, but it has since risen to 130.8 in 1996, showing that housing has become quite affordable once again.

6.16
Housing affordability index
Twenty percent downpayment on median priced home as percent of median family income, all buyers

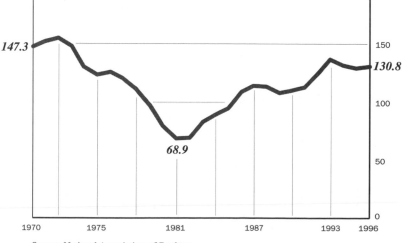

Source: National Association of Realtors.

Homeownership Rates.   What percentage of Americans own their own homes? In spite of the numerous changes in housing affordability since the 1970s, this percentage of homeowners in the nation has remained remarkably steady. In 1973, 64.4 percent of Americans owned homes. In 1996, 65.4 percent did. The figure has not moved under 64 percent or over 66 percent during the entire period. Part of the stability of these figures, of course, is that people own homes for long periods of time and homeowners do not shift that quickly. But, the figures also show that despite substantial pressures on incomes during much of this period, homebuying continued. The slight uptick in the figures for 1996 reflects increasing affordability. Small improvements in the 1990s can be seen for all groups, although minorities remain substantially below the homeownership rates of whites.

For the Young.   Although the proportion of Americans who own a home has remained stable, the nature of this population has changed. Today, fewer young people and more older people own homes, and it is far more difficult for young families to purchase homes today than it was in the past. Because the income of young workers has actually declined—in constant dollars—young families today can rarely afford to buy their own home. Since 1973, among those aged 25-29, home ownership declined by 22 percent, from a high of 43.6 percent in 1973 to 33.9 in 1995. For those under age 25, home ownership has declined by 39 percent, dropping from 23.4 to 14.2 per-

6.17
Homeownership by race and ethnicity
Percent of population owning a home

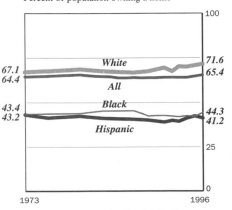

Source: Joint Center for Housing Studies,
Harvard University.

6.18
Homeownership of young adults
Percent of age group owning a home

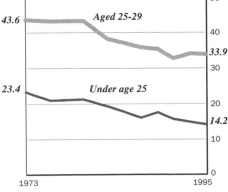

Source: Joint Center for Housing Studies,
Harvard University.

cent. While a home is not a necessity for young families, it is worth noting that the opportunity to own one came earlier in life for many families in the past than it does today.

Among Renters.   Like the situation for the young, the housing picture for renters has worsened. According to the Joint Center for Housing Studies at Harvard University, widening inequality has produced a sharp gap between high-income owners and low-income renters. The number of renter households with incomes of $10,000 or less, in constant dollars, has risen from 7 million to 10 million over the past twenty years, an increase of 43 percent.

Since 1975, unlike the homeownership situation, the renter cost burden—rent as a proportion of income—has failed to improve, both for the contracted rent, and for the gross rent which includes utilities, insurance, and taxes. Between 1975 and 1996, the average contract rent rose from 22 percent of income to 23.7 percent in 1996. Gross rent has risen from 25.3 percent to 27.1 percent of income.

Worst Case Needs.   The Department of Housing and Urban Development (HUD) regularly tracks what it calls "worst case needs," households of "very-low-income" renters who receive no federal housing assistance and either pay more than half of their income for housing and/or live in severely substandard housing.

HUD's most recent analysis, the 1997 report to Congress entitled "Rental Housing Assistance—The Crisis Continues," found that "despite robust economic growth between 1993 and 1995," the number of worst case needs remained at an "all-time high" of 5.3 million households, or a total of 12.5 million individuals. Approximately 1.5 million of these individuals were elderly, 4.5 million were children, and between 1.1 and 1.4 million were people with disabilities.

Between 1991 and 1995, according to HUD, worst case needs increased fastest among working households. Approximately 1.4 million households had incomes equivalent to what a full-time worker would earn at the minimum wage. This was an increase of 265,000 or 24 percent in worst case needs among those who work.

Another area of increasing difficulty is in the suburbs. Traditionally, worst case needs were most often found in central cities, but now one out of three occurs in the suburbs. Suburban worst case households have increased by 9 percent since 1991.

Worst case needs represent a significant problem for the nation. The 5.3 million households with worst case needs equal 4.9 percent of the nation's population and over one-seventh of all U.S. renters. That these problems should be so severe in the midst of an economic recovery is troubling, and according to HUD, means that "economic growth alone will not ameliorate the record-level housing needs among families with limited incomes. Not even families working full-time at the minimum wage can afford decent quality housing in the private rental market ."

Low-Cost Housing Availability.   One factor contributing to the rise in worst case
needs is the declining availability of low-cost housing. Finding low-cost housing represents one of the great hurdles facing young people and those with low incomes.
Overall, the number of people needing low-income housing has risen steadily since
the 1970s, while the supply of available low-cost housing has dwindled. The growing
gap between need and demand has made the task of finding low-cost shelter one of the
most insurmountable in the housing market.

According to the Center on Budget and Policy Priorities, in 1970 there was a surplus of 300,000 low-rent units. There were 6.2 million low-income renters compared
to 6.5 million low-income units. By 1995, the situation had dramatically reversed,
creating a shortage. There were now 10.5 million low-income renters but only 6.1
million units they could afford, a shortfall of 4.4 million units. The gap between units
and people is considered by many to be a crisis. It has contributed to rising costs for
rental housing because need exceeds supply, putting further pressures on low-income
Americans.

The Department of Housing and Urban Development reports that between 1993
and 1995 alone, the supply of low-cost housing declined by 9 percent. Even more severely, the supply of units available for "extremely-low-income renters" declined by
16 percent.

6.19
Low-income renters and low-rent units
In millions

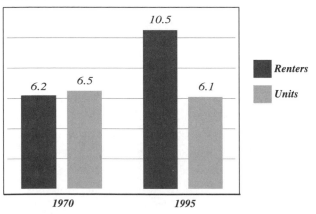

Source: Center on Budget and Policy Priorities.

Homelessness.   One of the most troubling problems to emerge in recent years is homelessness. Coupled with the high cost and shortage of low-income housing have been several other factors which have contributed to this problem, including continuing high poverty rates, deinstitutionalization of the mentally ill, low veteran's incomes, and an increase in low-wage jobs.

There are no comprehensive estimates of the numbers of homeless in America, and the reliability of homeless counts has been the subject of controversy. Estimates vary from 500,000-700,000 homeless people in shelters at a given "point-in-time" to telephone surveys during the early 1990s which produced estimates of 7 million people homeless "at some point" in their life. The Clinton Administration's estimates for the nation's homeless population was initially 4.95-9.32 million; a revision increased the top estimate to as many as 12 million persons. HUD cites estimates that families with children now exceed 30 percent of the homeless population.

A Decent Home For Every American.   The affordability of a single-family home has returned to the levels of the 1970s and the home-ownership situation has improved, but many related housing problems have worsened or failed to improve, including the decline in home ownership among the young, the cost and availability of affordable rental units, and the continuation of homelessness.

In 1949, this nation made a commitment to provide a decent home and suitable living environment for every American. This is a promise only partially fulfilled. Because home prices are once again declining, it is worthwhile to consider the needs of the low-cost housing market. That a substantial number of people are paying a high proportion of their income for housing—50 percent or more—is an unsolved problem that reverberates to other issues in the nation, including the purchase of adequate food, health care, clothing, educational resources, and recreation. The high cost of housing weakens the quality of life for many in the nation and is a problem that still needs to be addressed.

> *The Congress hereby declares that it is the continuing policy and*
> *responsibility of the government . . . to promote maximum*
> *employment, production, and purchasing power.*
> —Employment Act of 1946

Unemployment

■ Over time, the unemployment rate in America has paralleled the business cycle, rising and falling with recessions and recoveries. In 1996, the unemployment rate was a low 5.4 percent of the civilian labor force.

■ Youth and minorities continue to experience high rates of unemployment. In 1996, youth unemployment was 16.7 percent, three times the national average, while black unemployment was 10.5 percent, almost twice the national average.

■ The unemployment rate in the United states in 1996 was much better than in other industrial nations. Many had far higher unemployment figures of between 8 to 12 percent.

Work in America.   To be gainfully employed in America is to have a place in this society. The concept of work is threaded through the most fundamental beliefs of the nation, embodying an expectation of plentiful opportunity and fair rewards for those willing to invest their efforts.

Today, the benefits of work are open to many as the availability of jobs has risen. Yet, for others, work is still difficult to find, and unrewarding when found, with long hours spent for low wages and few or no benefits. The contingent work force has increased as well, shifting people in and out of temporary, part-time, and part-year jobs with little job security. The larger employment picture has improved with the growing economy, but many aspects are still troublesome.

Over the past two and one-half decades, the unemployment rate has basically mirrored the business cycle, rising during recessions and falling during economic recoveries. The unemployment rate in 1996 was a low 5.4 percent, only slightly higher than the 1970 rate of 4.9 percent, and far better than during the peaks of the 1980s, when unemployment reached a high of 9.7. Unemployment has continued to improve significantly with the growing economy, dropping below 5 percent for much of the most recent period.

Inching Up Over Time.   Between 1950 and 1980, each recessionary period had a larger impact on unemployment. The unemployment rate per decade rose steadily

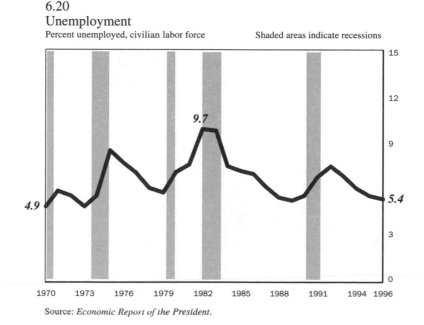

6.20
Unemployment
Percent unemployed, civilian labor force   Shaded areas indicate recessions

Source: *Economic Report of the President.*

from the 1950s through the 1980s, averaging 4.5 percent for the 1950s, 4.8 percent for the 1960s, 6.2 percent for the 1970s, and 7.3 percent for the 1980s. Between 1990 and 1996, average unemployment was 6.3 percent, a considerable improvement thus far over the 1980s, and a return to the levels of the 1970s.

Still Struggling.   While the average unemployment rate has dropped for the nation as a whole, groups such as youth and minorities continue to experience exceedingly high rates. Both of these problems have persisted and there has been little change in the gap over time.

Like the national average, minority and youth unemployment rates parallel the ups and downs of the business cycle, but at a far higher level. Also like the national average, both groups' unemployment rates today stand just slightly above where they were in 1970. In 1996, unemployment for youth was 16.7 percent; as in 1970, this was triple the national average. For blacks, the 1996 rate was 10.5 percent, almost double the national average. These are areas where progress still needs to be made.

Unemployment Insurance.   Unemployment Insurance was created in 1935 under the *Social Security Act.* Its purpose was to protect worker incomes during periods of job loss and to stabilize the economic system during recessions.

The Unemployment Insurance system protects far fewer of the unemployed today than it did in the past. According to the *Economic Report of the President,* "changes in the economy have . . . had profound effects on the UI [Unemployment Insurance] sys-

6.21
Average unemployment by decade
Percent unemployed

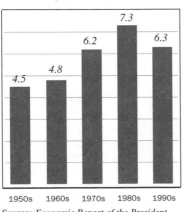

Source: *Economic Report of the President.*
Note: The 1990s are 1990 to 1996.

6.22
Unemployment among youth and minorities
Percent unemployed

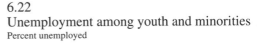
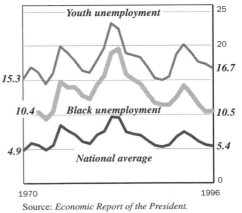

Source: *Economic Report of the President.*

tem. Most notably, the share of unemployed workers who received UI benefits has fallen dramatically . . . . This reduction has been attributed to demographic shifts in the workforce, a reduction in union membership, regional shifts in employment, and tightened State eligibility requirements."

Between 1975 and 1996, Unemployment Insurance coverage declined from 76 percent of the unemployed to 36 percent. This shift makes a period of unemployment a far more treacherous experience. Problems may be lessened during the current recovery, while jobs are relatively more available, but this situation may cause severe problems during a future economic downturn.

Unemployment Duration.   At the same time that Unemployment Insurance has declined, the length of time that people remain out of work has lengthened. In 1970, the average duration of unemployment was 8.6 weeks; in 1996, it was 16.7 weeks, almost double. Correspondingly, the proportion of persons unemployed 27 weeks or more has risen. According to the Bureau of Labor Statistics, the persistence of long-term unemployment is one aspect of the current recovery which differs markedly from previous recoveries.

Variations by State.   Although the nation as a whole has shown major improvements in its unemployment, rates differ fairly markedly between the states. Most states with higher rates in 1996 were in the West and South. The highest included New Mexico, Alaska, West Virginia, California, Louisiana, and Washington. The lowest

6.23
Insured employment
Percent of total employment

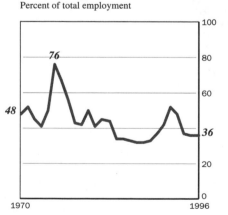

Source: U.S. House of Representatives,
House Ways and Means Committee, *Green Book.*

6.24
Average duration of unemployment
Mean duration in weeks

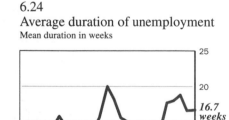

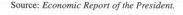

Source: *Economic Report of the President.*

states were mostly in the Midwest and included Nebraska, North and South Dakota, Utah, Wisconsin, and Iowa.

The Contingent Economy.   Many jobs today are "contingent," offering work that is temporary, part-time, part-year, contractual, self-employed, on-call, or day labor. People may have to work several of these jobs to make ends meet and may have to move in and out of these positions on a regular basis.

The contingent economy has not yet been defined in a standardized way. Statistics over time on this segment of the labor market are not currently available, but a recent study, entitled *Nonstandard Work, Substandard Jobs: Flexible Work Arrangements in the U.S.,* reports that 29 percent of the work force is currently employed in what they call nonstandard or contingent jobs, with 34.3 percent of females in such jobs and 25.3 percent of males. They further report that these jobs, overall, tend to be "inferior" to regular full-time work, offering lower pay, fewer benefits, and no job security.

International Rankings.   The proportion of the population unemployed in the United States in 1996 was far lower than in most other industrialized nations. Only Japan, with an unemployment rate of 3.4 percent in 1996 had a rate substantially

6.25
Unemployment
Selected states, 1996
Percent unemployed

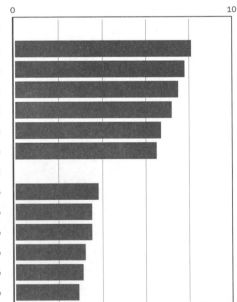

Highest states	
New Mexico	8.1%
Alaska	7.8%
W. Virginia	7.5%
California	7.2%
Louisiana	6.7%
Washington	6.5%
Lowest states	
Iowa	3.8%
Wisconsin	3.5%
Utah	3.5%
S. Dakota	3.2%
N. Dakota	3.1%
Nebraska	2.9%

Source: U.S. Bureau of Labor Statistics.

lower than the U.S., and its rate was rising while the U.S. unemployment rate has continued to fall. Most industrial nations ranged between 7 percent and 12 percent.

As the globalization of the economy speeds up, there will be numerous decisions to be made. It is likely that many nations will continue to experience high unemployment as they restructure their economies to address new needs and situations. The United States is currently well ahead of most other nations in keeping this particular problem in check.

When the Cycle Shifts. The U.S. has made substantial strides in improving its unemployment picture. Yet history suggests that the problem is cyclical and that the picture will likely shift once again. For those groups who still currently experience high unemployment, such as youth and minorities, the ground could become even less secure. The decline in Unemployment Insurance protection is a serious concern, as is the long duration of spells of unemployment. The rising proportion of contingent jobs is also an issue, creating a more volatile employment picture and poorer quality jobs. With an economy that is still changing rapidly, the nature of work as well as the experience of joblessness for specific groups will have to be vigilantly monitored.

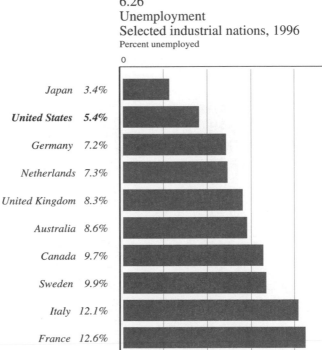

6.26
Unemployment
Selected industrial nations, 1996
Percent unemployed

Japan	3.4%
United States	5.4%
Germany	7.2%
Netherlands	7.3%
United Kingdom	8.3%
Australia	8.6%
Canada	9.7%
Sweden	9.9%
Italy	12.1%
France	12.6%

Source: U.S. Bureau of Labor Statistics.
Note: "Approximating U.S. concepts" series.

Chapter Seven

Judging The Nation's Social Performance

The previous three chapters represent a starting point in the task of framing the nation's social health. They make clear that a great deal has been missing from our public discourse over the past three decades. Much has occurred that has changed the nature and character of our society. Some of the changes have been for the better, many have not, but what is most important is that these movements have been cumulatively invisible to the public and to the makers of policy.

In effect, we carry in our minds a binocular view of our national state, whose two pictures have not focused into a coherent whole. The first picture, derived from economic and business indicators, is highly accessible and officially sanctioned. The second, the social health perspective, remains in the early stages of presentation and recognition. This is dangerous for democracy, because so important a part of the nation's progress and performance remains officially uncharted.

The Nation's Best as a Standard. In Chapter One we argued that developing a social health perspective would require the creation of standards against which the current performance of key indicators could be judged in order to make a rational assessment of how well we are doing as a nation. One approach to creating such a standard is to compare the current performance of each indicator with its best performance in the past. For example, the 1996 rate for child poverty was 19.8 percent. One might argue that this represents progress, since it is better than the previous year's rate. But, comparing our performance to a standard of the best we have ever done—14.2 percent in 1973—provides quite a different view. Judged from this perspective, our current performance is far less impressive.

Using the nation's best past performance as a standard does not necessarily point to where we would want the indicator to be or where our values suggest it should be. Rather, it represents what our society did achieve at one point in its recent history. Implicit in this standard of performance is the idea that if such a level has been reached before, it can be reached again. Thus, past achievement provides a benchmark against which to evaluate current performance and begin to assess future potential.

Over time, the performance of each indicator ranges between the outposts of its best and worst levels. Every year, the indicator either moves closer to its best level or further from it. A few indicators may reach new highs; others may fall to new lows. This approach places the performance of each indicator into perspective. How far is the indicator from its best performance? How much would each indicator have to improve in order to match its best past level? Given its pattern of performance over time, is it likely that such progress will occur in the future?

The following table presents the sixteen indicators that were discussed in Chapters Four to Six. It depicts each indicator's current performance as a proportion of its own "last best," ranging from 0 to 100 percent.

7.1
Indicator performance in 1996 as a percentage
of the "last best" standard

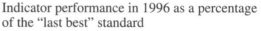

	Worst 0	20	40	60	80	Best 100

Improving Indicators
Infant mortality   100%
Life expectancy, aged 65   100%
Poverty, aged 65+   98%
High school dropouts   98%

Worsening Indicators
Youth suicide   34%
Violent crime   31%
Child poverty   28%
Inequality   5%
Wages   1%
Health care coverage   0%
Child abuse   0%

Shifting Indicators
Alcohol-related traffic fatalities   100%
Unemployment   90%
Teenage births   75%
Affordable housing   72%
Teenage drug use   52%

■ *Current indicator performance*

Source: Fordham Institute for Innovation in Social Policy

Chart 7.1 shows that several indicators now stand at their best point since the 1970s—a performance score of 100 percent. These include infant mortality, life expectancy, and alcohol-related traffic fatalities. Some are very close to their best, such as poverty among the elderly and high school dropouts—at 98 percent. Others are between their best and worst, such as teenage drug use—at 52 percent of its best. Two are at their worst levels ever—child abuse and health care coverage—with a performance score of 0.

Chart 7.2 provides a closer look at the performance of each indicator. It shows the current level of performance (from Chart 7.1), positive and negative performance since 1970—in number of years and average annual change—and the number of years each indicator did not change. The final column suggests each indicator's potential for future improvement.

7.2 Performance patterns in key social indicators, 1970-1996

Indicator	Current Performance	Positive Performance		Negative Performance		No Change Performance	Future Potential
	Percent	*# of Years*	*Average Annual Change*	*# of Years*	*Average Annual Change*	*# of Years*	
Improving Indicators							
Infant mortality	100	26	3.8%	0	0.0%	0	Very good
Life expectancy, aged 65	100	16	1.1%	4	1.0%	6	Very good
Poverty, aged 65+	98	17	6.5%	9	3.8%	0	Very good
HS dropouts	98	13	4.1%	10	2.5%	3	Very good
Worsening Indicators							
Youth suicide	34	11	2.9%	15	4.4%	0	Fair
Violent crime	31	10	3.3%	16	5.8%	0	Fair
Child poverty	28	12	3.1%	14	5.0%	0	Poor
Inequality	5	5	0.8%	19	1.2%	2	Poor
Wages	1	9	1.4%	17	1.6%	0	Poor
Health care coverage	0	5	2.2%	15	3.2%	0	Very poor
Child abuse	0	0	0.0%	18	9.1%	2	Very poor
Shifting Indicators							
Alcohol-related traffic fatalities	100	10	3.1%	6	3.9%	2	Good
Unemployment	90	17	8.3%	9	20.1%	0	Good
Teenage births	75	16	2.9%	9	2.9%	1	Good
Affordable housing	72	14	6.2%	12	7.4%	0	Fair
Teenage drug use	52	12	5.7%	9	6.9%	0	Poor

Table 7.2 reveals some important patterns. Without exception, each of the improving indicators has more years of positive than negative performance and each has an average positive rate of change that exceeds its average negative rate of change. One, the infant mortality rate, improved every year, by an average 3.8 percent. Life expectancy, with only a few negative years, is also now at its best. The poverty rate among the elderly and the nation's high school dropout rate show negative years, but are very close to the best this nation has achieved because their average positive rate of performance is far higher than their average negative rate. Given the consistent performance of these indicators, the prospects for continuing improvement reasonably can be considered very good.

Each of the worsening indicators has more years of negative performance and higher negative annual rates of change, a reverse of the pattern for those indicators that are improving. Among the worsening indicators, it is troubling to note that the best performance level for each was reached more than twenty years ago. Since that time, the nation has not shown the capacity to regain or even move significantly closer to the thresholds established in the 1970s. As noted, two indicators in this category now stand at their all-time worst levels: health care coverage and child abuse. In the years since 1970, health care coverage improved only five times and worsened fifteen times. Similarly, the nation's child abuse rate worsened eighteen times, remained the same twice, and has not shown even one year of improvement. In both of these areas, the distance needed to return to the peak performance levels of the past is great. Without substantial intervention, prospects for these indicators appear very poor.

The other worsening indicators—youth suicide, violent crime, child poverty, wages, and inequality—each have had numerous years of negative performance, remain far from their best performance, and show significantly higher average negative years than positive. Data from two of these indicators, however, show some encouraging signs and may indicate slightly better potential. The nation's teenage suicide rate shows the capacity to at least stabilize. Recent improvements in the violent crime rate have been substantial, with five of the ten improving years in the 1990s. No other indicator except infant mortality has shown improvement every year between 1992 and 1996.

The shifting indicators show a distinctive pattern, as well. Each has more years of positive than negative performance. But, the downturns, when they occurred, were more substantial than the upturns, and the negative changes equaled or outdistanced the positive, reflecting the fluctuations already noted in Chapter Six.

The proportion of alcohol-related traffic fatalities, for instance, is currently at its best recorded level. It has improved more often than it worsened, but when improvements occurred, changes were smaller than in the negative performing years. This indicator has been particularly sensitive to policy intervention, with the greatest advances occurring during periods when highway speed limits were reduced. The removal of these limits in parts of the country may adversely affect performance in the future, although other factors, such as minimum drinking age laws, may help to keep fatalities down.

Improvements in the nation's unemployment rate are clearly one of the significant achievements of the 1990s. Year to year, since 1970, unemployment has improved far more often than it worsened. But, as with alcohol-related traffic fatalities, the worsening years outpaced the improving ones. What we know, of course, about unemployment is its cyclical nature; the question before economists is how long the present boom period will last.

Trends for teenage drug use and teenage births have gone in opposite directions. Drug use improved during the 1980s, but worsened during the 1990s, with the nation's current performance at only 52 percent of its best, a poor prospect for the future. In contrast, the teenage birth rate rose significantly in the 1980s, alarming the nation. It has since shown the propensity to return to earlier improvements, a performance at 75 percent of its best. Like the teenage birth rate, the affordability of housing has, similarly, begun to return to its earlier, more positive levels. The continuation of this trend is greatly dependent on the swings of the economy.

Judging the current performance of these sixteen indicators against their best level achieved in the past, tells us much about how we are doing as a nation and where we may be headed. At present, only three of the indicators are at their best level since 1970, while many others are significantly below the standard of performance that has been achieved in the past. Some of the indicators have shown substantial improvement and the reasons for this need to be carefully examined. Others have shown decline or fluctuation, and these require our attention and analysis.

In the case of the indicators where performance is at its best, such as life expectancy and infant mortality, new best standards are continually being set. In essence, the bar of performance is being raised nearly every year. If that process can be sustained, the social health of the nation will be demonstrably improved.

It is important to remember, however, that while using the best level achieved in the past provides an objective standard, it does not necessarily give us a desirable one. Many would agree that in an ideal world there would be no infant mortality at all, nor any poverty among the elderly. This goal may be beyond our reach, but other standards might be considered. Perhaps we should be measuring our performance against the achievements of other nations. For infant mortality, for instance, we might aim to match the performance of Sweden which, at 3.5, is the lowest in the world, and considerably better than our own level of 7.3.

When we turn to indicators that are currently performing below even America's own best level of achievement, an international comparison becomes even more relevant. For instance, as noted previously, the nation's best child poverty rate was 14.2

percent, achieved in 1973. Although our current rate is considerably worse, even achieving our best rate would leave us trailing nearly all the other major industrial countries. Thus, regaining a rate of 14.2 percent would by no means be sufficient if we wished to match the performance of other industrial countries. Nevertheless, it would represent significant progress.

For the indicators currently performing at or near their worst level, the future looks particularly grim. Here, with each movement away from the best, with each worsening year of performance, new worst levels are being defined. How does one measure the effect on society when indicators such as child abuse or health care coverage continually fall to new lows? Just as setting a new best represents a threshold of progress, a new worst level may weaken the fabric of society in ways that are not yet understand.

Surely, the character of American society in a year when most social indicators are functioning close to their best levels of performance would be very different from a time when only a few were showing progress and most were near their worst level. Assessing social health in this way offers an approach to understanding more precisely the "feel" of our society, and helps explain what is happening to us in ways that business and economic indicators do not.

Perhaps a reasonable goal for social health would be for all indicators to regain the best performance level that each has achieved in the past. Is such a vision utopian or is it realistic? For some indicators, this objective has already been achieved. For infant mortality or life expectancy, the current performance *is* the best performance. For others, like poverty among the elderly, the current rate of 10.8 percent of the population in poverty would have to be lowered to 10.5; for the high school dropout rate, the current performance of 13.9 percent would have to be reduced to 12.7. These performance levels are within easy reach. For other indicators, the task would be far more difficult. To reach the nation's best past performance, the rate of violent crime, even with the recent years of improvement, would still need to be reduced from 634.1 per 100,000 to 363.5. The youth suicide rate would need to drop from 12.0 per 100,000 to 8.8. The level of improvement required for health care coverage and child abuse would be even more substantial.

The way the nation performs on each indicator is a product of public policies, resources, values, attitudes, and awareness. At some point in the past, these forces converged to produce our best rate of child poverty or youth suicide, in ways that we do not fully understand. But the question remains: can this society achieve those rates again? If we say we cannot, what does that imply about our sense of national progress? How do we regard our society if we assert that such a standard, attained in the past, is now beyond our grasp? On the other hand, if we maintain that such a level is reachable, how do we explain our current low levels of performance in many of these indicators? What are we saying about the nation's attitudes and resources, the range of available policy interventions, and the quality and richness of our public dialogue?

In the realm of business and economic indicators, continued growth and progress are *expected*. The entire economy is evaluated on the basis of growth and improvement. There is a continual effort to expand the Gross Domestic Product and to enhance corporate profits—in effect, to keep moving beyond the best that has been achieved. Can we apply the same assumption to the social sphere—that sustained progress is not only desirable but expected?

The question, "How are we doing?" is, of course, not the same question as "What should we do?" In the realm of business and economics there is frequently a good deal of controversy about the latter, but consensus on the first of these questions tends to be far firmer than in the social sphere. There is little argument about whether the stock market, the GDP, the Index of Leading Economic Indicators, or the Consumer Price Index is, in fact, up or down. A similar point of departure is very much needed with regard to social conditions. Agreeing on how to answer the first question is an essential prerequisite for making progress on the second.

What is most important is to start building a foundation for a new kind of public dialogue about the social conditions of the nation, based on analyzing the performance of social indicators. This analysis can ground the discussion, giving it a rationality that is not present when politics, ideology, and advocacy predominate. If we can forge some agreement about which indicators are important, which are performing better, which are not, and which we need to monitor most closely, we can begin to build the context for true dialogue.

It matters greatly to society that some indicators, such as youth suicide, child abuse, or inequality are worsening, their best performance long in the past, and that others, like elderly poverty, infant mortality, and alcohol-related traffic fatalities, are performing at or close to their best and are apparently responsive to policy or technology. This perspective offers a more factual and precise response than has been available in the past to the question, "How are we doing?"

It also offers a basis for future judgment, a way to monitor the progress of these indicators and to discuss the impact of their performance on society. Will the number of indicators that are performing well increase or decrease in the next year, or in the next five years? It should be important to our society and to our public dialogue when an indicator improves beyond what was achieved twenty years ago to set a new best, or falls below the worst level of the past. Such events should be monitored, reported, and widely discussed.

The news resonates through our society when the market falls one hundred points, or interest rates rise one-fourth of 1 percent. But bells never go off when the poverty of America's children reaches twenty percent or when significant movement occurs in the other indicators presented in Part Two. When one of these rises to a new best or falls to a new worst, the event is only rarely noted, much less discussed in a consistent and timely way. Yet these are milestones in the development of society, important signs of its social health, and they should be a regular and conspicuous part of public discussion.

The data presented in Part Two—the movement of these sixteen indicators over time, the ancillary trends that have been described, the measurement of these indicators' performance against the best the nation has achieved, and their prospects for future progress—begin to frame the social side of the American portrait, telling us where we are, where we have been, and to some degree where we are going. Other data may illuminate other important conditions, and there may be other performance criteria that can provide an even more precise perspective. But Part Two is a starting point, providing social conditions with a context and a meaning by which they can be assessed in the future.

The purpose of a social health perspective for the nation is to be able to conduct a discourse that is as sustained and engaged as the one we currently conduct about business and economics. Part Three presents a vision for the fuller development of this perspective.

Part Three

Pursuing A Practical Vision

Chapter Eight

Advancing the Field

We have learned—perhaps it is our greatest achievement—
to envisage the economy as a whole composed of many parts,
each of which influences and is influenced by every other part. . . .
Marshall's motto "The many in the one, and the one in the many"
puts the essential notion into words.
—Wesley C. Mitchell,
Empirical Research and the Development of Economic Science, *1946*

Part Two began the process of assessing the social health of the nation. It shaped a perspective that includes vital aspects of our progress that are absent from the official business-economic indicators. The data included represent an important part of what is needed to help enrich our public dialogue about social conditions. The final section of the book presents a series of initiatives designed to create a more fully developed concept of social health—one that can be measured, monitored, and communicated to the makers of policy and to the American people.

One set of initiatives, the subject of this chapter, involves defining and pursuing a new agenda for the advancement of the field of social health. Innovative concepts and ideas are necessary to break new ground; new tools are needed to move the work forward. Richer social and socioeconomic indicators need to be developed in areas such as employment, safety, income, health, housing, and education. New indicators need to be created to monitor the nation's progress in less explored areas such as our civil society, our diversity, our cohesion, our degree of political and social engagement, our public discourse, and our sense of mutuality. Ways need to be found to understand the broader meaning of these indicators for society, their subtle patterns of improvement and decline, their cumulative impact, and their thresholds of performance that serve as signs of danger or progress.

A second series of initiatives, the subject of the next chapter, addresses the need to improve the way the nation's social conditions are communicated to the public. Social information must be as vivid, as timely, and as significant as economic and business information. More creative use of the media must be developed to report social conditions with a greater sense of context and continuity. This will require innovative strategies and new partnerships between the world of research and the world of reporting, each informing the other and both informing the public.

Movement on both sets of initiatives is vital. Improving the tools and language of the field of social health will be of limited value without improving how we communicate the picture they portray. By the same token, innovations in reporting must be informed by advances in the field.

This chapter discusses three areas in which progress is needed in order to advance the field. First, new areas of social indicator research need to be investigated in order to create the innovative concepts and ideas required to allow a deeper view of the dynamics of social health. Second, new tools must be designed to gather and analyze new information. For example, a National Social Survey—a periodic census of social well-being—could tell us far more about the nation's social conditions than is possible to determine from current sources of data; similarly, a yearly official National Social Report like those issued in many other countries, would represent an annual benchmark of progress for the nation's deliberations. Finally, new formal mechanisms must be established in both the public and private sector to provide focus and continuity to the endeavor as a whole. These could include a National Conference on Social Health and Social Indicators and a National Association of Community Indicators Projects, each serving to establish connections among individuals in the field, many of whom are currently working in isolation. New structures of government, such as a Council of Social Advisors to the President, would also help to articulate and promote a better understanding of social health.

New Concepts and Ideas

All fields of knowledge, in order to advance, require a regular infusion of new energy. In the view of the philosopher of science, Thomas Kuhn, new paradigms are needed periodically to enrich the questions posed and the answers sought. These new approaches, however, must be informed by experience. Understanding the way that economic indicators and the analysis of business trends evolved can help to guide the process.

During the 1920s, when advances in economics were just beginning, the field lacked its current coherence. To advance the work, Wesley C. Mitchell, the economist who founded the National Bureau of Economic Research, recommended a fruitful approach. Begin with the data, Mitchell advised; monitor trends precisely and accurately and a greater cohesion would follow, insights would be gained, and a solid foundation would be created. Out of this approach came an understanding of business cycles, a deeper perspective on the nature of economic thresholds—recessions and recoveries—and the development of concepts such as leading and lagging indicators.

The power and impact of this process demonstrates its utility. Examining key data, systematically and over time, can provide clues to the underlying patterns, processes, and dynamics. Such a strategy can help forge a unity of meaning far easier to communicate and understand than the mere release of isolated statistics.

In the same manner, greater conceptual coherence can be achieved for social indicators if we understand more about the patterns that underlie social health. Part Two begins this process. It demonstrates the variety and richness of existing data and initiates the systematic exploration of social performance over time of a selected set of indicators. It presents a new standard of assessment—the nation's best past performance—a means by which to judge current performance and begin to assess future potential.

Part Two is a point of departure, a portion of the alphabet for a language that must be more completely evolved. Progress along these lines will help to further transform the mass of currently unnarrated social data into deeply revealing indicators of social health and significantly contribute to the public's understanding of the issues that affect us on a daily basis.

Key Questions. There are a number of provocative questions that can serve as place to begin. Are there chain reactions in social health? If drug abuse becomes more prevalent among ten-year olds, can generational increases in suicide, crime, or mental illness be expected to follow? Are there threshold points at which these chain reactions are likely to occur? Can they be identified? Is any single indicator a fulcrum for several others? Do wages serve that function, or meaningful employment? Can we create indicators of conditions that are more difficult to measure but no less significant, such as the presence of strong community ties, or a sense of belonging?

How much inequality can a democratic society absorb before visible and measurable impact takes place in other areas? How many medically uninsured families or abused children can a society tolerate before downward movement occurs in related indicators? By the same token, what positive movement can be expected in other indicators when there is a 5 percent improvement in the number of children in poverty or a 10 percent improvement in those who graduate high school, or a significant increase in those who have secure and meaningful employment?

Do "social recessions" exist? Are there identifiable periods of time when combinations of social indicators decline together in specific ways as in economic recessions? When many indicators worsen simultaneously, is this an identifiable "event" whose duration and intensity is of critical significance to the social health of the nation? Can it be monitored? The definition of an economic recession—two or more quarters with declining GDP—provides a benchmark indicating that action is required. Do such benchmarks exist in social health? Can the "last-best" standard of performance, introduced in Chapter Seven, provide a beginning point for this analysis?

Are there key indicators that predict social crises? Do leading social indicators exist that can anticipate significant changes in the state of social health? Can lagging or coincident indicators be identified? Can new instruments be devised to frame and communicate such indicators, as is done for the economy?

Are there indicators whose movement is central to the well-being of specific sectors of society? Of children? Of women? Of the aging? Of workers? Does the character of society or the social health of these groups alter when specific problems dramatically improve or worsen? Can such upturns or downturns in social health be attributed to specific changes in social policy, as is suggested by the change in performance in some of the indicators presented in Part Two?

Can more complete social indicators be conceived that use a combination of the empirical and the qualitative? There are, for example, almost fourteen million American children currently living in poverty. This statistic is striking, but much can also be learned from a view of the lives of just one or a few of these children. Alex Kotlowitz's book, *There are No Children Here*, is a good example, portraying the human toll of poverty, crime, and drugs in one housing project in Chicago. Jonathan Kozol's description of life in a few of the nation's schools is another, giving a clear picture of educational deprivation. The photographic depictions of the Depression are still vivid today, some evoking in a single picture a time, a place, and a condition. Statistics can tell us the magnitude of problems but other kinds of accounts reach us on a more human level. Can both perspectives be part of an advanced conception of social indicators? Can collaborative efforts between the social sciences and the humanities help to form such indicators?

Such questions are illustrative. Some are beginning to be addressed; others are still in their formative stage. Together they are meant to suggest the nature and scope of the work yet to be done. The development of creative approaches to these kind of questions will provide a sharper and fuller picture of social health.

New Tools

The field of social health can be advanced in part through the innovative use of existing data. This effort would be facilitated by the more frequent collection and more rapid release of such data. If issues such as teenage suicide or child abuse were reported quarterly, for example, a far more acute view of social change and the relationships among indicators would be possible. Social trends could be observed and understood as they were occurring, rather than months or even years after the fact. But, in order to fully address this agenda we will have to develop new tools. An important first step is the creation of an annual National Social Survey.

A National Social Survey.   The purpose of a National Social Survey would be to bring together the many concerns of social health in a single, holistic, and integrated instrument. The National Social Survey could probe more deeply the issues on which data are currently available, and generate information needed to develop new indicators reflecting aspects of society that have not as yet been systematically explored and monitored. It would constitute a "census of social well-being."

In Part One, we described national social surveys currently being conducted throughout Europe. The fifteen member nations of the European Union are now administering "harmonized" social surveys based on the Level of Living Survey initially developed in Sweden. They compare the social well-being of a variety of countries to assess the relative strengths and weaknesses of each.

The first report of these surveys was issued in 1997 by Eurostat, the statistical arm of the European Union. In it, the authors argue that only a national social survey can provide the kind of consistent approach necessary to advance the field. They note: "Most important, a comprehensive survey provides simultaneous measurement, and hence integrated data regarding several areas of interest for the same sample of persons, and for the same period or point in time."

These European nations have numerous other surveys that measure a wide variety of social concerns, but none provide the necessary focus. Existing surveys, the Eurostat report observes, have "not been developed for the kinds of purposes served by social indicators. Administrative registers have often been designed to serve the institutional need to count inputs, costs, and activities. . . . For all these reasons new kinds of comprehensive surveys have been developed, which capture social indicator characteristics." Numerous surveys exist in the United States as well, but none provide the deep and regular readings necessary to create a new view of the nation's social health.

The National Social Survey would include indicators that examine more thoroughly such issues as health, education, work, family, housing, inequality, safety, and leisure, complementing and deepening the existing social data about these subjects. In the area of work, for example, we need to know far more than the current rate of unemployment, the number of jobs created by the economy, or which categories of people are employed in what kinds of jobs. We need to develop indicators that monitor the satisfactions of work, the extent of economic security or insecurity that work now engenders, the effect of work on family life, and the degree to which jobs provide a sense of contributing to community and to society.

The National Social Survey would also provide a way to examine the social impact of globalization and the "new economy." The impact of downsizing, out-sourcing, the increasing number of hours in the typical work week, the rise of a part-time and contingent labor force, underemployment, bankruptcies, the growing use of credit, and the status of the two-earner family, are but a few of the areas that will need to be addressed.

Furthermore, new indicators could be developed to reveal insights about such subjects as our sense of community, the strength of our national discourse, the depth of our social participation, the state of race relations, the fear of crime, and the level of social capital. These areas are vital to our understanding the nation's social health, but are rarely monitored in a consistent way.

Such a survey would sharpen, as well, our view of the social health of specific sectors of society—the condition of women, children, minorities, and the aging. The interrelationships among these sectors of society would be captured, and as data accumulate, the finer connections would be better understood.

Like the Index of Consumer Confidence and the Index of Leading Economic Indicators, a National Social Survey would become a recognized barometer in areas vital to the quality of life. The dependability of health care, the time spent with our children, the changing nature of families, the pressures of our work life, the quality of our leisure, are clearly as important to a regular assessment of the state of the nation as durable goods or factory inventories.

The systematic publication of a National Social Survey could provide a frequent and familiar way to place social health on the national agenda. The regularity of the information, its accessibility, and its frequent presentation could create a variety of new avenues for discussion and help bring about a more informed public.

The survey would advance the field of social indicators as well. Gathering data about people's experiences in all of these areas can provide a new view of the society's level of social health and social performance and generate new kinds of indicators. Measuring these indicators frequently, and in relation to each other, would provide a perspective on the dynamics of society that is not possible with current instruments.

The central importance of the National Social Survey would be in its potential to help us see our social health in the way that Wesley Mitchell described the economy, as "a whole composed of many parts." The survey would represent a crucial foundation for progress in the field, generating new data from which other work could flow.

A National Social Report. Complementing the National Social Survey should be the development, yearly preparation, and ultimately the official recognition of an annual National Social Report for the United States. Such a document would be composed of selected, objective data providing a profile of the social health of the nation. As noted in Part One, nearly every developed nation in the world, as well as many developing countries have for many years released periodic reports that provide a regular forum for the consideration of national progress in addressing social conditions. Social reports are opportunities for national deliberation. The United States is the only developed nation in the world that does not issue such a public document.

Most of these reports are officially released through central statistical offices and are composed almost exclusively of objective government statistics. Since the United States does not have a central location for social statistics, the initial creation and release of a social report is more problematic than in other countries. Part Two of this document represents the beginning of such a report for the United States. Although it is not modeled on any particular document currently being released in other countries, it is designed to serve a similar purpose: to assemble, in accessible form, an array of social data that provide an objective picture of social conditions and progress. It represents a beginning effort to define a new perspective. Eventually, it should be expanded to incorporate advances in the field, utilize data generated from a National Social Survey, and employ new concepts to extend the reach of its analysis and presentations. As progress is made toward the development and recognition of such concepts as thresholds of performance, these too would be incorporated.

Ultimately, such a document should be officially established in the United States as it is in other countries. Like the *Economic Report of the President*, the Index of Leading Economic Indicators, or the many other recognized barometers, official recognition is crucial to its impact. It is the national acknowledgement of the importance of a social health perspective that will bring legitimacy to the findings and make them a consistent part of the national dialogue.

At present, such institutionalization is a long way off. But, as was the case with the creation of official economic reporting, the initial impetus can come from outside of government, where the development and annual publication of such a document will be of immediate importance to advancing the field and enriching the public discourse. If judged to be of value by the public and by the makers of policy, it might initiate a process leading to the eventual adoption by government.

New Structures of Continuity

New thinking requires the development of new structures for deliberation and interaction where energies can be renewed and ideas further advanced. These structures should occur both inside and outside of government, creating the kind of public-private partnership that is central to the monitoring of the economy. One immediate step in this direction would be the establishment of a yearly National Conference on Social Health and Social Indicators.

A Conference on Social Health and Social Indicators.   The purpose of such a Conference would be to provide a comprehensive view of the social health of the nation using the tools and data currently available; additionally, it would serve as a vehicle for the development of new approaches. Finally, the Conference would help to organize the energies needed to enhance the ideas and impact of the field.

The Conference would bring together participants from many disciplines and endeavors: from the research and academic worlds, from community projects which report on social conditions, from the humanities, the media, and government. A broad diversity of participants would provide a unique and continuing perspective on the nation's well-being.

The Conference would review key studies and reports issued during the course of the year related to social health and assess the results of new tools such as the National Social Survey and the National Social Report. Focal issues might include the state of children, women, the aging, work, the arts, culture, community, and political engagement. In-depth analyses would serve to deepen a social health perspective. The Conference would conclude with the release of a formal statement assessing the social state of the nation.

Convening such a conference on a regular basis would help to advance efforts to develop indicators and to monitor social health in the United States and around the world. As an annual benchmark, the conference could help build connections among efforts that are too often isolated and among participants now separated by the barriers of specialization. Most importantly, perhaps, it could serve as a vehicle by which new ideas about the well-being and progress of the nation could be formally proposed, explored, refined, and made public.

Once such a conference was established on a regular basis and began to provide the field with needed structure and continuity, it might expand to include interim quarterly sessions. Ultimately, such a body would begin to serve the kinds of functions that are carried out by the National Bureau of Economic Research and the Conference Board in periodically making official assessments of the economy. Their identification of warning signs as well as their determination of national recessions are used by the government and other institutions as official measurements of economic health.

A Council of Social Advisors to the President.   As the National Conference on Social Health and Social Indicators further evolved, it might serve as the basis for establishing an official governmental entity like a Council of Social Advisors to the President. The Council would assume a role similar to that of the Council of Economic Advisors, but it would be concerned with issues of social health. One of its major tasks would be the preparation and release of the National Social Report, adding the weight of governmental sanction to its contents, as is the case with the *Economic Report of the President.* The Council would be responsible for presenting the social health of the nation in the most objective manner possible, through the on-going analysis of key data, indicators, and trends. In performing this task, its members would consult with a wide network of knowledgeable analysts in government, the academic community, industry, and labor. Like the Council of Economic Advisors, the Council's major function would be to advise the president.

The Council of Social Advisors would function outside of the agencies that administer social programs, such as the Department of Health and Human Services and Housing and Urban Development. The Council, therefore, would not be caught up in these agency's agendas, nor would it need to defend their policy approaches and expenditures. Its purpose would be to provide a continuing picture of social conditions that cuts across bureaucratic lines.

Potentially, the Council could become an important resource in a number of areas. It could help to analyze the social health impact of present and proposed policies, assist in setting priorities for social expenditures, serve as a mechanism for communicating social concerns to the public, and offer informed comment on social issues as they arose.

In this way, the Council of Social Advisors would represent the kind of overview of social health for which we have argued throughout this book. No such entity currently exists in the federal government. Its creation would prove an important contribution, because it would both symbolize and promote the big picture.

A National Association of Community Indicators Projects.   An agenda for real progress in understanding social health and developing social indicators should also include the contributions of the community indicators movement. As described in Part One, much of the energy and activity today, particularly in America, is occurring at the community level, and these efforts can contribute to shaping the social side of the national portrait.

In attempting to provide new approaches to the question, "How are we doing?" many local projects have moved beyond the kind of thinking that separates problems into isolated arenas. They have come to reflect a holism that is lacking at the national level. They often combine social issues in unique ways, with an emphasis on long-term concerns, enhanced public education, and democratic dialogue. But like many advances in social indicators, particularly in the United States, much of the effort at the state and community level has occurred in isolation. Although information is exchanged and some approaches have been shared, no formal mechanism now exists to draw upon these individual centers of energy; no process yet has been created to give them a national voice or to maximize their contributions.

One step in this direction would be to establish a National Association of Community Indicators Projects. Such an organization could begin to provide the focus necessary to support current projects, encourage new ones, develop new resources, and strengthen the enterprise as a whole. Each project needs to know about the others, their successes, their problems, their ambitions, their constraints, the advances they have made, and the setbacks they have experienced.

Many questions would need to be addressed. Can the experiences, procedures, and outcomes of these various local projects be shared? Can "best practices" or strategies be identified? What similar problems have been confronted? How were they overcome? Are there standard ways to obtain commonly needed data? Are strategies of presentation easily shared? Can the many different approaches at the community level be compared? Are there ways in which a national organization could advocate for better data? Can common gaps in information be addressed by strategic efforts? What approaches have been employed to gain the attention of the press and policymakers? Can policy-makers at the local level be made more responsive to the efforts of these community indicators groups? How might knowledge of these projects be increased at the national level? How might their impact be enhanced?

The purpose of all of the initiatives suggested in this chapter—the research questions that need to be addressed, the National Social Survey, the National Social Report, the annual Conference on Social Health and Social Indicators, and the Association of Community Indicators Projects—is to further progress in the field. Such structures could help stimulate and facilitate work in relevant academic departments, research institutes, and in local communities bringing together separate efforts and supporting advances in the field.

Some of these goals are, of course, a long way off, as are the changes in thinking they can bring. But, if we are to enhance our capacity to understand and evaluate the conditions of our national life, they are ultimately necessary. Many can begin immediately. Their success in developing new knowledge and contributing to the national dialogue can pave the way for further advances. The agenda for progress presented in this chapter is intended as a point of departure.

Chapter Nine

The Tasks of Visibility:
A New Direction
for Social Reporting

Beyond the task of creating new indicators, concepts, tools, and language for the field, lies the need to make information about social conditions more available and accessible to the public. Social reporting helps to fulfill a basic requirement of a democratic society; it enriches public discourse and encourages political and civic involvement. In order to contribute to this very fundamental process, information must be consistently reported and it must be made available in a form that is useful to the general public and to those who make policy.

The most important channels by which this society communicates social information are:

- the federal government through its capacity to collect and release social data

- the print and electronic media

Each contributes much to the public dialogue, but there is also much that can be improved. In the following pages, we will consider new approaches within each arena which could serve to improve the way social conditions are currently reported in the United States.

The Federal Government: The Most Important Source

The collection and distribution of clear, objective information about the conditions of society lies at the heart of the government's dialogue with its people. In effect, one of government's basic responsibilities is to tell us about one another. The obligation to provide such information is written into the Constitution; Article I, Section 3, requires that a national census be carried out every ten years to assess the "numbers" of the American population.

Today, the federal government does far more than count heads. The statistics it gathers and the thousands of studies it conducts make it the most important and reliable source of social data in the country. The government surveys the nation's health, education, housing, income, employment, inequality, poverty, birth, death, disease, migration, as well as countless other facets of American life.

As described in Part One, the public's capacity to make use of this information is limited by the fact that it is often released in an unnarrated form. This is particularly apparent when compared with the way in which economic indicators are collected, interpreted, analyzed, and reported. Social data are often issued without a context that would give them meaning. Studies and surveys are generally reported under many different definitions and auspices. Data are released infrequently and often with a significant lag time. Furthermore, reports are not generally prepared in a form that is conducive to policy deliberation, media reporting, or public understanding; the degree of detail is useful mostly to academic experts. The nation's dialogue about social conditions has been hurt as a result.

Much of the problem can be alleviated through the kind of advances in the field of social health and social indicators presented in the last chapter. As these questions are addressed, pathways to the explanation and use of current social data will be clearer. But progress should not await the completion of these developments; rather, it should accompany them. There is much that can be done with the data and tools that we now have. We need to create a system of social reporting appropriate both to the public dialogue and to the making of public policy.

Using the Information in a New Way. As we have noted, most nations have governmental statistical offices that report social information. According to Franz Rothenbacher, in his review of international social reporting, "Central Statistical Offices have the highest potential for social reporting because they have the infrastructure, the resources, and the technical know-how in all fields of statistics. . . . They have the statistical data at hand and can integrate the statistics into information systems." Central statistical offices often serve as central clearinghouses for social data, providing releases to the public, the media, and the academy.

The United States needs a similar structure which draws on the many studies conducted by federal agencies in such areas as health, education, labor, population, and human services. Such a structure should not duplicate the work of government surveys, but assist in communicating their most significant findings. Instead of releasing whole surveys, which are often difficult to decipher and to report, this new entity would stress the publication of vital indicators of social performance thus providing the "big picture" required for meaningful discourse, a view that each individual federal agency cannot currently provide. This would give the media and public officials a way to unscramble the frequently disjointed and even conflicting information that is often released.

This new structure would select from a large array of key statistics, make decisions about their importance, and establish a system of distribution and release that would provide information in a clear and accessible form. It would examine, as well, the gaps in the available data and move toward improvements in the consistency and frequency of reporting. It is important to emphasize that the focus should not be on changing the agencies that collect the data. Rather, the focus should be on the information which they provide and the form in which it is presented to the public.

Such a change in the release of social data would need to address numerous issues. Can key government data be collected and released more frequently to increase public awareness and policy relevance? Could a set of the most important data be selected, agreed upon, and released on a far more regular basis? Would it be possible to issue a quarterly survey of selected data that provided a clearer picture of improving or deteriorating social conditions? Could indicators that are closely related be reported together, to provide a timely and official view of the state of children or women or work, for example? Could these new data serve as the basis for a more timely National Social Report than is possible with the data that are currently available?

Could guides be developed to help the public and the media better understand the meaning, nature, and location of social data. Economic indicators have such maps, as well as stable calendars of release dates. Could social data do this as well?

Can the myriad sources of data be better coordinated to relate a more vivid picture? Could multiple measures of the same problem be sorted and refined? Could related measures be better grouped to reflect upon each other, clarifying rather than confounding our grasp of issues?

Such questions are meant to suggest paths that merit pursuit. Part Two began the effort by selecting, from the vast array of information, a set of indicators keyed to social performance. But the full project—a thoughtful system of context and narration for all government studies that report social conditions—needs to be undertaken if we are to achieve a more rational and accessible system.

Ultimately, this effort, perhaps in cooperation with the private sector, could assist the nation in gaining a firmer understanding of its social health. If the provision of clearly and thoughtfully portrayed information were to become a priority, we would be taking a vital step in gaining greater insight into the nation's social state.

The Media: Telling the Story

Each night on television, throughout the day on radio, and in the daily newspapers, there is a weather report, a sports report, an economic report, a business report, and a political report. Polls, indexes, statistics, predictions, and trends give us a precise portrayal of key developments in these well-defined fields. These reports combine information into a "beat," in the parlance of the print media, or "segment," in the language of the electronic media. What is missing in the national media, however, as noted in Part One, is the idea of a "social report."

A "Beat" or "Segment" for Social Health.   Social health needs to be as much an ongoing story in the media as are many other national concerns. Because stories about social issues lack their own beat or segment, they are currently submerged in the coverage of other topics. Some are treated as local news, some as science, some as political, and many are viewed solely from an economic or financial perspective. Many are stories about individual cases. The placement of social issues is often arbitrary, reflecting little effort to combine related concerns into a greater whole and little attempt to provide continuity as new developments occur. The social context, the meaning for society, the trends, the relationship to other issues, are generally not included.

Part Two presented a different perspective. Yet, the profound social changes it described often took place without sustained public attention. This weakens democracy. It is as if the Vietnam War had been fought with no press coverage, no chance for the country to understand what was happening, and no opportunity to make a judgment about it.

Social health, because of its absence from the media, has little place in the accountability of elected officials. While a slippage from 3.8 percent to 2.0 percent in quarterly economic growth during an election year might prove lethal for a president, a 10 percent decline in social health, affecting the the lives of a majority of the population cannot even be conceived, much less discussed. A president or governor is only rarely called to account when there is a significant increase in child abuse, teen suicide, or the number of families who do not have health insurance during his or her term of office. Nor is such an official praised when the rate of child poverty falls. The data are not released promptly enough or prominently enough to bring about a public response.

In a democracy, problems generally are not addressed until they are recognized and understood by the public. Yet, many social conditions have worsened for a generation without significant public knowledge. If the social health of the nation were constantly before us, if information and trends were portrayed widely, dependably, and precisely, like the standard business indicators or even weather and sports, then our performance in this neglected area might find its way into enlightened policy debate more often. This would reinforce the idea that our level of social health is as important in evaluating public officials as the size of the deficit or the growth of the GDP.

Such a result would strengthen us. The public might eventually conclude that both government and the media were more focused on issues more representative of its interests. We might then take a step toward becoming a healthier and more democratic society.

As we have noted, the field itself must make progress, and government reporting should be far better organized. Publishing a series of recognized social indicators, with significant benchmarks or thresholds to interpret their performance, would provide clear evidence that the nation had measured up to a particular standard or had failed to do so. Even the simple reporting of the same indicators each quarter would allow consistent comparisons. Are we doing better or worse?

This kind of regularly issued performance data, which is not now available, is far easier for the media to cover than are isolated studies on unrelated topics. It would provide editors, producers, and reporters with the kind of information they need to tell an on-going story. It would begin to build a context within which the media could frame the coverage of individual cases.

These advances in the field can make an important contribution to the way the media covers the social conditions of the nation. But, there is much that can be done now in both the print and electronic media to make better use of the data that is currently available. Such efforts would greatly enhance the coverage of social issues, institutionalize a more focused system of analysis, and better inform the public.

In the print media, a section for newspapers and national news magazines needs to be developed as a "social report." Such a section could present both objective information and survey data. Appearing on a regular basis, the section might cover key aspects of social health such as the status of women, work, wages, housing, or children. As new findings are released, they could be presented in the context of long-term trends as well as with an exploration of their significance and broader meaning. Some reports might be a combination of trends in important indicators and the human stories that illustrate them.

Such a section would be similar in scope, depth, and frequency to the business report or the arts section of most daily papers, serving to inform readers about social health as a whole. It could help to promote the idea of an important aspect of society that is neither the economy nor the polity, but is closer to the actual conditions of people's lives.

To add greater relevance to specific localities, the idea could be developed at the state or local level as well. Community issues could be addressed in the context of larger national trends, with expert commentary to supplement, enliven, and humanize the presentation. Eventually, such reports could be deepened, as advances in the field brought about more innovative social data and more refined tools of analysis.

Most importantly, the new section should appear frequently and predictably, its indicators and trends selected carefully to communicate a sense of the whole rather than fragmented parts. Such a social report could present a consistent, rational, and timely portrait of the nation's social health.

An equally vital effort could be undertaken in the electronic media. The goals would be the same, although the material would be communicated differently. Here, a social health segment could be created as a regular portion of the national news. Network news, cable news, or radio news programs might all become involved. As with the print media, such an effort would bring together key aspects of social health and social indicators, producing a regularly scheduled segment similar to those in business, politics, or sports.

At present, political and economic commentators appear frequently on the electronic media. Political commentary ranges from extensive presentation and analysis of poll data, to the interpretation of the behavior of political figures, sometimes descending to the level of gossip. Economic commentary, generally more sober, interprets the available statistics, identifying trends and forecasting the future movement of the stock market and other signs of the nation's economic condition. It is rare to see comparable social commentary, presenting issues of social health such as those that have been the focus of this book. The presentation of such commentary would add continuity and depth to the public's understanding of public issues.

In order to develop an innovative approach to the coverage of social health in the media, critical questions would need to be confronted. Could a distinctive style of coverage be developed, different from the presentation of traditional business and economic indicators? Are there ways in which long-term trends can become a more important part of social-issue stories? Can the vital interconnections between social issues be accessibly and meaningfully portrayed? Given the fact, for example, that the public is well informed about the connections among unemployment, inflation, and interest rates, could the broader meaning of inequality, the deterioration of our schools, or the decline in our civil life be portrayed with equal clarity? How could improvements in government data help the national news media to cover social issues more comprehensively? How could the results of such new tools as a National Social Report or a National Social Survey be utilized?

Could social reporting become a specialty within journalism? Can schools of journalism contribute new approaches, and perhaps develop courses of study in social health issues? Might there be a special cable channel devoted to the coverage of social issues, similar to the History Channel, the Weather Channel, or the many sports and business channels? Could there eventually be a publication in the social sphere equivalent to *Business Week, Money*, or even the *Wall Street Journal*?

As social reporting projects develop within the media, they could serve as models for further efforts at the local, regional, state, and national levels, demonstrating how to provide continuity and context, how to reduce the sensational and crisis-driven character of news, and how to enrich the public dialogue. Over time they might help to stimulate deliberation over ways to represent and report the broadest aspects of social health. For example, the media could evaluate, from a social health perspective, such events as the budgetary process, a national election, or a president's State of the Union address.

Beyond the production of actual media reports is another immediate need: an ongoing dialogue between those who research social data and those who report it. Researchers and reporters move in vastly different worlds, but they have important objectives in common. An on-going discourse between these groups ultimately would strengthen both endeavors.

Such a dialogue might be a regular aspect of the National Conference on Social Health and Social Indicators, which was proposed in the previous chapter. The Conference would be an ideal forum in which to explore the way social problems and social indicators are being reported and the consequences for the public of that reporting. New approaches to media news reporting might emerge from such a discussion.

From a dialogue between these groups, those who conduct research might gain a better understanding of the possibilities and constraints of the world of media, where the sense of timing is more urgent, the language of reporting more concise, and the constraints of space more limiting. The reverse is true as well. Members of the media might come to better understand the difficulties in collecting, analyzing, and interpreting social data, the complexities of the findings, and their longer-term implications. Such a dialogue might help to further the development of social analysis and interpretation in the media in order to balance the prevalence of economic and political commentary. If social reporting is to be improved, the void that now exists between these two worlds must be bridged.

Such efforts in the print and electronic media would be greatly enhanced by the initiatives discussed earlier: the development of a clearer and more accessible conceptual language, the evolution of new tools and the creation of a more coherent government information system for the preparation and release of social data. These advances would help the media tell a more complete story about the nation's quality of life.

Visible Progress

The initiatives presented in this part of the book seek both to enrich the field of social health and social indicators, and to improve how they are reported to the American people. Together, they represent an approach that draws on many sectors of society, including the research and academic communities, the agencies of the federal government, the media—both print and electronic- and the community indicators movement that is emerging in states and localities across the country. These initiatives are both tangible and attainable, and their realization would represent progress toward an improved public dialogue about the nature and direction the nation's social health, and perhaps toward the beginnings of a politics that is more connected to everyday life.

The strengthening of the concepts and tools of the field and the enrichment of the nation's social reporting could help to promote the idea that the conditions that define us are not only a series of individual achievements or failures but also the products of social dynamics that can be recognized, discussed, and addressed. If this were to occur, it would reinforce the belief that public access to facts matters, that facts provide a firm ground on which different sectors of the same society can come together in order to deliberate, and that such deliberation lies at the core of democracy.

Some of the initiatives presented in this chapter are long-term efforts; others can be achieved more quickly. What is most important is that each be viewed as part of a larger enterprise. This enterprise, if pursued as a whole, would do much to address our need to know how we are doing and our ability to deliberate about what should be done. Together they would begin to complete the official national portrait.

Epilogue

One of the most significant developments of the latter part of the twentieth century is the growth and predominance of global capitalism. National boundaries remain, but the movement of international capital has blurred them. In effect, global capitalism has achieved a measure of what was envisioned in the first half of the century with the founding of the League of Nations and the United Nations: a tempering of nationalism and greater communication between countries.

But much of the on-going international communication is financial. The concepts and numbers are in dollar terms, as are the data required to compete and survive. We monitor and report the international impact of markets and investments; we need to know quickly how fluctuations in Hong Kong affect investments in New York. The language of traditional economic and business indicators—the stock market, the GDP, the balance of trade—have become an international language.

These developments will help shape the twenty-first century. But like any movement of this magnitude, the expansion of global capitalism poses serious challenges and raises new problems. One of the most important is how its concepts and tools dominate the way we officially view and discuss progress and performance. Increasingly, they have come to determine the way we frame a fundamental question of democracy: "How are we doing?"

An underlying argument of this book concerns the need to create a different kind of dialogue, one which reflects the true and changing conditions of the quality of life and achieves a deeper and broader view of the human condition. This dialogue must rest on a foundation that is as strong, durable, rational, and precise as that which supports our discourse about the economy.

This new dialogue need not stand in opposition to well-established business and economic barometers. Rather, it should accompany them, serving as balance, helping to place them in a more human perspective, and adding richness and depth to our official concerns. In the long run, the development and refinement of such a dialogue will not diminish our economic system, but will strengthen and sustain it, helping to democratize the economic transitions and transformation of the coming century, charting their effects on our lives, and adding a picture of their human impact and consequence.

An ongoing dialogue about the social health of the nation, based on social indicators, would move beyond the measurement of money lost and regained, growth upward and downward, inflation present and predicted in monthly, quarterly and yearly intervals. It would concern the essential condition of society, telling us about the way people live, participate, relate, and prosper. A fully realized concept of social health would be a pathway to the soul and center of society. It would give us a view of who we are in ways close to our core.

Such a concept would monitor what is human and indelible: how long we live, how safe we feel, how educated we are, and to whom and with what result we turn when we are in need. It would reflect the essential character and nature of society: the status of children; the resilience of youth; the wages, housing, and health insurance of families; the ability of the aging to pay medical bills. Social health is about who we really are and to what we must attend.

The absence of an agreed-upon concept of social health that is openly monitored and frequently reported leaves a vacuum that is easily filled. Because the assets and liabilities of social health have been difficult to ground, frame, and measure, they are sometimes susceptible to ideologues and spin doctors who take carefully chosen, poll-tested fragments of our concern—our feeling that something is not right—and with shrill or smoothly deceptive rhetoric erode our public discourse.

The creation of a clear concept of social health and a mechanism to measure it would help to provide a sense that our nation's social well-being is open to rational deliberation and can be altered to a more desired state. In a democracy, the determination of this state should reflect a genuine contest of values and philosophy emerging from all sides of the political spectrum. But this is not possible unless basic social conditions are accountably and accurately charted, and discussion is far more grounded in fact and analysis than is currently the case.

The trends in social health in this book are retrospective. We look back on their beginnings in 1970 and trace them to the present. Some are positive, but many are disappointing. Because they are not short-term fluctuations, but long-term trends, they represent what have come to be established aspects of our society, conditions present for a long time and likely to continue. We are therefore compelled to read them forward as well. They give us a sense of the future.

The ultimate impact on the character of our society and its people of these and related trends is very difficult to know in its entirety. But it is clear their impact is great and lasting. It must be discussed and debated with grounding, rationality, and openness. Whether a democratic society can continue to absorb such trends that affect so many of the population and still maintain its essential character is a question that requires our concerted attention. If such questions remain outside of our discourse we have chosen a perilous direction for our country.

The case for new thinking about social conditions in this book, the trends it has presented, and the initiatives it has proposed, are all intended as the beginning point for a new dialogue. *The Social Health of the Nation* is part of a process which is gaining momentum in a large number of America's communities, in many other countries, and in international organizations as well. It is a process which seeks a more complete answer to the question, "How are we doing?" It is toward a deeper understanding of the "we" in that question—the same word that begins the United States Constitution—that this book is dedicated.

List of Charts and Indicators

Chapter 5: Indicators of Worsening Performance

Chapter Six: Indicators of Shifting Performance

Chapter Seven: Judging the Nation's Social Performance

Appendices

Note: 1997 data is provided where available or preliminary;
all analyses in the text are based on data through 1996

Infant mortality

	Infant mortality				Maternal mortality		
	Number **All**		**Rate**				**Rate**
		All	**White**	**Black**	**All**	**White**	**Black**
1970	74,667	20.0	17.8	32.6	21.5	14.4	59.8
1971	67,981	19.1	17.1	30.3	18.8	13.0	48.3
1972	60,182	18.5	16.4	29.6	18.8	14.3	40.7
1973	55,581	17.7	15.8	28.1	15.2	10.7	38.4
1974	52,776	16.7	14.8	26.8	14.6	10.0	38.3
1975	50,525	16.1	14.2	26.2	12.8	9.1	31.3
1976	48,285	15.2	13.3	25.5	12.3	9.0	29.5
1977	46,976	14.1	12.3	23.6	11.2	7.7	29.2
1978	45,945	13.8	12.0	23.1	9.6	6.4	25.0
1979	45,665	13.1	11.4	21.8	9.6	6.4	25.1
1980	45,526	12.6	10.9	22.2	9.2	6.7	21.5
1981	43,305	11.9	10.3	20.8	8.5	6.3	20.4
1982	42,401	11.5	9.9	20.5	7.9	5.8	18.2
1983	40,627	11.2	9.6	20.0	8.0	5.9	18.3
1984	39,580	10.8	9.3	19.2	7.8	5.4	19.7
1985	40,030	10.6	9.2	19.0	7.8	5.2	20.4
1986	38,891	10.4	8.8	18.9	7.2	4.9	18.8
1987	38,408	10.1	8.5	18.8	6.6	5.1	14.2
1988	38,910	10.0	8.4	18.5	8.4	5.9	19.5
1989	39,655	9.8	8.1	18.6	7.9	5.6	18.4
1990	38,351	9.2	7.6	18.0	8.2	5.4	22.4
1991	36,766	8.9	7.3	17.6	7.9	5.8	18.3
1992	34,628	8.5	6.9	16.8	7.8	5.0	20.8
1993	33,466	8.4	6.8	16.5	7.5	4.8	20.5
1994	31,710	8.0	6.6	15.8	8.3	6.2	18.5
1995	29,583	7.6	6.3	15.1	7.1	4.2	22.1
1996	28,487	7.3	6.1	14.7	7.6	5.1	20.3
(1997)	(27,691)	(7.1)	(6.0)	(13.7)	n/a	n/a	n/a

Infant mortality—Number of deaths in the first year of life. Source: National Center for Health Statistics; 1997 data is preliminary.

Infant mortality rate, all, by race, deaths in the first year of life per 1,000 live births. Source: National Center for Health Statistics. Note: 1970-1979 by race of child, 1980-1997 by race of mother; 1997 data is preliminary.

Note: The 1996 Hispanic infant mortality rate was 5.9 deaths per 1,000 live births. According to the National Center for Health Statistics, because of methodological difficulties, Hispanic infant mortality rates are underreported using the same methods that produce black and white rates. An alternate method, the "linked file," produces what is considered a more reliable rate of 6.1 infant deaths per 1,000. For a discussion see: K. D. Peters, K. D. Kochanek, S. L. Murphy, *Deaths: Final Data for 1996,* National Vital Statistics Reports, vol. 47, no. 9 (Hyattsville, Maryland: National Center for Health Statistics, 1998), "Hispanic infant mortality" and Technical Notes. See also: M. F. MacDorman, J. O. Atkinson, *Infant Mortality Statistics From the 1996 Period Linked Birth/Infant Data Set,* Monthly Vital Statistics Report, vol. 46, no. 12, supp. (Hyattsville, Maryland: National Center for Health Statistics, 1998).

Maternal mortality rate—deaths per 100,000; deaths are those assigned to complications of pregnancy, childbirth, and the puerperium, category numbers 630-670 of the Ninth Revision, International Classification of Disease, 1975. Source: National Center for Health Statistics. Note 1970-1988 by race of child, 1989-1996 by race of mother.

n/a: data not available.

Infant mortality, continued

	Low birthweight			Late or no prenatal care		
	All	**White**	**Black**	**All**	**White**	**Black**
1970	7.9	6.9	13.9	7.9	6.3	16.6
1971	7.7	6.6	13.4	7.2	5.8	14.6
1972	7.7	6.5	13.7	7.0	5.5	13.2
1973	7.6	6.4	13.3	6.7	5.4	12.4
1974	7.4	6.3	13.2	6.2	5.0	11.4
1975	7.4	6.3	13.2	6.0	5.0	10.5
1976	7.3	6.2	13.1	5.7	4.8	9.9
1977	7.1	6.0	12.9	5.6	4.7	9.6
1978	7.1	6.0	13.0	5.4	4.5	9.3
1979	6.9	5.8	12.7	5.1	4.3	8.9
1980	6.8	5.7	12.7	5.1	4.3	8.9
1981	6.8	5.7	12.7	5.2	4.3	9.1
1982	6.8	5.6	12.6	5.5	4.5	9.6
1983	6.8	5.7	12.8	5.6	4.6	9.7
1984	6.7	5.6	12.6	5.6	4.7	9.6
1985	6.8	5.7	12.7	5.7	4.8	10.2
1986	6.8	5.7	12.8	6.0	5.0	10.6
1987	6.9	5.7	13.0	6.1	5.0	11.1
1988	6.9	5.7	13.3	6.1	5.0	10.0
1989	7.0	5.7	13.5	6.4	5.2	11.9
1990	7.0	5.7	13.3	6.1	4.9	11.3
1991	7.1	5.8	13.6	5.8	4.7	10.7
1992	7.1	5.8	13.3	5.2	4.2	9.9
1993	7.2	6.0	13.3	4.8	3.9	9.0
1994	7.3	6.1	13.2	4.4	3.6	8.2
1995	7.3	6.2	13.1	4.2	3.5	7.6
1996	7.4	6.3	13.0	4.0	3.3	7.3
(1997)	(7.5)	(6.5)	(13.0)	(4.0)	(3.3)	(7.3)

Low birthweight infants—percent of all births 5 lb. 8 oz. or less. Source: National Center for Health Statistics; 1997 data is preliminary.

Late or no prenatal care—percent of all births, care beginning in the third trimester or not at all. Source: National Center for Health Statistics, 1997 data is preliminary.

High school dropouts

	Status dropouts % of persons, aged 18-24, not enrolled in school, not finished high school				Event dropouts % of H.S. students who drop out of school each year	High school completion % of 25-29 year olds who have finished high school
	All	**White**	**Black**	**Hispanic**	**All**	**All**
1970	17.3	15.2	33.3	n/a	5.7	75.4
1971	17.0	15.4	28.8	n/a	5.4	77.2
1972	16.6	15.2	26.2	40.4	6.2	79.8
1973	15.7	14.2	26.5	38.9	6.3	80.2
1974	15.9	14.5	25.1	37.1	6.7	81.9
1975	15.6	13.9	27.3	34.9	5.8	83.1
1976	15.9	14.7	24.2	36.5	5.9	84.7
1977	15.8	14.7	23.9	38.7	6.5	85.4
1978	15.9	14.6	24.6	39.2	6.7	85.3
1979	16.3	14.9	25.5	39.2	6.7	85.6
1980	15.6	14.4	23.5	40.3	6.0	85.4
1981	15.6	14.7	21.7	38.5	5.9	86.3
1982	15.6	14.6	22.0	37.0	5.4	86.2
1983	15.4	14.3	21.5	37.5	5.2	86.0
1984	14.8	14.1	18.4	34.2	5.0	85.9
1985	13.9	13.5	17.6	31.5	5.2	86.1
1986	13.9	13.4	16.8	34.4	4.3	86.1
1987	14.5	14.2	17.0	32.8	4.1	86.0
1988	14.6	14.2	17.7	39.6	4.8	85.7
1989	14.4	14.1	16.4	37.7	4.5	85.5
1990	13.6	13.5	15.1	37.3	4.0	85.7
1991	14.2	14.2	15.6	39.6	4.0	85.4
1992	12.7	12.2	16.3	33.9	4.3	86.3
1993	13.1	12.7	16.4	32.8	4.3	86.7
1994	13.3	12.7	15.5	34.7	5.0	86.1
1995	13.9	13.6	14.4	34.7	5.4	86.8
1996	12.8	12.5	16.0	34.5	4.7	87.3

Status dropouts—population 18-24 years old not enrolled in school, who have not finished high school.
Source: U.S. Bureau of the Census.

Event dropouts—percent of tenth, eleventh, twelfth graders who drop out of school each year.
Source: U.S. Bureau of the Census.

High school completion—percent of 25-29 year olds who have finished high school.
Source: U.S. Bureau of the Census.

High school dropouts, cont.

	Scholastic Assessment Test (SAT-1) Scores						College completion			
	Verbal All	Math All	Verbal Male	Fem.	Math Male	Fem.	All	White	Black	Hisp.
1970	537	512	536	538	531	493	16.4	17.3	7.3	n/a
1971	532	513	531	534	529	494	16.9	17.9	6.4	n/a
1972	530	509	531	529	527	489	19.0	19.9	8.3	n/a
1973	523	506	523	521	525	489	19.0	19.9	8.1	n/a
1974	521	505	524	520	524	488	20.7	22.0	7.9	5.7
1975	512	498	515	509	518	479	21.9	22.8	10.7	8.8
1976	509	497	511	508	520	475	23.7	24.6	13.0	7.4
1977	507	496	509	505	520	474	24.0	25.3	12.6	6.7
1978	507	494	511	503	517	474	23.3	24.5	11.8	9.6
1979	505	493	509	501	516	473	23.1	24.3	12.4	7.3
1980	502	492	506	498	515	473	22.5	23.7	11.6	7.7
1981	502	492	508	496	516	473	21.3	22.4	11.6	7.5
1982	504	493	509	499	516	473	21.7	22.7	12.6	9.7
1983	503	494	508	498	516	474	22.5	23.4	12.9	10.4
1984	504	497	511	498	518	478	21.9	23.1	11.6	10.6
1985	509	500	514	503	522	480	22.2	23.2	11.5	11.1
1986	509	500	515	504	523	479	22.4	23.5	11.8	9.0
1987	507	501	512	502	523	481	22.0	23.0	11.4	8.7
1988	505	501	512	499	521	483	22.5	23.5	12.2	11.4
1989	504	502	510	498	523	482	23.4	24.4	12.7	10.1
1990	500	501	505	496	521	483	23.2	24.2	13.4	8.1
1991	499	500	503	495	520	482	23.2	24.6	11.0	9.2
1992	500	501	504	496	521	484	23.6	25.0	11.3	9.5
1993	500	503	504	497	524	484	23.7	24.7	13.2	8.3
1994	499	504	501	497	523	487	23.3	24.2	13.7	8.0
1995	504	506	505	502	525	490	24.7	26.0	15.3	8.9
1996	505	508	507	503	527	492	27.1	28.1	14.6	10.0

Scholastic Assessment Test (SAT-1) Scores, scores recentered in 1996. Source: National Center for Education Statistics.

College completion—percent of 25-29 year olds with 4 years of college or more. Source: U.S. Bureau of the Census.

n/a: data not available

Poverty among those aged 65 and over

	Number in poverty aged 65 and over (in thousands)	Percent in poverty aged 65 and over				Percent in poverty:		
	All	**All**	**White**	**Black**	**Hispanic**	**Under age 18**	**Aged 18-64**	**All ages**
1970	4,793	24.6	22.6	48.0	n/a	14.9	9.0	12.6
1971	4,273	21.6	19.9	39.3	n/a	15.1	9.3	12.5
1972	3,738	18.6	16.8	39.9	n/a	14.9	8.8	11.9
1973	3,354	16.3	14.4	37.1	24.9	14.2	8.3	11.1
1974	3,085	14.6	12.8	34.3	28.9	15.1	8.3	11.2
1975	3,317	15.3	13.4	36.3	32.6	16.8	9.2	12.3
1976	3,313	15.0	13.2	34.8	27.7	15.8	9.0	11.8
1977	3,177	14.1	11.9	36.3	21.9	16.0	8.8	11.6
1978	3,233	14.0	12.1	33.9	23.2	15.7	8.7	11.4
1979	3,682	15.2	13.3	36.2	26.8	16.0	8.9	11.7
1980	3,871	15.7	13.6	38.1	30.8	17.9	10.1	13.0
1981	3,853	15.3	13.1	39.0	25.7	19.5	11.1	14.0
1982	3,751	14.6	12.4	38.2	26.6	21.3	12.0	15.0
1983	3,625	13.8	11.7	36.0	22.1	21.8	12.4	15.2
1984	3,330	12.4	10.7	31.7	21.5	21.0	11.7	14.4
1985	3,456	12.6	11.0	31.5	23.9	20.1	11.3	14.0
1986	3,477	12.4	10.7	31.0	22.5	19.8	10.8	13.6
1987	3,563	12.5	10.6	32.4	27.5	19.7	10.6	13.4
1988	3,481	12.0	10.0	32.2	22.4	19.0	10.5	13.0
1989	3,312	11.4	9.6	31.0	20.7	19.0	10.2	12.8
1990	3,658	12.2	10.1	33.8	22.5	19.9	10.7	13.5
1991	3,781	12.4	10.3	33.8	20.8	21.1	11.4	14.2
1992	3,928	12.9	11.0	33.5	22.1	21.6	11.9	14.8
1993	3,755	12.2	10.7	28.0	21.4	22.0	12.4	15.1
1994	3,663	11.7	10.2	27.4	22.6	21.2	11.9	14.5
1995	3,318	10.5	9.0	25.4	23.5	20.2	11.4	13.8
1996	3,428	10.8	9.4	25.3	24.4	19.8	11.4	13.7
(1997)	(3,376)	(10.5)	(9.0)	(26.0)	(23.8)	(19.2)	(10.9)	(13.3)

Number and percent in poverty. Source: U.S. Bureau of the Census, Note: For under 18, related children in families.

n/a: data not available

Life expectancy

	Life expectancy at age 65					Life expectancy at birth				
		White		Black			White		Black	
	All	**Male**	**Fem.**	**Male**	**Fem.**	**All**	**Male**	**Fem.**	**Male**	**Fem.**
1970	15.2	13.1	17.1	12.5	15.7	70.8	68.0	75.6	60.0	68.3
1971	15.2	13.2	17.2	12.7	15.8	71.1	68.3	75.8	60.5	68.9
1972	15.2	13.1	17.2	12.4	15.8	71.2	68.3	75.9	60.4	69.1
1973	15.3	13.2	17.3	12.5	15.7	71.4	68.5	76.1	60.9	69.3
1974	15.6	13.5	17.7	12.7	16.2	72.0	69.0	76.7	61.7	70.3
1975	16.1	13.8	18.2	13.1	16.7	72.6	69.5	77.3	62.4	71.3
1976	16.1	13.8	18.2	13.1	16.7	72.9	69.9	77.5	62.9	71.6
1977	16.4	14.0	18.5	13.3	16.9	73.3	70.2	77.9	63.4	72.0
1978	16.4	14.1	18.5	13.3	17.1	73.5	70.4	78.0	63.7	72.4
1979	16.7	14.4	18.8	13.5	17.3	73.9	70.8	78.4	64.0	72.9
1980	16.4	14.2	18.4	13.0	16.8	73.7	70.7	78.1	63.8	72.5
1981	16.6	14.4	18.7	13.4	17.2	74.1	71.1	78.4	64.5	73.2
1982	16.8	14.5	18.8	13.5	17.5	74.5	71.5	78.7	65.1	73.6
1983	16.7	14.5	18.7	13.2	17.2	74.6	71.6	78.7	65.2	73.5
1984	16.8	14.6	18.7	13.2	17.2	74.7	71.8	78.7	65.3	73.6
1985	16.7	14.5	18.7	13.0	16.9	74.7	71.8	78.7	65.0	73.4
1986	16.8	14.7	18.7	13.0	17.0	74.7	71.9	78.8	64.8	73.4
1987	16.9	14.8	18.8	13.0	17.0	74.9	72.1	78.9	64.7	73.4
1988	16.9	14.8	18.7	12.9	16.9	74.9	72.2	78.9	64.4	73.2
1989	17.1	15.1	18.9	13.0	16.9	75.1	72.5	79.2	64.3	73.3
1990	17.2	15.2	19.1	13.2	17.2	75.4	72.7	79.4	64.5	73.6
1991	17.4	15.4	19.2	13.4	17.2	75.5	72.9	79.6	64.6	73.8
1992	17.5	15.5	19.3	13.5	17.4	75.8	73.2	79.8	65.0	73.9
1993	17.3	15.4	19.0	13.4	17.1	75.5	73.1	79.5	64.6	73.7
1994	17.4	15.6	19.1	13.6	17.2	75.7	73.3	79.6	64.9	73.9
1995	17.4	15.7	19.1	13.6	17.1	75.8	73.4	79.6	65.2	73.9
1996	17.5	15.8	19.1	13.9	17.2	76.1	73.9	79.7	66.1	74.2
(1997)	(17.6)	(15.9)	(19.1)	(14.2)	(17.4)	(76.5)	(74.3)	(79.8)	(67.3)	(74.7)

Life expectancy at age 65—expected additional years of life. Source: National Center for Health Statistics; 1997 data is preliminary.

Life expectancy at birth—expected years of life. Source: National Center for Health Statistics; 1997 data is preliminary.

Child abuse

	Estimated number of child abuse reports	Child abuse reporting rate (per 1,000)	Number of child abuse fatalities	Estimated number of sexual abuse reports
1976	669,000	10.1	n/a	n/a
1977	838,000	12.8	n/a	n/a
1978	836,000	12.9	n/a	12,000
1979	988,000	15.4	n/a	27,000
1980	1,154,000	18.1	n/a	37,000
1981	1,225,000	19.4	n/a	35,000
1982	1,262,000	20.1	n/a	57,000
1983	1,477,000	23.6	n/a	74,000
1984	1,727,000	27.3	n/a	100,000
1985	1,928,000	30.6	810	127,000
1986	2,086,000	32.8	1,002	132,000
1987	2,157,000	34.0	1,042	324,000
1988	2,265,000	35.0	1,092	385,000
1989	2,435,000	38.0	1,095	390,000
1990	2,559,000	40.0	1,099	384,000
1991	2,684,000	42.0	1,233	429,000
1992	2,909,000	45.0	1,129	408,000
1993	2,967,000	45.0	1,216	331,000
1994	3,074,000	46.0	1,278	366,000
1995	3,120,000	46.0	1,248	329,000
1996	3,126,000	47.0	1,046	301,000

Estimated number of child abuse reports and rate per 1,000: Sources: 1976-1986, American Association for Protecting Children; 1987-1996, National Committee to Prevent Child Abuse.

Number of fatalities. Source: National Committee to Prevent Child Abuse.

Estimated number of sexual abuse reports. Source: National Committee to Prevent Child Abuse.

n/a: data not available

Child poverty

	Number in poverty under age 18 (in thousands)	Percent in poverty under age 18				Percent in poverty under age 6
	All	All	White	Black	Hispanic	All
1970	10,235	14.9	10.5	41.5	n/a	16.6
1971	10,344	15.1	10.9	40.4	n/a	16.9
1972	10,082	14.9	10.1	42.7	n/a	16.1
1973	9,453	14.2	9.7	40.6	27.8	15.7
1974	9,967	15.1	11.0	39.6	28.6	16.9
1975	10,882	16.8	12.5	41.4	33.1	18.2
1976	10,081	15.8	11.3	40.4	30.1	17.7
1977	10,028	16.0	11.4	41.6	28.0	18.1
1978	9,722	15.7	11.0	41.2	27.2	17.2
1979	9,993	16.0	11.4	40.8	27.7	17.8
1980	11,114	17.9	13.4	42.1	33.0	20.5
1981	12,068	19.5	14.7	44.9	35.4	22.0
1982	13,139	21.3	16.5	47.3	38.9	23.3
1983	13,427	21.8	17.0	46.2	37.7	24.6
1984	12,929	21.0	16.1	46.2	38.7	23.4
1985	12,483	20.1	15.6	43.1	39.6	22.6
1986	12,257	19.8	15.3	42.7	37.1	21.6
1987	12,275	19.7	14.7	44.4	38.9	22.4
1988	11,935	19.0	14.0	42.8	37.3	22.6
1989	12,001	19.4	14.1	43.2	35.5	22.5
1990	12,715	19.9	15.1	44.2	37.7	23.0
1991	13,658	21.1	16.1	45.6	39.8	24.0
1992	14,521	21.6	16.5	46.3	38.8	25.0
1993	14,961	22.0	17.0	45.9	39.9	25.6
1994	14,610	21.2	16.3	43.3	41.1	24.5
1995	13,999	20.2	15.5	41.5	39.3	23.7
1996	13,764	19.8	15.5	39.5	39.9	22.7
(1997)	(13,422)	(19.2)	(15.4)	(36.8)	(36.4)	(21.6)

Poverty of related children in families under age 18, numbers and rates for all, white, black, Hispanic; rates under 6. Source: U.S. Bureau of the Census.

n/a: data not available

Youth suicide

		Suicide aged 15-24				Suicide aged 15-19	Suicide aged 20-24
	All	**White Male**	**White Female**	**Black Male**	**Black Female**	**All**	**All**
1970	8.8	13.9	4.2	10.5	3.8	5.9	12.2
1971	9.3	14.4	4.5	9.7	4.8	6.5	12.4
1972	10.1	15.4	4.5	14.7	4.7	6.8	13.8
1973	10.5	17.3	4.3	12.7	3.3	6.9	14.6
1974	10.8	17.6	4.7	11.1	3.4	7.1	14.9
1975	11.7	19.3	4.9	12.7	3.2	7.5	16.3
1976	11.5	18.8	4.8	13.0	3.7	7.2	16.1
1977	13.3	22.4	5.4	13.0	3.7	8.7	18.2
1978	12.1	20.4	4.9	13.0	2.7	7.9	16.5
1979	12.4	20.5	4.9	14.0	3.3	8.4	16.4
1980	12.3	21.4	4.6	12.3	2.3	8.5	16.1
1981	12.2	21.1	4.9	11.2	2.4	8.6	15.7
1982	12.1	21.2	4.5	11.3	2.3	8.7	15.2
1983	11.8	20.4	4.5	11.5	2.7	8.6	14.6
1984	12.4	21.8	4.7	11.2	2.4	8.9	15.5
1985	12.8	22.3	4.7	13.3	2.0	9.9	15.4
1986	12.9	23.1	4.7	11.4	2.3	10.1	15.5
1987	12.7	22.2	4.6	12.9	2.5	10.2	15.0
1988	12.9	22.7	4.5	14.5	2.6	11.1	14.6
1989	13.0	22.5	4.3	16.6	2.9	11.1	14.9
1990	13.2	23.2	4.2	15.1	2.3	11.1	15.1
1991	13.1	23.0	4.2	16.4	1.6	11.0	14.9
1992	13.0	22.7	3.8	18.0	2.2	10.8	14.9
1993	13.5	23.1	4.3	20.1	2.7	10.9	15.8
1994	13.8	24.1	3.8	20.6	2.7	11.1	16.4
1995	13.3	23.5	3.9	18.0	2.2	10.5	16.2
1996	12.0	20.9	3.8	16.7	2.3	9.7	14.5

Suicide rates per 100,000, aged 15-24; by race and gender, aged 15-19, 20-24. Source: National Center for Health Statistics.

Health care coverage

	Number of uninsured all persons (millions)	Percent of population uninsured						
		All	**Male**	**Female**	**White**	**Black**	**Hispanic**	**Under 18**
1976	23.2	10.9	n/a	n/a	n/a	n/a	n/a	n/a
1977	23.8	11.1	n/a	n/a	n/a	n/a	n/a	n/a
1978	24.3	11.3	n/a	n/a	n/a	n/a	n/a	n/a
1979	24.4	11.0	n/a	n/a	n/a	n/a	n/a	n/a
1980	24.6	10.9	n/a	n/a	n/a	n/a	n/a	n/a
1981	27.1	12.0	n/a	n/a	n/a	n/a	n/a	n/a
1982	28.9	12.6	n/a	n/a	n/a	n/a	n/a	n/a
1983	30.6	13.2	n/a	n/a	n/a	n/a	n/a	n/a
1984	31.9	13.7	n/a	n/a	n/a	n/a	n/a	n/a
1985	32.6	13.8	n/a	n/a	n/a	n/a	n/a	n/a
1986	32.7	13.7	n/a	n/a	n/a	n/a	n/a	n/a
1987	31.0	12.9	14.1	11.7	11.7	19.9	30.7	12.9
1988	32.7	13.4	14.7	12.2	12.3	19.6	31.8	13.1
1989	33.4	13.6	14.8	12.4	12.5	19.2	33.4	13.3
1990	34.7	13.9	15.4	12.5	12.9	19.7	32.5	13.0
1991	35.4	14.1	15.8	12.4	12.9	20.7	31.5	12.7
1992	38.6	15.0	16.9	13.3	13.9	20.2	32.9	12.7
1993	39.7	15.3	17.1	13.6	14.2	20.5	31.6	13.7
1994	39.7	15.2	16.6	13.7	14.0	19.7	33.7	14.2
1995	40.6	15.4	16.8	14.0	14.2	21.0	33.3	13.8
1996	41.7	15.6	17.1	14.2	14.4	21.7	33.6	14.8
(1997)	(43.4)	(16.1)	(17.6)	(14.8)	(15.0)	(21.5)	(34.2)	(15.0)

Number and percent of uninsured, all. Sources: 1976-1986, estimated percentages based on the number of uninsured from the Center for National Health Program Studies, Harvard University/Cambridge Hospital, published and unpublished data, as a proportion of All Persons, U.S., U.S. Bureau of the Census, calculations by the Fordham Institute for Innovation in Social Policy; 1987-1997, U.S. Bureau of the Census.

Percent of male, female, white, black, Hispanic origin, and persons under 18 uninsured. Source: U.S. Bureau of the Census.

n/a: data not available

Wages

	Average weekly earnings (1982$)	Percent distribution of year-round full-time workers earning less than $14,640 (low earnings) in 1996$		
		All Ages	**Aged 18-24**	**High School Graduate**
1970	$298.08	n/a	n/a	n/a
1971	$303.12	n/a	n/a	n/a
1972	$315.44	n/a	n/a	n/a
1973	$315.38	n/a	n/a	n/a
1974	$302.27	n/a	n/a	n/a
1975	$293.06	n/a	n/a	n/a
1976	$297.37	n/a	n/a	n/a
1977	$300.96	n/a	n/a	n/a
1978	$300.89	n/a	n/a	n/a
1979	$291.69	12.1	22.9	13.1
1980	$274.65	13.1	26.4	14.5
1981	$270.63	14.4	29.3	16.5
1982	$267.26	14.0	28.4	16.0
1983	$272.52	15.0	34.0	17.9
1984	$274.73	14.6	33.4	16.8
1985	$271.16	15.9	36.9	18.9
1986	$271.94	15.5	35.5	18.5
1987	$269.16	14.5	34.5	17.6
1988	$266.79	15.1	34.5	18.1
1989	$264.22	14.1	33.9	17.4
1990	$259.47	15.8	38.2	19.3
1991	$255.40	15.7	39.5	19.8
1992	$254.99	16.5	42.3	20.9
1993	$254.87	16.2	41.4	20.3
1994	$256.73	16.2	42.5	20.3
1995	$255.07	16.1	42.6	20.9
1996	$255.51	15.3	43.1	19.4
(1997)	($260.89)	n/a	n/a	n/a

Average weekly earnings, 1982$, total private, private nonagricultural industries, includes production or nonsupervisory workers. Source: Economic Report of the President; 1997 data is preliminary.

Percent distribution of year-round full-time workers earning less than $14,640 (low earnings). Source: U.S. Bureau of the Census.

n/a: data not available

Wages, cont.

	Median income 1996$			Median earnings 1996$	
	All families	**Married couple families wife in paid labor force**	**Married couple families wife not in paid laborforce**	**Male**	**Female**
1970	$37,485	$46,637	$35,346	$34,062	$20,222
1971	$37,441	$46,790	$35,472	$34,216	$20,361
1972	$39,282	$49,109	$37,303	$36,052	$20,860
1973	$40,059	$50,650	$37,955	$37,184	$21,059
1974	$39,004	$49,038	$36,976	$35,863	$21,071
1975	$38,301	$48,123	$35,601	$35,618	$20,950
1976	$39,510	$49,476	$36,798	$35,540	$21,393
1977	$39,744	$50,317	$37,395	$36,310	$21,395
1978	$41,003	$51,391	$37,554	$36,564	$21,734
1979	$41,530	$52,712	$37,542	$36,074	$21,523
1980	$40,079	$51,243	$36,169	$35,483	$21,346
1981	$38,986	$50,931	$35,394	$35,281	$20,899
1982	$38,459	$49,798	$34,956	$34,592	$21,359
1983	$38,721	$50,578	$34,483	$34,469	$21,920
1984	$39,917	$52,352	$35,611	$35,062	$22,319
1985	$40,443	$53,123	$35,807	$35,281	$22,783
1986	$42,171	$54,895	$36,939	$36,156	$23,237
1987	$42,775	$56,284	$36,794	$35,836	$23,357
1988	$42,695	$56,644	$36,102	$35,384	$23,351
1989	$43,290	$57,276	$36,374	$34,583	$23,749
1990	$42,440	$56,154	$36,332	$33,226	$23,795
1991	$41,401	$55,490	$33,646	$33,892	$23,677
1992	$40,900	$55,664	$33,744	$33,770	$23,904
1993	$40,131	$55,598	$32,811	$33,016	$23,613
1994	$41,059	$56,438	$33,036	$32,665	$23,509
1995	$41,810	$57,471	$33,331	$32,426	$23,161
1996	$42,300	$58,381	$33,748	$32,144	$23,710

Median income, 1996$, all families, married couple families, wife in paid labor force, wife not in paid labor force. Source: "Type of Family—Families (All Races) by Median and Mean Incomes: 1947 to 1996," U.S. Bureau of the Census.

Median earnings, male, female, year-round full-time workers. Source: "Persons (all races) 15 Years Old and Over by Median Earnings and Sex: 1960-1996," U.S. Bureau of the Census.

Inequality

	Gini Index	Share of aggregate income received by:		
		Bottom fifth	**Middle three-fifths**	**Top fifth**
1970	0.353	5.4	53.6	40.9
1971	0.355	5.5	53.4	41.1
1972	0.359	5.5	53.3	41.4
1973	0.356	5.5	53.4	41.1
1974	0.355	5.7	53.7	40.6
1975	0.357	5.6	53.8	40.7
1976	0.358	5.6	53.8	40.7
1977	0.363	5.5	53.6	40.9
1978	0.363	5.4	53.5	41.1
1979	0.365	5.4	53.2	41.4
1980	0.365	5.3	53.6	41.1
1981	0.369	5.3	53.5	41.2
1982	0.380	5.0	52.9	42.2
1983	0.382	4.9	52.9	42.4
1984	0.383	4.8	52.7	42.5
1985	0.389	4.8	52.2	43.1
1986	0.392	4.7	51.9	43.4
1987	0.393	4.6	51.5	43.8
1988	0.395	4.6	51.4	44.0
1989	0.401	4.6	50.8	44.6
1990	0.396	4.6	51.2	44.3
1991	0.397	4.5	51.4	44.2
1992	0.404	4.3	51.0	44.7
1993	0.429	4.1	48.9	47.0
1994	0.426	4.2	49.0	46.9
1995	0.421	4.4	49.1	46.5
1996	0.425	4.2	48.9	46.8
(1997)	(0.429)	(4.2)	(48.6)	(47.2)

Gini Index. Source: "Gini Ratios for Families, by Race and Hispanic Origin of Householder: 1947-1997," U.S. Bureau of the Census.

Share of Aggregate Income. Source: "Share of Aggregate Income Received by Each Fifth and Top 5 Percent of Families: 1947-1997," U.S. Bureau of the Census.

Inequality, cont.

	Mean income of families, 1996$		
	Bottom fifth	**Top fifth**	**Top five percent**
1970	$11,640	$86,325	$131,450
1971	$11,653	$86,572	$132,000
1972	$12,160	$92,299	$141,500
1973	$12,472	$93,073	$140,462
1974	$12,697	$90,337	$131,766
1975	$12,192	$88,425	$129,713
1976	$12,494	$90,701	$132,750
1977	$12,430	$92,869	$135,388
1978	$12,612	$96,020	$140,708
1979	$12,717	$97,918	$144,942
1980	$12,222	$93,888	$133,470
1981	$11,847	$92,822	$129,703
1982	$11,168	$94,847	$135,702
1983	$11,007	$96,286	$138,825
1984	$11,358	$99,711	$144,164
1985	$11,474	$103,558	$154,758
1986	$11,793	$108,567	$164,867
1987	$11,750	$111,692	$174,847
1988	$11,797	$112,655	$176,020
1989	$11,975	$117,249	$187,822
1990	$11,804	$113,328	$177,817
1991	$11,213	$110,049	$170,283
1992	$10,720	$110,492	$173,962
1993	$10,575	$120,544	$208,055
1994	$10,997	$122,395	$209,979
1995	$11,598	$122,980	$210,912
1996	$11,388	$125,627	$217,355

Mean income of families. Source: "Mean Income of Families Received by Each Fifth and Top 5 Percent of Families (All Races): 1966 to 1996," U.S. Bureau of the Census.

Violent crime

	All violent crimes	Murder	Rape	Robbery	Assault
1970	363.5	7.9	18.7	172.1	164.3
1971	396.0	8.6	20.5	188.0	178.8
1972	401.0	9.0	22.5	180.7	188.8
1973	417.4	9.4	24.5	183.1	200.5
1974	461.1	9.8	26.2	209.3	215.8
1975	487.8	9.6	26.3	220.8	231.1
1976	467.8	8.8	26.6	199.3	233.2
1977	475.9	8.8	29.4	190.7	247.0
1978	497.8	9.0	31.0	195.8	262.1
1979	548.9	9.7	34.7	218.4	286.0
1980	596.6	10.2	36.8	251.1	298.5
1981	594.3	9.8	36.0	258.7	289.7
1982	571.1	9.1	34.0	238.9	289.2
1983	537.7	8.3	33.7	216.5	279.2
1984	539.2	7.9	35.7	205.4	290.2
1985	556.6	7.9	37.1	208.5	302.9
1986	617.7	8.6	37.9	225.1	346.1
1987	609.7	8.3	37.4	212.7	351.3
1988	637.2	8.4	37.6	229.9	370.2
1989	663.1	8.7	38.1	233.0	383.4
1990	731.8	9.4	41.2	257.0	424.1
1991	758.1	9.8	42.3	272.7	433.3
1992	757.5	9.3	42.8	263.6	441.8
1993	746.8	9.5	41.1	255.9	440.3
1994	713.6	9.0	39.3	237.7	427.6
1995	684.6	8.2	37.1	220.9	418.3
1996	634.1	7.4	36.1	202.4	388.2
(1997)	(610.8)	(6.8)	(35.9)	(186.1)	(382.0)

Violent crime indexes, rate per 100,000 population; violent crime offenses are murder, forcible rape, robbery, and aggravated assault. Source: Federal Bureau of Investigation, Uniform Crime Reports.

Violent crime, cont.

	Number	Rate per 100,000 resident population			Total adults on probation, in jail, prison and on parole
		All	**Male**	**Female**	
1970	196,429	96	191	5	n/a
1971	198,061	95	189	6	n/a
1972	196,092	93	185	6	n/a
1973	204,211	96	191	6	n/a
1974	218,466	102	202	7	n/a
1975	240,593	111	220	8	n/a
1976	262,833	120	238	9	n/a
1977	2854,56	129	255	10	n/a
1978	294,396	132	261	10	n/a
1979	301,470	133	264	10	n/a
1980	315,974	139	275	11	1,840,400
1981	353,167	154	304	12	2,006,600
1982	394,374	171	337	14	2,192,600
1983	419,820	179	354	15	2,475,100
1984	443,398	188	370	16	2,689,200
1985	480,568	202	397	17	3,011,500
1986	522,084	217	426	20	3,239,400
1987	560,812	231	453	22	3,459,600
1988	603,732	247	482	24	3,714,100
1989	680,907	276	535	29	4,055,600
1990	739,980	297	575	32	4,348,000
1991	789,610	313	606	34	4,535,600
1992	846,277	332	642	36	4,762,600
1993	932,074	359	698	41	4,944,000
1994	1,016,691	389	753	45	5,141,300
1995	1,085,363	411	796	48	5,335,100
1996	1,138,984	427	819	51	5,475,000

Incarceration rates
Sentenced Prisoners in State and Federal Institutions

Number and rate, per 100,000 resident population of sentenced prisoners in state and federal institutions on December 31. Source: Bureau of Justice Statistics.

Adults on probation, in jail or prison, and on parole. Source: Bureau of Justice Statistics.

n/a: data not available

Drug abuse

	Drug abuse—annual prevalence						
	12th graders any illicit drug	12th graders marijuana use	10th graders any illicit drug	8th graders any illicit drug	College students any illicit drug	12-17 year olds any illicit drug	18-25 year olds any illicit drug
1975	45.0	40.0	n/a	n/a	n/a	n/a	n/a
1976	48.1	44.5	n/a	n/a	n/a	n/a	n/a
1977	51.1	47.6	n/a	n/a	n/a	n/a	n/a
1978	53.8	50.2	n/a	n/a	n/a	n/a	n/a
1979	54.2	50.8	n/a	n/a	n/a	24.3	45.5
1980	53.1	48.8	n/a	n/a	56.2	n/a	n/a
1981	52.1	46.1	n/a	n/a	55.0	n/a	n/a
1982	49.4	44.3	n/a	n/a	49.5	n/a	n/a
1983	47.4	42.3	n/a	n/a	49.8	n/a	n/a
1984	45.8	40.0	n/a	n/a	45.1	n/a	n/a
1985	46.3	40.6	n/a	n/a	46.3	20.7	37.4
1986	44.3	38.8	n/a	n/a	45.0	n/a	n/a
1987	41.7	36.3	n/a	n/a	40.1	n/a	n/a
1988	38.5	33.1	n/a	n/a	37.4	14.9	29.1
1989	35.4	29.6	n/a	n/a	36.7	n/a	n/a
1990	32.5	27.0	n/a	n/a	33.3	14.1	26.1
1991	29.4	23.9	21.4	11.3	29.2	13.1	26.6
1992	27.1	21.9	20.4	12.9	30.6	10.4	24.1
1993	31.0	26.0	24.7	15.1	30.6	11.9	24.2
1994	35.8	30.7	30.0	18.5	31.4	15.5	24.6
1995	39.0	34.7	33.3	21.4	33.5	18.0	25.5
1996	40.2	35.8	37.5	23.6	34.2	16.7	26.8
(1997)	(42.4)	(38.5)	(38.5)	(22.1)	(34.1)	n/a	n/a

Annual prevalence, any illicit drug, twelfth graders, tenth graders, eighth graders, college students, marijuana use by twelfth graders. Source: *Monitoring the Future Study,* The University of Michigan and the Department of Health and Human Services.

Annual prevalence, any illicit drug, 12-17 year olds, 18-25 year olds. Source: *National Household Survey on Drug Abuse*, U.S. Department of Health and Human Services, Public Health Service, Substance Abuse and Mental Health Services Administration, Office of Applied Statistics.

n/a: data not available

Teenage births

	Total births aged 15-19	Birth rates aged 15-19			
		All	White	Black	Hispanic
1970	644,708	68.3	57.4	140.7	n/a
1971	627,942	64.5	53.6	134.5	n/a
1972	616,280	61.7	51.0	129.8	n/a
1973	604,096	59.3	49.0	123.1	n/a
1974	595,466	57.5	47.9	116.5	n/a
1975	582,252	55.6	46.4	111.8	n/a
1976	558,744	52.8	44.1	104.9	n/a
1977	559,154	52.8	44.1	104.7	n/a
1978	543,407	51.5	42.9	100.9	n/a
1979	549,472	52.3	43.7	101.7	n/a
1980	552,161	53.0	45.4	97.8	n/a
1981	527,392	52.2	44.9	94.5	n/a
1982	513,758	52.4	45.0	94.3	n/a
1983	489,286	51.4	43.9	93.9	n/a
1984	469,582	50.6	42.9	94.1	n/a
1985	467,485	51.0	43.3	95.4	n/a
1986	461,905	50.2	42.3	95.8	n/a
1987	462,312	50.6	42.5	97.6	n/a
1988	478,353	53.0	44.4	102.7	n/a
1989	506,503	57.3	47.9	111.5	100.8
1990	521,826	59.9	50.8	112.8	100.3
1991	519,577	62.1	52.8	115.5	106.7
1992	505,415	60.7	51.8	112.4	107.1
1993	501,093	59.6	51.1	108.6	106.8
1994	505,488	58.9	51.1	104.5	107.7
1995	499,873	56.8	50.1	96.1	106.7
1996	491,577	54.4	48.1	91.4	101.8
(1997)	(489,211)	(52.9)	(46.8)	(89.5)	(99.1)

Total Births. Source: National Center for Health Statistics; 1997 data is preliminary.

Birth Rates—Live births per 1,000 women. Source: National Center for Health Statistics; 1997 data is preliminary.

Note: White and Black rates differ from those in Chart 6.6 because of the additional breakdown there by Hispanic origin.

n/a: data not available

Teenage births, cont.

	Birth rates—unmarried—aged 15-19			
	All	**White**	**Black**	**Hispanic**
1970	22.4	10.9	96.9	n/a
1971	22.3	10.3	98.6	n/a
1972	22.8	10.4	98.2	n/a
1973	22.7	10.6	94.9	n/a
1974	23.0	11.0	93.8	n/a
1975	23.9	12.0	93.5	n/a
1976	23.7	12.3	89.7	n/a
1977	25.1	13.4	90.9	n/a
1978	24.9	13.6	87.9	n/a
1979	26.4	14.6	91.0	n/a
1980	27.6	16.5	87.9	n/a
1981	27.9	17.2	85.0	n/a
1982	28.7	18.0	85.1	n/a
1983	29.5	18.7	85.5	n/a
1984	30.0	19.3	86.1	n/a
1985	31.4	29.8	87.6	n/a
1986	32.3	21.8	88.5	n/a
1987	33.8	23.2	90.9	n/a
1988	36.4	25.3	96.1	n/a
1989	40.1	28.0	104.5	n/a
1990	42.5	30.6	106.0	65.9
1991	44.8	32.8	108.5	72.4
1992	44.6	33.0	105.9	72.9
1993	44.5	33.6	102.4	74.6
1994	46.4	36.2	100.9	82.6
1995	44.4	35.5	92.8	78.7
1996	42.9	34.5	89.2	74.5

Birth Rates—Live births per 1,000 women. Source: National Center for Health Statistics.

Alcohol-related traffic fatalities

	Number of traffic crashes	Number of traffic crash fatalities	Number of alcohol-related traffic crash fatalities	Percent of all traffic crash fatalities which are alcohol-related	Number of alcohol-related traffic crash fatalities	Percent of all traffic crash fatalities which are alcohol-related
	Alcohol Epidemiological Data System				**Fatal Accident Reporting System**	
1977	42,064	47,715	17,414	36.5	n/a	n/a
1978	44,433	50,327	18,362	36.5	n/a	n/a
1979	45,212	51,084	20,245	39.6	n/a	n/a
1980	45,271	51,077	21,114	41.3	n/a	n/a
1981	43,979	49,268	20,662	41.9	n/a	n/a
1982	38,899	43,721	18,622	42.6	25,165	57.3
1983	37,971	42,584	17,847	41.9	23,646	55.5
1984	39,622	44,241	18,523	41.9	23,758	53.7
1985	39,196	43,825	18,040	41.2	22,716	51.8
1986	41,090	46,082	20,038	43.5	24,045	52.2
1987	41,435	46,386	19,918	42.9	23,641	51.0
1988	42,130	47,087	19,303	41.0	23,626	50.2
1989	40,718	45,555	18,381	40.3	22,404	49.2
1990	39,779	44,529	18,279	41.0	22,084	49.5
1991	36,895	41,462	16,231	39.1	19,887	47.9
1992	34,942	39,250	14,684	37.4	17,858	45.5
1993	35,747	40,115	14,225	35.5	17,473	43.5
1994	36,254	40,716	13,693	33.6	16,580	40.7
1995	37,241	41,817	13,881	33.2	17,274	41.3
1996	n/a	n/a	n/a	n/a	17,126	40.9

Alcohol Epidemiological Data System, Number of Traffic Crashes, Number of Traffic Crash Fatalities, Number of Alcohol-Related Traffic Crash Fatalities and Percent of All Traffic Crash Fatalities Which Are Alcohol-Related. Source: National Institute on Alcohol Abuse and Alcoholism, Division of Biometry and Epidemiology.

Fatal Accident Reporting System, Number of Alcohol-Related Traffic Crash Fatalities and Percent of All Traffic Crash Fatalities Which Are Alcohol-Related. Source: U.S. Department of Transportation, National Highway Traffic Safety Administration, National Center for Statistics and Analysis, Research and Development.

Note: The two systems use the same database but the Alcohol Epidemiological Data System employs a more "conservative" definition. The Fatal Accident Reporting System includes non-driver drinking as an indicator of alcohol involvement.

n/a: data not available

Affordable housing

	Housing affordability index composite all buyers	Housing affordability index first time buyers	Homeowner— cost as % of income after-tax mortgage payment	Renter— contract rent as % of income	Renter— gross rent as % of income
1970	147.3	n/a	n/a	n/a	n/a
1971	151.9	n/a	n/a	n/a	n/a
1972	154.8	n/a	n/a	n/a	n/a
1973	147.9	n/a	n/a	n/a	n/a
1974	130.3	n/a	n/a	n/a	n/a
1975	123.5	n/a	20.1	22.0	25.3
1976	125.8	n/a	20.1	21.8	25.2
1977	120.6	93.7	22.5	21.8	25.4
1978	111.4	83.8	24.5	21.8	25.4
1979	97.2	73.4	28.3	21.7	25.4
1980	79.9	59.8	31.6	21.8	25.7
1981	68.9	49.9	34.1	21.9	26.0
1982	69.5	50.6	34.3	22.3	26.6
1983	83.2	59.4	28.6	22.6	27.1
1984	89.1	64.9	27.9	22.8	27.3
1985	94.8	68.3	26.3	23.2	27.6
1986	108.9	75.6	24.2	23.8	28.0
1987	114.2	78.9	23.9	23.8	27.8
1988	113.5	79.0	24.8	23.7	27.5
1989	108.1	75.3	27.2	23.9	27.7
1990	110.2	77.5	26.5	23.8	27.5
1991	112.9	75.0	24.8	24.0	27.6
1992	124.7	81.8	21.9	23.5	27.1
1993	136.9	89.2	20.4	23.8	27.4
1994	131.8	83.9	21.3	23.9	27.5
1995	129.3	80.2	22.0	23.9	27.3
1996	130.8	80.4	21.9	23.7	27.1

Housing affordability index—degree to which the typical family can afford the monthly mortgage payment on a typical home, varies between 0 and 100, with 100 equal to typical family with median income having exactly enough to qualify for an 80 percent mortgage, 20 percent down payment, on a median priced home with a 25 percent qualifying ratio. Composite index is weighted average of fixed rate and adjustable rate mortgages. First-time buyers includes heads of household 23-44, adjusted for a lower median income, with a 10 percent downpayment. Source: National Association of Realtors.

Homeowner cost as percent of income, after-tax mortgage payment. Source: Joint Center for Housing Studies, Harvard University.

Contract rent and gross rent (contract rent plus fuel and utilities, property taxes, and insurance) as percent of income. Source: Joint Center for Housing Studies, Harvard University.

n/a: data not available

Unemployment

	Unemployment rates					
	All civilian workers	Male	Female	White	Black	Youth both sexes, 16-19
1970	4.9	4.4	5.9	4.5	n/a	15.3
1971	5.9	5.3	6.9	5.4	n/a	16.9
1972	5.6	5.0	6.6	5.1	10.4	16.2
1973	4.9	4.2	6.0	4.3	9.4	14.5
1974	5.6	4.9	6.7	5.0	10.5	16.0
1975	8.5	7.9	9.3	7.8	14.8	19.9
1976	7.7	7.1	8.6	7.0	14.0	19.0
1977	7.1	6.3	8.2	6.2	14.0	17.8
1978	6.1	5.3	7.2	5.2	12.8	16.4
1979	5.8	5.1	6.8	5.1	12.3	16.1
1980	7.1	6.9	7.4	6.3	14.3	17.8
1981	7.6	7.4	7.9	6.7	15.6	19.6
1982	9.7	9.9	9.4	8.6	18.9	23.2
1983	9.6	9.9	9.2	8.4	19.5	22.4
1984	7.5	7.4	7.6	6.5	15.9	18.9
1985	7.2	7.0	7.4	6.2	15.1	18.6
1986	7.0	6.9	7.1	6.0	14.5	18.3
1987	6.2	6.2	6.2	5.3	13.0	16.9
1988	5.5	5.5	5.6	4.7	11.7	15.3
1989	5.3	5.2	5.4	4.5	11.4	15.0
1990	5.6	5.7	5.5	4.8	11.4	15.5
1991	6.8	7.2	6.4	6.1	12.5	18.7
1992	7.5	7.9	7.0	6.6	14.2	20.1
1993	6.9	7.2	6.6	6.1	13.0	19.0
1994	6.1	6.2	6.0	5.3	11.5	17.6
1995	5.6	5.6	5.6	4.9	10.4	17.3
1996	5.4	5.4	5.4	4.7	10.5	16.7
(1997)	(4.9)	(4.9)	(5.0)	(4.2)	(10.0)	(16.0)

Unemployment—civilian unemployment rate, percent, monthly data, seasonally adjusted, all civilian workers, by gender, race, and age. Source: *Economic Report of the President.*

n/a: data not available

Notes

Introduction

Page 4. "The presidential campaigns of recent years illustrate this point.": For a discussion of this issue and an analysis of gaming versus governing strategies, see, Thomas E. Patterson, *Out of Order* (New York: Alfred A. Knopf, 1993), Chapter 2, "Of Schemas—Gaming and Governing," 53-93.

Page 4. "By most standard macroeconomic indicators". . .: *Economic Report of the President,* Transmitted to the Congress, February 1995, together with the Annual Report of the Council of Economic Advisors (Washington, D.C., February 1995), 19, 46.

Page 4. "Economic performance during the past 3 years has been exceptional.": *Economic Report of the President,* Transmitted to the Congress, February 1996, together with the Annual Report of the Council of Economic Advisors (Washington, D.C., February 1996), 41.

Page 4. "Economic growth has been strong and sustainable.": *Economic Report of the President,* Transmitted to the Congress, February 1997, together with the Annual Report of the Council of Economic Advisors (Washington, D.C., February 1997), 23.

Page 5. "The past year saw the nation's economy turn in its best performance in a generation.": *Economic Report of the President,* Transmitted to the Congress, February 1998, together with the Annual Report of the Council of Economic Advisors (Washington, D.C., February 1998), 19.

Page 5. "If there were a Council of Social Advisors". . .: These ideas were first proposed in the 1960s. See: U.S. Senate Sub-committee on Government Research of the Committee on Government Operations, *Full Opportunity and Social Accounting Act: [Seminar] Hearings on S. 843, A Bill to Promote the Public Welfare and to Create a Council of Social Advisors, A Social Report of the President, and a Joint Committee on the Social Report, HR 10261,* 90th Cong., 1st sess., June 26, 1967, Part I (Washington, D.C., 1968). For further discussion of this issue see Part One of this book, Chapter Two, and Part Three, Chapter Eight.

Page 5. "On the whole, long-term trends in social performance may be viewed as less than encouraging.": For a detailed discussion of each of the social indicators mentioned, see Part Two of this book, Chapters Four, Five, and Six. Note: These analyses are based on data through 1996; 1997 data is provided in the Appendix where available or preliminary.

Page 7. "To achieve this, the following initiatives are needed:" The initiatives proposed in this section were presented by the staff of the Fordham Institute for Innovation in Social Policy to the members of the Working Group on Social Indicators, either in plenary or task-group session. They were discussed and refined by the Working Group.

Part One: Seeking the Social Side of the Portrait

Chapter One: How Are We doing?

The Dominance of the "Economy."

Page 12. "The previous year's events are documented in great detail, as are trends over time". . .: Economic indicators dating back to 1929 include, "Changes in Consumer Price Indexes for Commodities and Services," "Bond Yields and Interest Rates," and "Civilian Population and Labor Force." Most indicators date back to at least 1959.

Page 12. "Every six weeks, the nation focuses on another important set of economic indicators". . .: The Beige Book (so-called unofficially, because of the color of its cover) is published every six weeks by the Federal Reserve Board. Officially, it is called *The Current Economic Condition.* It covers twelve economic districts: Atlanta, Boston, Chicago, Cleveland, Dallas, Kansas City, Minneapolis, New York, Philadelphia, Richmond, Saint Louis, and San Francisco.

Page 12. "Social data are collected once a year at best". . . : Examples of indicators which are published on delays of two to four years include teenage suicide, aged 15-19. The five-year age group comes later than the ten-year age group, 15-24, which is published on a more timely basis. The high school dropout rate, published by the Census Bureau, is also often published on a two-year, or more, delay. Most international social indicators are on a two-year, or more, delay.

Page 14. "Problems such as hunger, homelessness, and illiteracy are still not reliably measured or tracked.": Estimates of these problems exist, but no consistent year-by-year monitoring of these problems is done. For hunger and homelessness estimates, see for example: The United States Conference of Mayors, *A Status Report on Hunger and Homelessness in America's Cities: 1996, A 29 City Survey* (Washington, D.C., December 1996). For a discussion of illiteracy, see Jonathan Kozol, *Illiterate America* (Garden City, New York: Anchor Press, 1985).

Page 14. "Some data are published under several auspices". . .: An example of this is high school dropouts, issued by the Census Bureau for 18-24 year-olds, and by the Department of Education for 16-24 year-olds. See: Current Population Survey, Education and Social Stratification Branch, *School Enrollment—Social and Economic Characteristics of Students: October 1996 (Update)* (Washington, D.C.: U.S. Bureau of the Census, June 1998), detailed tables and documentation for P20-500; Marilyn M. McMillen and Phillip Kaufman, National Center for Education Statistics, *Dropout Rates in the United States: 1996*, NCES 98-250 (Washington, D.C.: U.S. Department of Education, Office of Educational Research and Improvement, December 1997). For a detailed discussion of these issues see: Sandra Opdycke, "Social Reporting in the United States: The Role of Government and the Media" (a Working Paper prepared for the Working Group on Social Indicators, a project supported by the Ford Foundation), Fordham Institute for Innovation in Social Policy (Tarrytown, New York, 1998).

Page 14. "This approach applies even to our major print media.": This is an extract from a larger study of media coverage of social problems conducted by the Fordham Institute for Innovation in Social Policy. For this project, 1,080 stories were identified in *The New York Times* and *USA Today* during 1996 that dealt with seven social indicators. For a complete discussion of the findings and methodology, see: Sandra Opdycke, "Social Reporting in the United States: The Role of Government and the Media" (a Working Paper prepared for the Working Group on Social Indicators, a project supported by the Ford Foundation), Fordham Institute for Innovation in Social Policy (Tarrytown, New York, 1998).

Changing the Picture.

Page 17. "Recessions have a working definition". . .: See, for example, Robert E. Hall, "The Business Cycle Dating Process," *NBER Reporter* (Washington, D.C.: National Bureau of Economic Research, Winter 1991/2).

Page 18. "In the social sphere" . . . : For data on health insurance and child poverty, see Part Two of this book, Chapter Five.

Page 18. "By the same token, how do we know we are doing well?": For data on violent crime, teenage births, and alcohol-related traffic fatalities, see Part Two of this book, Chapters Five and Six.

Chapter Two: Part of a Tradition

Page 21. "In a democracy, social reporting has a very special function". . .: Joachim Vogel, "Social Indicators: A Swedish Perspective," *Journal of Public Policy* vol. 9, no. 4 (1989), 441.

American Initiatives in Social Reporting.

Page 21. "Periodically, throughout this century". . .: See, Upton Sinclair, *The Jungle* (New York: Viking, 1946); John Steinbeck, *The Grapes of Wrath* (New York: Viking, 1939); Michael Harrington, *The Other America: Poverty in the United States* (New York: Macmillan, 1962).

Page 22. "In 1913, Julia Lathrop. . . observed, [the information] was 'scattered through numerous volumes'". . .: Julia Lathrop, U.S. Children's Bureau, *Handbook of Federal Statistics of Children, Part I* (Washington, D.C.: U.S. Children's Bureau, 1913), 7, in The Papers of Julia Lathrop, Special Collections, Vassar College Library, Poughkeepsie, New York.

Page 22. "As the 1920s drew to a close, the need emerged once again for a systematic and sustained assessment of the state of the nation.": See, President's Research Committee on Social Trends, *Recent Social Trends in the United States* (New York:

McGraw Hill, 1934); also see, Martin Bulmer, "The Methodology of Early Social Indicator Research: William Fielding Ogburn and 'Recent Social Trends,' 1933," *Social Indicators Research,* vol. 13 (1983) 109-30.

Page 22. "The meaning of the present study of social change". . .: President's Research Committee on Social Trends, *Recent Social Trends in the United States* (New York: McGraw Hill, 1934), xiii.

Page 22. "During the 1930s, as the Depression deepened, federal mechanisms were established". . .: See, for example, George Martin, *Madam Secretary, Frances Perkins* (Boston: Hougton Mifflin, 1976); Hank O' Neal, *A Vision Shared: A Classic Portrait of America and its People, 1935-1943* (New York: St. Martin's Press, 1976); Edward Steichen, *The Bitter Years: 1935-1941, Rural America as Seen by the Photographers of the Farm Security Administration* (New York: Museum of Modern Art, 1962).

Page 23. "NASA, the nation's newly created space agency, commissioned the American Academy of Arts and Sciences". . .: See, Raymond Bauer, ed., *Social Indicators* (Cambridge, Mass.: M.I.T. Press, 1966).

Page 23. "Raymond Bauer, the project director, wrote that 'for many of the important topics'". . .: Raymond Bauer, "Detection and Anticipation of Impact: The Nature of the Task," in *Social Indicators,* ed. Raymond Bauer (Cambridge, Mass.: M.I.T. Press, 1966), 20.

Page 23. "Bauer proposed the term 'social indicators'". . .: See, Heinz-Herbert Noll and Wolfgang Zapf, "Social Indicator Research: Societal Monitoring and Social Reporting," in *Trends and Perspectives in Empirical Social Research,* ed. Ingwer Borg and Peter Mohler (New York: Walter de Gruyter, 1994), 1. See also, Raymond Bauer, ed., *Social Indicators* (Cambridge, Mass.: M.I.T. Press, 1966).

Page 23. "In 1966, building on Bauer's work, the federal government took a first step". . .: See, U.S. Department of Health, Education, and Welfare, *Toward A Social Report* (Washington, D.C., 1969).

Page 23. "President Lyndon Johnson directed the Department of Health, Education, and Welfare to explore". . .: U.S. Department of Health, Education, and Welfare, *Toward A Social Report* (Washington, D.C., 1969), iii.

Page 23. "The resulting study, *Toward a Social Report,* was viewed as a 'preliminary step toward the evolution of a regular system of social reporting.'": U.S. Department of Health, Education, and Welfare, *Toward A Social Report* (Washington, D.C., 1969), iii.

Page 23. "In 1967, the Annals of the American Academy of Political and Social Science published two volumes of essays on social indicators.": See, Bertram Gross, ed., "Social Goals and Indicators for American Society," *Annals of the American Academy of Political and Social Science,* Part I (May 1967), and Part II (September 1967); see also, R. D. Lambert, ed., "America in the Seventies: Some Social Indicators," *Annals of the American Academy of Political and Social Science* (January 1978); C. Taeuber, ed., "America Enters the Eighties: Some Social Indicators," *Annals of the American Academy of Political and Social Science* (January 1981).

Page 23. "In the same year, then Senator Walter Mondale". . .: See, U.S. Senate Subcommittee on Government Research of the Committee on Government Operations, *Full Opportunity and Social Accounting Act, Hearings on S. 843, A Bill to Promote the Public Welfare and to Create a Council of Social Advisors, A Social Report of the President, and a Joint Committee on the Social Report, HR 10261,* 90th Cong., 1st Session, June 26, 1967, Part I (Washington, D.C., 1968).

Page 23. "*Social Indicators* reports were issued in 1973, 1976, and 1980 but were discontinued". . .: See, U.S. Bureau of the Census, *Social Indicators* (Washington, D.C, 1973); U.S. Bureau of the Census, *Social Indicators 1976* (Washington, D.C., 1977); U.S. Bureau of the Census, *Social Indicators III* (Washington, D.C., 1981).

Page 24. "However, studies on specific issue areas are published regularly". . .: See, for example, U.S. Department of Justice, Federal Bureau of Investigation, Uniform Crime Reports, *Crime in the United States 1996,* Uniform Crime Reports, September 28, 1997 (Washington, D.C., 1997); U.S. Department of Justice, Bureau of Justice Statistics, *Sourcebook of Criminal Justice Statistics 1997,* Kathleen Maguire and Ann L. Pastore, eds. (Washington, D.C., 1998); National Center for Health Statistics, *Health United States 1996-97 and Injury Chartbook* (Hyattsville, Maryland: National Center for Health Statistics, 1997); U.S. Department of Education, Office of Educational Research and Improvement, National Center for Education Statistics, *The Condition of Education 1997,* NCES 97-388, by Thomas M. Smith, et al. (Washington, D.C., June 1997).

Page 24. "The federal government has made available several new on-going studies. . . .": See U.S. Department of Health and Human Services, Office of the Assistant Secretary for Planning and Evaluation, *Trends in the Well-Being of America's Chil-*

dren and Youth: 1996 (Washington, D.C., 1996); Federal Interagency Forum on Child and Family Statistics, *America's Children: Key National Indicators of Well-Beings, 1997* (Washington, D.C., 1997). See also: U.S. Department of Education, Office of Educational Research and Improvement, National Center for Education Statistics, *Youth Indicators 1996, Trends in the Well-Being of American Youth* (Washington, D.C., September 1996); U.S. Department of Health and Human Services, Public Health Service, Health Resources and Services Administration, Maternal and Child Health Bureau, *Child Health USA '95*, DHHS Publication No. HRSA-M-DSEA-96-5 (Washington, D.C., September 1996).

Page 24. "Because of the troubling status of children, numerous reports on youth also have been generated outside of government.": See, The Annie E. Casey Foundations, *Kids Count Data Book: State Profiles of Child Well-Being, 1997* (Baltimore, Maryland: Annie E. Casey Foundations, 1997); Children's Defense Fund, *The State of the Nation's Children Yearbook, 1997* (Washington, D.C.: Children's Defense Fund, 1997).

Page 24. "In 1993, the Genuine Progress Indicator (GPI) was issued by Redefining Progress. . . 'the economy that people experience.'" : See, Clifford Cobb, Ted Halstead, and Jonathan Rowe, "If the Economy is Up, Why is America Down?" *Atlantic Monthly,* vol. 276, no. 4 (October 1995), 59. See also: Redefining Progress, *The Genuine Progress Indicator: Summary of Data and Methodology* (San Francisco: Redefining Progress, 1995).

Page 24. "Car wrecks, divorces, disease, crime". . .: Jonathan Rowe, "Replace the GDP," *Washington Monthly* (January 1, 1996), internet download.

Page 24. "Environmental problems play particular havoc. . . 'The factory pollutes the water: the GDP goes up'". . . : Jonathan Rowe, "Replace the GDP," *Washington Monthly* (January 1, 1996), internet download.

Page 25. "To correct this form of accounting, the GPI seeks". . .: Clifford Cobb, Ted Halstead, and Jonathan Rowe, "If the Economy is Up, Why is America Down?" *Atlantic Monthly,* vol. 276, no. 4 (October 1995), 59. See also: Redefining Progress, *The Genuine Progress Indicator: Summary of Data and Methodology* (San Francisco: Redefining Progress, 1995).

Page 25. "A second measure is the *Index of Social Health*". . .: See, Fordham Institute for Innovation in Social Policy, *The 1998 Index of Social Health, Monitoring the Social Well-Being of the Nation, Special Section: The Elderly in Poverty* (Tarrytown, New York, 1998). See also: Marc Miringoff, "Toward a National Standard of Social Health: The Need for Progress in Social Indicators," *American Journal of Orthopsychiatry* vol. 65, no. 4 (October 1995), 462-67; Marc Miringoff and Marque-Luisa Miringoff, "America's Social Health: The Nation's Need to Know," *Challenge* (Fall 1995), 19-24. Marque-Luisa Miringoff, Marc Miringoff, and Sandra Opdycke, "The Growing Gap Between Standard Economic Indicators and the Nation's Social Health," *Challenge* (July-August 1996), 17-22; Marc Miringoff, Marque-Luisa Miringoff, and Sandra Opdycke, "Monitoring the Nation's Social Performance: The Index of Social Health," in *Children, Families, and Government, Preparing for the Twenty-First Century,* ed. Edward F. Zigler, Sharon Lynn Kagan, and Nancy W. Hall (New York: Cambridge University Press, 1996); Marc L. Miringoff and Marque-Luisa Miringoff, "Context and Connection in Social Indicators: Enhancing What we Measure and Monitor," in *Indicators of Children's Well-Being,* ed. Robert M. Hauser, Brett V. Brown, and William R. Prosser (New York: Russell Sage Foundation, 1997).

Page 26. "In 1996, the Index stood at 43". . .: Fordham Institute for Innovation in Social Policy, *The 1998 Index of Social Health, Monitoring the Social Well-Being of the Nation, Special Section: The Elderly in Poverty* (Tarrytown, New York, 1998).

Page 26. "The Index approach has been applied to subgroups within populations, such as children and women". . .: See, Fordham Institute for Innovation in Social Policy, *The Index of Social Health 1989: Measuring the Social Well-Being of the Nation. Special Focus: The Social Health of America's Children and Youth* (Tarrytown, New York, Fall 1989); Fordham Institute for Innovation in Social Policy, *The Index of Social Health 1990: Measuring the Social Well-Being of the Nation. Special Focus: The Social Health of Women* (Tarrytown, New York, Fall 1990); Fordham Institute for Innovation in Social Policy, in cooperation with *The Bangor Daily News, The Index of Social Health of Maine* (Tarrytown, New York, 1990); *The Index of Social Health of New Jersey* (Newark: *The Star-Ledger,* December 10, 1991); Fordham Institute for Innovation in Social Policy, *The Index of Social Health 1992: Monitoring the Social Well-Being of the Nation. Special Focus: The Social Health of America's Children* (Tarrytown, New York, Fall 1992); Fordham Institute for Innovation in Social Policy, in cooperation with UNICEF, *The Social Health of the Children of Europe* (Tarrytown, New York, Fall 1993).

Page 26. "In 1997, the State of Connecticut passed a law". . .: PL 97310 of the State of Connecticut states, "The Commission on Children shall develop, within available appropriations, an annual social health index report to the State of Connecticut to monitor the social health of its citizens and assist the state in analyzing and publicizing social health issues and in evaluating the state's progress in addressing these issues." *The Social State of Connecticut* has been published for the past five years, funded by the Connecticut Commission on Children and the Graustein Memorial Fund. It incorporates an Index of the Social

Health of the State. See: Fordham Institute for Innovation in Social Policy, *The Social State of Connecticut, '98* (Tarrytown, New York, 1998).

Page 26. "Most recently, an Index of the Social Health of Canada". . .: See, Applied Research Branch, Strategic Policy, Human Resources Development Canada, *Measuring Social Well-Being: An Index of Social Health for Canada,* R-97-9E, by Satya Brink and Alan Zeesman (Quebec: Human Resources Development Canada, 1997).

Advances in Other Nations.

Page 27. "Social reporting performs an important function". . .: Joachim Vogel, Statistics Sweden, *Living Conditions and Inequality in the European Union 1997* (European Commission, 1997), 8.

Page 27. "The idea was first proposed". . . : See, U.S. Department of Health, Education, and Welfare, *Toward A Social Report* (Washington, D. C., 1969).

Page 27. "The first comprehensive national social report was developed in England.": For a discussion of its origins, see Tom Griffin, "'Social Trends'—The Annual Social Report from the Central Statistical Office" (text which formed the basis of a talk at the Social Research Association, distributed February 13, 1990; property of Her Britannic Majesty's Government CSO [EBS] [90] 2) [unpublished/unclassified]; Government Statistical Service, Office for National Statistics, *Social Trends 27,* 1997 Edition, ed. Jenny Church (London, 1997).

Page 29. "In addition to the establishment of national social reports, one of the most important recent advances has been the development of social surveys. The first of these was the Swedish Level of Living Survey.": See, Joachim Vogel, Lars-G. Andersson, Uno Davidsson, Lars Häll, *Inequality in Sweden: Trends and Current Situation, Living Conditions 1975-1985* (Stockholm: Statistics Sweden, 1988). Question examples come from the survey, "Living Conditions, ULF 82, National Central Bureau of Statistics" (unpublished). See also: Joachim Vogel, "Social Indicators: A Swedish Perspective," *Journal of Public Policy,* vol. 9, no. 4 (1989), 439-44; Joachim Vogel, "Inequality in Sweden: Trends and Current Social Situation," in *Generating Equality in the Welfare State: The Swedish Experience,* ed. Inga Persson (Norwegian University Press, 1991); Michael Tahlin, "Politics, Dynamics, and Individualism—The Swedish Approach to Level of Living Research," *Social Indicators Research,* vol. 22 (1990), 155-80; Robert Parke, "Review: Sweden, Central Bureau of Statistics, Social Report on Inequality in Sweden," *Social Indicators Research,* vol. 14 (1984), 477-80.

Page 29. "The combined result was an important multinational study". . .: See Joachim Vogel, *Social Report for the Nordic Countries: Living Conditions and Inequality in the Late 1980s* (Copenhagen: Nordic Statistical Secretariat, 1991).

Page 29. "More recently the Level of Living approach has been adopted throughout the European Union". . .: See Joachim Vogel, Statistics Sweden, *Living Conditions and Inequality in the European Union 1997* (European Commission, 1997). See also: Joachim Vogel, "The Future Direction of Social Indicator Research," *Social Indicators Research,* vol. 42, no. 2 (October 1997), 103-17; Joachim Vogel, "Social Indicators and Social Reporting: Traditions and Current Options for the Development of Comparative Social Indicators for the European Union, *Statistical Journal of the United Nations,* ECE 11 (1994), 241-60; Statistical Office of the European Communities, Working Party on "Social Indicators and Social Reporting," Meeting on 20 and 21 February 1995, "The Social Indicator Tradition" (December 1995; unpublished); Statistical Office of the European Communities, Working Party on "Social Indicators and Social Reporting," Meeting on 20 and 21 February 1995, "Options for Integrated and Comparative Statistics on Living Conditions" (December 1995; unpublished).

Page 30. "According to its authors, 'the primary use of European social indicators and social reporting'". . .: Joachim Vogel, Statistics Sweden, *Living Conditions and Inequality in the European Union 1997* (European Commission, 1997), 7.

Page 30. "Other social reports, based on available data rather than survey data". . .: UNICEF publishes its annual *Progress of Nations;* The World Health Organization publishes its *World Health Statistics Annual;* The World Bank publishes its *World Development Report,* and OECD publishes reports on selected areas, such as *Education at a Glance: OECD Indicators,* and *Employment Outlook.* The Department of Economic and Social Information and Policy Analysis of the United Nations also publishes an annual *Demographic Yearbook.*

Page 30. "One important advance was made by the United Nations Development Programme". . .: See United Nations Development Programme (UNDP), *Human Development Report 1990* (New York: Oxford University Press, 1990).

Page 30. "a new yardstick of human progress". . .: United Nations Development Programme (UNDP), *Human Development Report 1993* (New York: Oxford University Press, 1993), 10.

Page 30. "Three core indicators are included in the Human Development Index. . . 'a measure of development much more comprehensive than GNP alone.'": United Nations Development Programme (UNDP), *Human Development Report 1993* (New York: Oxford University Press, 1993), 10.

Page 30. "there is no automatic link between income and human development". . .:United Nations Development Programme (UNDP), *Human Development Report 1993* (New York: Oxford University Press, 1993), 11-12.

Pages 30. "No country treats its women as well as it treats its men". . .: United Nations Development Programme (UNDP), *Human Development Report 1993* (New York: Oxford University Press, 1993), 16. The gender-related development index has been expanded and in 1998 assessed 163 countries. The findings, however, were the same. According to the *Human Development Report 1998,* "The human development achievements of women fall below those for men in every country. . .." United Nations Development Programme (UNDP), *Human Development Report 1998* (New York: Oxford University Press, 1998), 31.

Page 30. "The Human Development Index has had considerable international impact.": See, for example: United Nations Development Programme (UNDP), *Human Development Report 1993* (New York: Oxford University Press, 1993), 19.

New Stirrings at the Local Level.

Page 31. "We've been playing the football game without a scoreboard". . .: Florida Commission on Government Accountability to the People, *The Florida Benchmarks Report: Questions and Answers* (Tallahassee, Florida: Executive Officer of the Governor, 1996), 4.

Page 31. "In many localities, both in America and throughout the world". . .: The material from this section comes primarily from Sandra Opdycke, "The Community Indicator Movement and Social Reporting" (a Working Paper prepared for the Working Group on Social Indicators, a project supported by the Ford Foundation, Fordham Institute for Innovation in Social Policy (Tarrytown, New York, 1998).

Page 32. "Some work toward the development and recognition of regular 'benchmarks' or 'milestones'". . .: See, for example, *Oregon Benchmarks* and *Minnesota Milestones.* Seattle has made famous its report, *Indicators of Sustainable Community,* and Jacksonville and Duval Counties in Florida have developed "quality of life" indicators. See Chart 2.3.

Page 32. "Some of the most intractable public health problems". . .: World Health Organization Regional Office for Europe, "Healthy Cities for a Better Life in Europe" (April 7, 1996), internet download.

Page 32. "At present, about 1,100 cities around the world". . .: World Health Organization Regional Office for Europe, "What is the Healthy Cities Project?", internet download.

Page 32. "In the Roaring Fork-Grand Valley region of Colorado". . .: Colin Laird, personal communication with Sandra Opdycke, Fordham Institute for Innovation in Social Policy (Tarrytown, New York, January 31, 1997).

Page 32. "Floridians set a comparable goal". . .: Florida Commission on Government Accountability to the People, *The Florida Benchmarks Report* (Tallahassee, Florida: Executive Officer of the Governor, 1996), 5.

Page 32. "Alexis de Tocqueville, traveling through America during the 1830s". . .: See, Alexis de Tocqueville, *Democracy in America,* trans. George Lawrence, ed. J. P. Mayer (Garden City, New York: Doubleday, 1969).

Page 32. "For example, in St. Paul, Minnesota". . .: Amherst H. Wilder Foundation, *Social Outcomes for Our Community: Entering the 21st Century, Twin Cities East Metropolitan Area, Minnesota* (St. Paul, Minnesota: Amherst H. Wilder Foundation, 1996), 2.

Page 33. "As the report from Alberta, Canada, explains". . .: Alberta Treasury, *Measuring Performance: A Reference Guide* (Edmonton, Alberta: Alberta Treasury, 1996), 3.

Page 33. "The report from Portland/Multnomah County, Oregon, explains". . .: Portland Multnomah Progress Board, *Benchmarks: Progress Measured One Step At a Time: 1996 Annual Report, Community Benchmarks* (Portland, Oregon: Portland Multnomah Progress Board, 1996), 4.

Page 33. "In Hawaii, too, spokespersons stress the appeal of a common vision". . .: Banks Lowman, "Future Bound," *Honolulu Weekly* (December 27, 1995).

Page 33. "Citizens of Oakland, California, too, appear willing". . .: Urban Strategies Council, *Chance 2: Prospects for Oakland's Infants, Children and Youth in the 1990s and Beyond* (Oakland, California: Urban Strategies Council, 1995), 3.

Page 33. "Participants in Greater Rochester, New York". . .: Center for Governmental Research, Inc., *The State of a Greater Rochester* (Rochester, New York: Goals for a Greater Rochester, 1993), 244.

Page 33. "The project coordinator in Hamilton County, Tennessee, observes". . .: Steve White, Metropolitan Council for Community Services, Chattanooga, Tennessee, via personal communication, June 20, 1997.

Page 35. "In Pasadena, California, participants note". . .: Pasadena City Health Department, *The Quality of Life in Pasadena: An Index for the 90s and Beyond* (Pasadena, California: Pasadena City Health Department, 1996), 3.

Page 35. "In Florida, 'The Commissioners were shocked to find'". . .: Florida Commission on Government Accountability to the People, *The Florida Benchmarks Report: Questions and Answers* (Tallahassee, Florida: Executive Officer of the Governor, 1996), 2.

Renewing the National Effort.

Page 36. "The many new efforts being conducted at the local level are important". . .: See, for example, David S. Sawicki and Patrice Flynn, "Neighborhood Indicators: A Review of the Literature and an Assessment of Conceptual and Methodological Issues," *Journal of the American Planning Association,* vol. 62, no. 2 (Spring 1996), 165-83; Steve Waddell, "Lessons from the Healthy Cities Movement for Social Indicator Development," *Social Indicators Research,* vol. 34 (1995), 213-35.

Part Two: Framing a Social Health Perspective for the Nation

Chapter Three: There's Something Else Out There

Page 39. "Ian Miles, for example, a development analyst, observes". . .: Ian Miles, *Social Indicators for Human Development* (New York: St. Martin's Press, 1985), 36, 38. See also: Giovanni Andrea Cornia, Richard Jolly, Frances Stewart, eds., *Adjustment with a Human Face: Protecting the Vulnerable and Promoting Growth,* vol. I of A Study by UNICEF (Oxford: Clarendon Press, 1989).

Page 39. "Senator Robert F. Kennedy framed this idea". . .: Edwin O. Guthman and C. Richard Allen, eds., *RFK, Collected Speeches* (New York: Viking, 1993), 330.

Page 39. "This view is reflected in a comparison of the Fordham Institute's Index of Social Health to the GDP.": See Fordham Institute for Innovation in Social Policy, *The 1998 Index of Social Health, Monitoring the Social Well-Being of the Nation, Special Section: The Elderly in Poverty* (Tarrytown, New York, 1998).

Page 40. "When we inquire about the prosperity of a nation or a region of the world". . .: Martha Nussbaum and Amartya Sen, *The Quality of Life* (Oxford: Clarendon Press, 1993), 1-2. See also, Amartya Sen, "The Economics of Life and Death," *Scientific American,* vol. 268, no. 5 (May 1993), 40-47; Amartya Sen, "Mortality as an Indicator of Economic Success and Failure," (Innocenti Lectures, Inaugural Lecture 1995, UNICEF, Instituto degli Innocenti, Florence, Italy, March 3, 1995).

Page 41. "This 'system shift,' as Joachim Vogel writes, . . . 'has inevitably led to growing social inequality'". . .: Joachim Vogel, "The Future Direction of Social Indicator Research," *Social Indicators Research,* vol. 42, no. 2 (October 1997), 111.

Page 41. "These problems are reflected in public-opinion data.": See, *CBS News/New York Times Survey* (January 24-25, 1998).

Chapter Four: Indicators of Improving Performance

Infant Mortality.

Page 48. "The infant mortality rate has been called.". . : Dennis Wrong, *Population and Society* (New York: Random House, 1967), 31.

Page 49. The Nation Continues to Improve.
Infant mortality rates, deaths in the first year of life per 1,000 live births: For 1970, 1975-1996, see K. D. Peters, K. D. Kochanek, S. L. Murphy, *Deaths: Final Data for 1996,* National Vital Statistics Reports, vol. 47, no. 9 (Hyattsville, Maryland: National Center for Health Statistics, 1998), Table 25. For 1971-1974, see National Center for Health Statistics, "Infant and Neonatal Mortality Rates, by Race: Birth Registration States or United States, 1915-1983," National Vital Statistics Reports, vol. 34, no. 13 (Hyattsville, Maryland: National Center for Health Statistics, 1986), Table 2-1.

Number of infant deaths, 1996: K. D. Peters, K. D. Kochanek, S. L. Murphy, *Deaths: Final Data for 1996,* National Vital Statistics Reports, vol. 47, no. 9 (Hyattsville, Maryland: National Center for Health Statistics, 1998), 12.

Page 49. Causes of Reduction.
Leading causes of infant deaths: K. D. Peters, K. D. Kochanek, S. L. Murphy, *Deaths: Final Data for 1996,* National Vital Statistics Reports, vol. 47, no. 9 (Hyattsville, Maryland: National Center for Health Statistics, 1998), 13.

See also: Centers for Disease Control, "Trends in Infant Mortality Attributable to Birth Defects—United States, 1980-1995," *Morbidity and Mortality Weekly Report,* vol. 47, no. 37 (Massachusetts Medical Society, September 25, 1998), 773-78.

Page 50. An Unequal Distribution.
Infant mortality rates by race, deaths in the first year of life per 1,000 live births (1970-1979, by race of child; 1980-1996, by race of mother): For 1970, 1975-1996, see K. D. Peters, K. D. Kochanek, S. L. Murphy, *Deaths: Final Data for 1996,* National Vital Statistics Reports, vol. 47, no. 9 (Hyattsville, Maryland: National Center for Health Statistics, 1998), Table 25. For 1971-1974 see Vital Statistics of the United States 1992, Volume 2, Mortality, Part A (Washington, D.C.), Table 2-2.

Note: The 1996 Hispanic infant mortality rate was 5.9 deaths per 1,000 live births. According to the National Center for Health Statistics, because of methodological difficulties, Hispanic infant mortality rates are underreported using the same methods that produce black and white rates. An alternate method, the "linked file," produces what is considered a more reliable rate of 6.1 infant deaths per 1,000. For a discussion see: K. D. Peters, K. D. Kochanek, S. L. Murphy, *Deaths: Final Data for 1996,* National Vital Statistics Reports, vol. 47, no. 9 (Hyattsville, Maryland: National Center for Health Statistics, 1998), "Hispanic infant mortality" and Technical Notes.

See also: M. F. MacDorman, J. O. Atkinson, *Infant Mortality Statistics From the 1996 Period Linked Birth/Infant Data Set,* Monthly Vital Statistics Report, vol. 46, no. 12, supp. (Hyattsville, Maryland: National Center for Health Statistics, 1998).

Year 2000 goal, infant mortality: National Center for Health Statistics, *Healthy People 2000 Review, 1997* (Hyattsville, Maryland: Public Health Service, 1997), 134.

Page 50. Poverty and Infant Mortality.
Relationship between poverty and infant mortality: Centers for Disease Control, "Poverty and Infant Mortality—United States, 1988," Morbidity and Morality Weekly *Report,* vol. 44, no. 49 (Massachusetts Medical Society, December 15, 1995), 922-27.

Page 51. Low Birthweight—No Advance.
Low birthweight rates and numbers, infants 5 lb. 8 oz. or less: For 1970-1980, see unpublished data, National Center for Health Statistics, "Percent low and very low birthweight by race of mother, 1970-1994," (Hyattsville, Maryland). For 1981-1996 see S. J. Ventura, J. A. Martin, S. C. Curtin, T. J. Matthews, *Report of Final Natality Statistics, 1996,* Monthly Vital Statistics Report, vol. 46, no. 11, supp. (Hyattsville, Maryland: National Center for Health Statistics, 1998), Table 44.

Low birthweight effect in first twenty-eight days: U.S. Department of Health and Human Services, Office of the Assistant Secretary for Planning and Evaluation, *Trends in the Well-Being of America's Children and Youth: 1996* (Washington, D.C., 1996), 92.

Low birthweight compared to full-size births: S. J. Ventura, J. A. Martin, S. C. Curtin, T. J. Matthews, *Report of Final Natality*

Statistics, 1995, Monthly Vital Statistics Report, vol. 45, no. 11, supp. 2 (Hyattsville, Maryland: National Center for Health Statistics, 1997), 16.

See also: Center for the Future of Children, *The Future of Children: Low Birth Weight,* vol. 5, no. 1 (Spring 1995).

Page 51. Low Birthweight—Differences by State.
Low birthweight, selected states, 1996, infants 5 lb. 8 oz. or less: S. J. Ventura, J. A. Martin, S. C. Curtin, T. J. Matthews, *Report of Final Natality Statistics, 1996,* Monthly Vital Statistics Report, vol. 46, no. 11, supp. (Hyattsville, Maryland: National Center for Health Statistics, 1998), Table 46.

Page 52. Progress in Prenatal Care.
Percent of women with late or no prenatal care, care beginning in the third trimester, or not at all: For 1970-1994, National Center for Health Statistics, unpublished data. For 1995 see S. J. Ventura, J. A. Martin, S. C. Curtin, T. J. Matthews, *Report of Final Natality Statistics, 1995,* Monthly Vital Statistics Report, vol. 45, no. 11, supp., 2 (Hyattsville, Maryland: National Center for Health Statistics, 1997), Table 34. For 1996, see S. J. Ventura, J. A. Martin, S. C. Curtin, T. J. Matthews, *Report of Final Natality Statistics, 1996,* Monthly Vital Statistics Report, vol. 46, no. 11, supp. (Hyattsville, Maryland: National Center for Health Statistics, 1998), Table 34.

"functions as a gateway". . .: S. J. Ventura, J. A. Martin, S. C. Curtin, T. J. Matthews, *Report of Final Natality Statistics, 1996,* Monthly Vital Statistics Report, vol. 46, no. 11, supp. (Hyattsville, Maryland: National Center for Health Statistics, 1998), 15.

"sentinel health event": Centers for Disease Control, "State-Specific Trends Among Women Who Did Not Receive Prenatal Care—United States, 1980-1992," Morbidity and Mortality Weekly *Report,* vol. 43, no. 50 (Massachusetts Medical Society, December 23, 1994), 942.

Page 52. Maternal Mortality.
Maternal mortality rates, deaths per 100,000; deaths are those assigned to complications of pregnancy, childbirth, and the puerperium; category numbers 630-670 of the Ninth Revision, International Classification of Disease, 1975 (1970-1988 by race of child, 1989-1996 by race of mother): Unpublished data, Mortality Statistics Branch, Division of Vital Statistics, Centers for Disease Control, National Center for Health Statistics.

See also: Centers for Disease Control, "Maternal Mortality—United States, 1982-1996," Morbidity and Mortality W*eekly Report,* vol. 47, no. 34 (Massachusetts Medical Society, September 4, 1998), 705-711.

Page 53. Our Standing in the World.
Infant mortality rates, selected industrial nations, 1996: For industrial nations see, United Nations, Department of Economic and Social Affairs, *Demographic Yearbook 1996* (New York: United Nations, 1998), Table 4; for U.S. infant mortality rate see S. J. Ventura, J. A. Martin, S. C. Curtin, T. J. Matthews, *Report of Final Natality Statistics, 1996,* Monthly Vital Statistics Report, vol. 46, no. 11, supp. (Hyattsville, Maryland: National Center for Health Statistics, 1998), Table 25.

Note: Nations included are those defined by UNICEF as "industrialized countries." See: UNICEF, *The State of the World's Children 1997* (New York: Oxford University Press, 1997), 101.

High School Dropouts.

Page 54. "Nations have increasingly turned to formal education". . . : U.S. Department of Education, National Center for Education Statistics, *Educational Indicators: An International Perspective,* NCES 96-003, by Nancy Matheson, Laura Hersh Salganik, Richard P. Phelps, Marianne Perie, Nabeel Alsalam, and Thomas M. Smith (Washington, D.C., 1996), 13.

Page 55. Progress Made.
Status dropouts—population 18-24 years old not enrolled in school, who have not finished high school: U.S. Bureau of the Census, Current Population Survey, Education and Social Stratification Branch, *School Enrollment—Social and Economic Characteristics of Students: October 1996* (Update) (Washington, D.C., June 1998), detailed tables and documentation for P20-500, Table A-5.

Event dropouts—population of tenth, eleventh, and twelfth graders who drop out of school each year: U.S. Bureau of the Census, Current Population Survey, Education and Social Stratification Branch, *School Enrollment—Social and Economic Characteristics of Students: October 1996* (Update) (Washington, D.C., June 1998), detailed tables and documentation for P20-500, Table A-4.

For high school completion rates, see: U.S. Department of Commerce, Economics and Statistics Administration, *Educational Attainment in the United States: March 1997,* Current Population Reports, Population Characteristics, by Jennifer Day and Andrea Curry, internet download.

For dropout rates developed by the Department of Education, slightly different than those from the Census Bureau, see: U.S. Department of Education, Office of Educational Research and Improvement, National Center for Education Statistics, *Dropout Rates in the United States: 1996,* NCES 98-250, by Marilyn M. McMillen and Phillip Kaufman (Washington, D.C., December 1997); U. S. Department of Education, Office of Educational Research and Improvement, National Center for Education Statistics, *The Condition of Education 1997,* NCES 97-388, by Thomas M. Smith, et al. (Washington, D.C., June 1997).

Page 55. Differences Between Groups.
Status dropouts by race, ethnicity, and population, 18-24 years old not enrolled in school, who have not finished high school: U.S. Bureau of the Census, Current Population Survey, Education and Social Stratification Branch, *School Enrollment—Social and Economic Characteristics of Students: October 1996* (Update) (Washington, D.C., June 1998), detailed tables and documentation for P20-500, Table A-5.

Page 56. School Infrastructure.
"Schools in unsatisfactory condition": General Accounting Office (GAO), *School Facilities: America's Changing Schools Report Differing Conditions,* GAO/HEHS-96-103 (Washington, D.C., June 14, 1995), internet download.

See also: William H. Honan, "14 Million Pupils in Unsuitable or Unsafe Schools, Report Says," New *York Times* (February 2, 1995), A21.

Page 56. The High Costs of Dropping Out.
Unemployment by educational attainment, aged 25-64, March 1996: See unpublished data, Bureau of Labor Statistics, "Labor Force Status of Civilian Noninstitutional Population by Age, Sex, Race, Hispanic Origin, and Years of School Completed" (Washington, D.C., March 1996).

Health insurance by educational attainment: Employee Benefit Research Institute, EBRI, "Sources of Health Insurance and Characteristics of the Uninsured, Issue Brief Appendix" (Washington, D.C., 1996), Table 6 .

Average earnings by educational attainment: U.S. Department of Commerce, Economics and Statistics Administration, Educational Attainment *in the United States: March 1997,* Current Population Reports, Population Characteristics, by Jennifer Day and Andrea Curry, Table C, internet download.

Page 57. School Achievement.
Scholastic Assessment Test-1 score averages for college-bound high-school seniors, by sex: For 1966-1967 to 1996-1997, see U.S. Department of Education, Office of Educational Research and Improvement, National Center for Education Statistics, *Digest of Education Statistics, 1997,* Table 129, internet download.

Page 58. College Completion.
College completion rates: U.S. Bureau of the Census, Education and Social Stratification Branch, "Percent of People 25 Years Old and Over Who Have Completed High School or College by Race, Hispanic Origin, and Gender, Selected Years, 1940-1997," internet download.

Page 58. International Standing.
High school graduation rates, selected industrial nations, 1996: Organization for Economic Cooperation and Development (OECD), Centre for Educational Research and Innovation, Indicators of Education Systems, *Education at a Glance, OECD Indicators* (Paris, 1998), 14.

See also: Ethan Bronner, "Long a Leader, U.S. Now Lags in High School Graduate Rate, New York *Times* (November 24, 1998), 1.

Page 59. Education: A Vital Necessity.
For a general discussion, see: U.S. Department of Education, Office of Educational Research and Improvement, National Center for Education Statistics, *Education and the Economy: An Indicators Report,* NCES 97-269, by Paul T. Decker, et al. (Washington, D.C., April 1997); Michelle Fine, *Framing Dropouts: Notes on the Politics of an Urban Public High School* (Albany: State University of New York Press, 1991).

Poverty Among Those Aged 65 and Over.

Page 60. "Every qualified individual". . .: *The Social Security Act of 1935,* H.R. 7260, Title II, Federal Old-Age Benefits.

Page 61. Far Fewer Than in the Past.
Poverty rates and numbers, aged 65 and over: U.S. Bureau of the Census, Current Population Reports, *Poverty in the United States: 1996,* Series P60-198, by Leatha Lamison-White (Washington, D.C., 1997), C-5.

See also: Center on Budget and Policy Priorities, *Poverty and Income Trends: 1996,* by Lynette Rawlings (Washington, D.C., March 1998).

Page 61. Compared to Younger Adults.
Poverty rates, aged 65 and over, and aged 18-64: U.S. Bureau of the Census, Current Population Reports, *Poverty in the United States: 1996,* Series P60-198, by Leatha Lamison-White (Washington, D.C., 1997), C-5.

Page. 62. Uneven Progress.
Poverty rates among those aged 65 and over by race/ethnicity, gender, and age, 1996: U.S. Bureau of the Census, Current Population Reports, *Poverty in the United States: 1996,* Series P60-198, by Leatha Lamison-White (Washington, D.C., 1997), Table 2.

Page 63. Close to the Poverty Line.
Poverty thresholds, near-poor, and low-income elderly: U.S. Bureau of the Census, Current Population Reports, *Poverty in the United States: 1996,* Series P60-198, by Leatha Lamison-White (Washington, D.C., 1997), Table 2. See also: U.S. Bureau of the Census, Current Population Reports, Special Studies, *65+ in the United States,* P23-190 (Washington, D.C., 1996), 4-21.

Page 64. Special Pressures—Out-of-Pocket Health Costs.
Out-of-pocket health costs: AARP Public Policy Institute and the Lewin Group, *Out-of-Pocket Health Spending by Medicare Beneficiaries Age 65 and Older: 1997 Projections* (Washington, D.C.: American Association of Retired Persons, 1997), i.

See also: AARP Public Policy Institute and the Urban Institute, *Coming Up Short: Increasing Out-of-pocket Health Spending by Older Americans* (Washington, D.C.: American Association of Retired Persons, April 1994); Families USA Foundation, *The Health Cost Squeeze on Older Americans* (Washington, D.C., February 1992).

Page 64. A Different View—The International Context.
Elderly poverty, selected industrial nations, ca. 1990: Timothy Smeeding, "Financial Poverty in Developed Countries: The Evidence from LIS," *Luxembourg Income Study,* Working Paper No. 155, Final Report to the UNDP (Syracuse, New York, April 1997).

Page 65. To Be Old and Poor.
For a general discussion of the state of the elderly in America, see U.S. Bureau of the Census, Current Population Reports, Special Studies, *65+ in the United States,* P23-190 (Washington, D.C., 1996).

Life Expectancy.

Page 66. "The most powerful impact of biomedical change". . .: Daniel Callahan, "Bioethics: Private Choice and Common Good," *The Hastings Center Report,* vol. 24, no. 3 (May-June 1994), 29.

Page 67. A Lifetime Indicator.
Life expectancy at age 65: For 1970-1979, see National Center for Health Statistics, *Health, United States,* 1983 (Hyattsville, Maryland, 1984), 181. For 1980-1989, see National Center for Health Statistics, *Health, United States, 1992* (Hyattsville, Maryland, 1993), 44. For 1990-1995, see National Center for Health Statistics, *Health, United States, 1996-1997* (Hyattsville, Maryland, 1997), 108. For 1996, see K. D. Peters, K. D. Kochanek, S. L. Murphy, *Deaths: Final Data for 1996,* National Vital Statistics Reports, vol. 47, no. 9 (Hyattsville, Maryland: National Center for Health Statistics, 1998), 21.

Life expectancy at birth: For 1970-1996, see K. D. Peters, K. D. Kochanek, S. L. Murphy, *Deaths: Final Data for 1996,* National Vital Statistics Reports, vol. 47, no. 9 (Hyattsville, Maryland: National Center for Health Statistics, 1998), 22.

Page 68. The Nation Grows Older.
Population aged 65 and over, 1900-2030: U.S. Bureau of the Census, Current Population Reports, Special Studies, *65+ in the United States,* P23-190 (Washington, D.C., 1996), 2-3.

Page 68. Differences in Life Expectations.
Life expectancy at age 65, by race and gender: For 1970-1979, see National Center for Health Statistics, *Health, United States, 1983* (Hyattsville, Maryland, 1984), 181. For 1980-1989, see National Center for Health Statistics, *Health, United States, 1992* (Hyattsville, Maryland, 1993), 44; for 1990-1995, see National Center for Health Statistics, *Health, United States, 1996-1997* (Hyattsville, Maryland, 1997), 108. For 1996, see K. D. Peters, K. D. Kochanek, S. L. Murphy, *Deaths: Final Data for 1996,* National Vital Statistics Reports, vol. 47, no. 9 (Hyattsville, Maryland: National Center for Health Statistics, 1998), 21.

Life expectancy at birth, by race and gender: For 1970-1996, see K. D. Peters, K. D. Kochanek, S. L. Murphy, *Deaths: Final Data for 1996,* National Vital Statistics Reports, vol. 47, no. 9 (Hyattsville, Maryland: National Center for Health Statistics, 1998), 22.

Page 69. In Different Parts of the Nation.
Life expectancy, selected U.S. counties, males: C. J. L. Murray, C. M. Michaud, M. T. McKenna, J. S. Marks, *U.S. Patterns of Mortality by County and Race: 1965-1994* (Cambridge, Mass: Harvard Center for Population and Development Studies/Centers for Disease Control, 1998), Tables 4b, 4d; "U.S. Male Life Expectancies," *Society,* vol. 35, no. 3 (March-April, 1998), internet download.

See also: C. J. L. Murray and L. C. Chen, "In Search of a Contemporary Theory for Understanding Mortality Change," *Social Science and Medicine,* vol. 36, no. 2 (1993), 143; Ruth Larson, "Wealth, Education Help Americans Live Longer: Survey Demonstrates Relationship Between Higher Income, Education, and Longer Life," *Insight on the News,* vol. 14, no. 32 (August 31, 1998), 40; "Black Men in D.C. Have Shorter Life Expectancy: Study Finds Black Men in Washington, D.C. Have Life Expectancy of Only 57.9 Years," *Jet,* vol. 93, no. 5 (December 22, 1997), 18; "Study Finds 'Life Gap' in U.S." *Harvard Public Health Review,* (1998), internet download.

Page 70. Closing the Gap Internationally.
Life expectancy at birth, selected industrial nations, 1996: UNICEF, *The State of the World's Children, 1998* (New York: Oxford University Press, 1998), Table 1.

Note: Nations included are those defined by UNICEF as "industrialized countries." See: UNICEF, *The State of the World's Children 1997* (New York: Oxford University Press, 1997), 101.

Page 70. Human Capital.
For a discussion of the demographic revolution, see: Alan Pifer and Lydia Bronte, *Our Aging Society* (New York: W. W. Norton, 1986); William C. Cockerham, *This Aging Society* (Englewood Cliffs, N.J.: Prentice Hall, 1991).

Chapter Five: Indicators of Worsening Performance

Child Abuse.

Page 74. "Public Law 104-235, Section 111, defines child abuse and neglect as"... : *Child Abuse Prevention and Treatment Act,* as amended October 1996, Public Law 104-235; 42, U.S.C. 5106g.

For a discussion of the reauthorization of this law, see National Clearinghouse on Child Abuse and Neglect Information, "What is Child Maltreatment?" internet download.

See also the original law: *Child Abuse Prevention and Treatment Act,* PL 92-247, 42USC S101, January 31, 1974 (S1191).

Page 75. A Public Issue.
Child abuse rates, estimated number of children reported for maltreatment, per 1,000, and numbers: For 1976-1986, see American Association for Protecting Children, The American Humane Association, *Highlights of Official Aggregate Child Neglect and Abuse Reporting, 1987* (Denver, Colorado, 1989), 6. For 1987-1996, see The National Center on Child Abuse

Prevention Research, a program of The National Committee to Prevent Child Abuse, *Current Trends in Child Abuse Reporting and Fatalities: The Results of the 1996 Annual Fifty State Survey* (Chicago, April 1997), 5.

"A recent study by the Department of Health and Human Services". . . .: See U.S. Department of Health and Human Services, Administration for Children and Families, Administration on Children, Youth, and Families, National Center on Child Abuse and Neglect, *The Third National Incidence Study of Child Abuse and Neglect (NIS-3),* prepared by Andrea Sedlak and Diane Broadhurst (Washington, D.C., September 1996), 8-17. They note: "The fact that the seriously injured group has quadrupled during the seven years since the NIS-2, and now comprises more than one-half million children, appears to herald a true rise in the scope and severity of child abuse and neglect in the United States."

See also: U.S. Department of Health and Human Services, "New State Reports Show Continued High Level of Confirmed Cases of Child Abuse and Neglect," Press Release (Washington, D.C., April 8, 1997).

Page 75. Types of Abuse.
Child abuse by maltreatment type, 1996, percent of cases, prevalence of neglect, physical abuse, sexual abuse, and emotional abuse: U.S. Department of Health and Human Services, Children's Bureau, *Child Maltreatment 1996: Reports from the States to the National Child Abuse and Neglect Data System* (Washington, D.C., 1998), 3-7. Note: Categories include both indicated and substantiated cases, unknown category not included in percentages, calculations by the Fordham Institute for Innovation in Social Policy, Tarrytown, New York.

For a discussion of severe forms of physical abuse, see: National Clearinghouse on Child Abuse and Neglect Information, "Frequently Asked Questions About Child Fatalities," internet download; U.S. Department of Health and Human Services, Administration for Children and Families, A Report of the U.S. Advisory Board on Child Abuse and Neglect, *A Nation's Shame: Fatal Child Abuse and Neglect in the United States* (Washington, D.C., April 1995).

Page 76. Abuse Fatalities.
Estimate of approximately 1,000 deaths per year: The National Center on Child Abuse Prevention Research, a program of The National Committee to Prevent Child Abuse, *Current Trends in Child Abuse Reporting and Fatalities: The Results of the 1996 Annual Fifty State Survey* (Chicago, April 1997), 14.

Estimate of approximately 2,000 deaths per year: U.S. Department of Health and Human Services, Administration for Children and Families, *A Nation's Shame: Fatal Child Abuse and Neglect in the United States, A Report of the U.S. Advisory Board on Child Abuse and Neglect* (Washington, D.C., April 1995), xxiii. The Board reports that even this figure is a "conservative" estimate.

For further discussion of underreporting, see: David E. Nelson, Grant Higginson, and Joyce Grant-Worley, "Physical Abuse Among High School Students: Prevalence and Correlation with Other Health Behaviors," *Archives of Pediatric and Adolescent Medicine*, vol. 149 (November 1995), 1254; David Stoesz and Howard Jacob Karger, "Suffer the Children: How Government Fails Its Most Vulnerable Citizens—Abused and Neglected Kids, *Washington Monthly,* vol. 28, no. 6 (June 1996), 20.

Page 77. Who are the Victims and Perpetrators?
Child abuse victims by age, gender, race, and ethnicity, 1996, percent of cases: U.S. Department of Health and Human Services, Children's Bureau, *Child Maltreatment 1996: Reports from the States to the National Child Abuse and Neglect Data System* (Washington, D.C., 1998), 3-9, 3-10, 3-11. Note: Unknown category not included in percentages, calculations by the Fordham Institute for Innovation in Social Policy, Tarrytown, New York.

Fatalities by age: The National Center on Child Abuse Prevention Research, a program of The National Committee to Prevent Child Abuse, *Current Trends in Child Abuse Reporting and Fatalities: The Results of the 1996 Annual Fifty State Survey* (Chicago, April 1997), 16.

Perpetrators of abuse: U.S. Department of Health and Human Services, Children's Bureau, *Child Maltreatment 1996: Reports from the States to the National Child Abuse and Neglect Data System* (Washington, D.C., 1998), 3-13. Note: Unknown category not included in percentages, calculations by the Fordham Institute for Innovation in Social Policy, Tarrytown, New York.

Domestic violence: For a summary of recent studies and discussion, see Linda Spears, "Domestic Violence is a Child Welfare Issue," in *Child Abuse and Neglect: Selected Readings* (Washington, D.C.: Child Welfare League of America, 1996).

For Bureau of Justice Statistics on Domestic Violence, see for example U.S. Department of Justice, Office of Justice Programs, Bureau of Justice Statistics, *Special Report: Murder in Families,* by John M. Dawson and Patrick A. Langan (Washington, D.C., July, 1994); U.S. Department of Justice, Office of Justice Programs, Bureau of Justice Statistics, *Selected Findings, Violence Between Intimates,* NCJ 149259 (Washington, D.C., November, 1994).

Page 78. Reporting and Substantiation.
Sources of child abuse reports, 1996, percent of cases: U.S. Department of Health and Human Services, Children's Bureau, *Child Maltreatment 1996: Reports from the States to the National Child Abuse and Neglect Data System* (Washington, D.C., 1998), 3-4.

Substantiation rates: The National Center on Child Abuse Prevention Research, a program of The National Committee to Prevent Child Abuse, *Current Trends in Child Abuse Reporting and Fatalities: The Results of the 1996 Annual Fifty State Survey* (Chicago, April 1997), 5.

Decline in percentage of investigated cases: U.S. Department of Health and Human Services, Administration for Children and Families, Administration on Children, Youth, and Families, National Center on Child Abuse and Neglect, *The Third National Incidence Study of Child Abuse and Neglect (NIS-3),* prepared by Andrea Sedlak and Diane Broadhurst (Washington, D.C., September 1996), 7-16.

"Triage policies" and their effects: Child Welfare League of America: *Child Abuse and Neglect: A Look at the States: The CWLA Stat Book,* by Patrick A Curtis, Jennifer D. Boyd, Mary Liepold, and Michael Petit (Washington, D.C., 1995), 12.

Page 79. Understanding the Problem.
For a discussion of sexual abuse problems in developing nations see for example: Alan Guttmacher Institute, *Into a New World: Young Women's Sexual and Reproductive Lives* (New York, 1998).

Child Poverty.

Page 80. "All other industrial nations do more". . .: UNICEF, *The Progress of Nations 1996,* internet download. Study cited is: Lee Rainwater and Timothy Smeeding, "Doing Poorly: The Real Income of American Children In a Comparative Perspective" *Luxembourg Income Study,* Working Paper No. 127 (Syracuse, New York, August 1995).

Page 81. A Special Problem.
Child poverty rates and numbers, percent, related children in families under age 18, in poverty: U.S. Bureau of the Census, Current Population Reports, *Poverty in the United States: 1996,* P60-198, by Leatha Lamison-White (Washington, D.C., 1997), C-5.

See also: Center on Budget and Policy Priorities, *Poverty and Income Trends: 1996,* by Lynette Rawlings (Washington, D.C., March 1998).

Page 81. The Two Ends of the Life Cycle.
Under 6 child poverty rates, related children in families under age 6, percent in poverty: For 1970-1995 see Historical Poverty Table—Persons, "Poverty Status of Related Children Under 6 Years of Age: 1969-1995," internet download. For 1996, see U.S. Bureau of the Census, Current Population Reports, *Poverty in the United States: 1996,* P60-198, by Leatha Lamison-White (Washington, D.C., 1997), Table 2.

Aged 65 and over, percent in poverty: U.S. Bureau of the Census, Current Population Reports, *Poverty in the United States: 1996,* P60-198, by Leatha Lamison-White (Washington, D.C., 1997), C-5.

Page 82. Profiling the Nation's Poor Children.
Child poverty by race/ethnicity and age, 1996, percent in poverty: U.S. Bureau of the Census, Current Population Reports, *Poverty in the United States: 1996,* P60-198, by Leatha Lamison-White (Washington, D.C., 1997), Table 2.

Page 83. Extreme Poverty.
"there has been a striking increase in the percentage of children raised in extreme poverty". . .: U.S. Department of Health and Human Services, Office of the Assistant Secretary for Planning and Evaluation, *Trends in the Well-Being of America's Children and Youth: 1996* (Washington, D.C., 1996), 38.

Page 83. Internationally, the U.S. Compares Poorly.
Child poverty, selected industrial nations, ca. 1990: Timothy Smeeding, "Financial Poverty in Developed Countries: The Evidence from LIS," *Luxembourg Income Study,* Working Paper No. 155, Final Report to the UNDP (Syracuse, New York, April 1997).

Page 84. Tax and Transfer Programs.
"safety nets for children are weakest in U.S.": UNICEF, *The Progress of Nations, 1996*, internet download. Note: Years are variable, ranging from the oldest, Switzerland in 1982, to 1992 in Sweden, Belgium, and Denmark.

For data and discussion of tax and transfer programs internationally, see: Lee Rainwater and Timothy Smeeding, "Doing Poorly: The Real Income of American Children In a Comparative Perspective," *Luxembourg Income Study,* Working Paper No. 127 (Syracuse, New York, August 1995).

Page 85. A Different Kind of Deficit.
For a discussion of investment in children and human deficits, see National Center for Children in Poverty, "Investing in Children: Closing the Real Deficit—Policy Point of View," by Harold W. Watts, *Child Poverty News and Issues,* vol. 5, no. 2 (Summer 1995), internet download.

Youth Suicide.

Page 86. "At each moment of its history. . . each society has a definite aptitude for suicide": Emile Durkheim, *Suicide: A Study in Sociology,* ed. George Simpson (New York: Free Press, 1951), 48.

Page 87. Deaths among The Young.
Youth suicide rates, deaths per 100,000, aged 15-24: For 1950, see National Center for Health Statistics, unpublished data. For 1970-91, see National Center for Health Statistics, "Death Rates from Suicide for Ages 15-24 Years, by Race and Sex: United States, 1960-1991," unpublished data. For 1992, see K. D. Kochanek and B. L. Hudson, *Advance Report of Final Mortality Statistics, 1992,* Monthly Vital Statistics Report, vol. 43, no. 6 (Hyattsville, Maryland: National Center for Health Statistics, 1995). For 1993, see P. Gardner and B. L. Hudson, *Advance Report of Final Mortality Statistics, 1993,* Monthly Vital Statistics Report, vol. 44, no. 7 (Hyattsville, Maryland: National Center for Health Statistics, 1996). For 1994, see G. K. Singh, K. D. Kochanek, M. F. MacDorman, *Advance Report of Final Mortality Statistics, 1994,* Monthly Vital Statistics Report, vol. 45, no. 3 (Hyattsville, Maryland: National Center for Health Statistics, 1996). For 1995, see R. N. Anderson, K. D. Kochanek, S. L. Murphy, *Report of Final Mortality Statistics, 1995,* Monthly Vital Statistics Report, vol. 45, no. 11 (Hyattsville, Maryland: National Center for Health Statistics, 1997). For 1996, see K. D. Peters, K. D. Kochanek, S. L. Murphy, *Deaths: Final Data for 1996,* National Vital Statistics Reports, vol. 47, no. 9 (Hyattsville, Maryland: National Center for Health Statistics, 1998).

Page 87. Male and Female, Black and White.
"Females attempt suicide more often, but males are more likely to complete it": For a discussion of this issue, see Jorg J. Pahl, "The Rippling Effects of Suicide," *USA Today Magazine,* vol. 125, no. 2616 (September 1996), 62.

Rising rates of suicides among black youth: See Centers for Disease Control, "Suicide Among Black Youths—United States, 1980-1995," Morbidity and Mortality Weekly *Report,* vol. 47, no. 10 (Massachusetts Medical Society, March 20, 1998), 193-96; Fern Shen, "Where Suicide Rates are Soaring: The Death Trend for Young African American Males Poses a Complex Puzzle for Social Scientists," *The Washington Post National Weekly Edition* (July 29-August 4, 1996), 31.

Youth suicide rates by race and gender, deaths per 100,000, aged 15-24: For 1970-1991, see National Center for Health Statistics, "Death Rates from Suicide for Ages 15-24 Years, by Race and Sex: United States, 1960-1991," unpublished data. For 1992, see K. D. Kochanek, B. L. Hudson, *Advance Report of Final Mortality Statistics, 1992,* Monthly Vital Statistics Report, vol. 43, no. 6 (Hyattsville, Maryland: National Center for Health Statistics, 1995). For 1993, see P. Gardner, B. L. Hudson, *Advance Report of Final Mortality Statistics, 1993,* Monthly Vital Statistics Report, vol. 44, no. 7 (Hyattsville, Maryland: National Center for Health Statistics, 1996). For 1994, see G. K. Singh, K. D. Kochanek, M. F. MacDorman, *Advance Report of Final Mortality Statistics, 1994,* Monthly Vital Statistics Report, vol. 45, no. 3 (Hyattsville, Maryland: National Center for Health Statistics, 1996). For 1995, see R. N. Anderson, K. D. Kochanek, S. L. Murphy, *Report of Final Mortality Statistics, 1995,* Monthly Vital Statistics Report, vol. 45, no. 11 (Hyattsville, Maryland: National Center for Health Statistics, 1997). For 1996, see K. D. Peters, K. D. Kochanek, S. L. Murphy, *Deaths: Final Data for 1996,* National Vital Statistics Reports, vol. 47, no. 9 (Hyattsville, Maryland: National Center for Health Statistics, 1998).

Page 88. Suicidal Thoughts and Attempts.
High-school students, suicidal thoughts and attempts: Centers for Disease Control, "Youth Risk Behavior Surveillance—United States, 1995," Morbidity and Mortality Weekly *Report,* vol. 45, no. SS-4 (Massachusetts Medical Society, September 27, 1996).

College students, suicidal thoughts and attempts: Centers for Disease Control, "Youth Risk Behavior Surveillance, National College Health Risk Behavior Survey—United States, 1995," *Morbidity and Mortality Weekly Report,* vol. 46, no. SS-6 (Massachusetts Medical Society, November 14, 1997).

See also: Gallup Organization, *Teenage Suicide Study* (Princeton, New Jersey, 1994), Executive Summary; Centers for Disease Control, "Fatal and Nonfatal Suicide Attempts Among Adolescents—Oregon, 1988-1993," Morbidity and Mortality Weekly *Report,* vol. 44, no. 16 (Massachusetts Medical Society, April 28, 1995).

Page 89. International Standing.
Youth suicide rates, selected industrial nations, 1992-1995, deaths per 100,00, aged 15-24: For industrial nations, see World Health Organization, *1995 World Health Statistics Annual* (Geneva, 1996); World Health Organization, *1996 World Health Statistics Annual* (Geneva, 1997); for the U.S., see S. J. Ventura, J. A. Martin, S. C. Curtin, T. J. Matthews, *Report of Final Natality Statistics, 1995,* Monthly Vital Statistics Report, vol. 45, no. 11, supp. 2 (Hyattsville, Maryland: National Center for Health Statistics, 1997).

Note: Nations included are those defined by UNICEF as "industrialized countries." See UNICEF, *The State of the World's Children 1997* (New York: Oxford University Press, 1997), 101. Denmark omitted because data not available.

Youth suicide rates, aged 15 and under, 26 industrialized countries: See Centers for Disease Control, "Rates of Homicide, Suicide, and Firearm-Related Death Among Children—26 Industrialized Countries," Morbidity and Mortality Weekly *Report,* vol. 46, no. 5 (Massachusetts Medical Society, February 7, 1997) 101-105.

Page 91. Year 2000 Goal.
Year 2000 goal, youth suicide: National Center for Health Statistics, *Healthy People 2000 Review, 1997* (Hyattsville, Maryland: Public Health Service, 1997), 80.

Youth Suicide rate, deaths per 100,000, aged 15-19: For 1970-1978, see National Institute of Mental Health, *Mental Health, 1985* (Washington, D.C.). For 1979-1993, see National Center for Health Statistics, "Death Rates for 282 Selected Causes, By 5-Year Age Groups, Color, And Sex, United States, 1979-1993," Trend C, Table 292A, unpublished data. For 1994, see National Center for Health Statistics, "Death Rates for 72 Selected Causes, By 5-Year Age Groups, Race, and Sex: United States 1994," Table 210, unpublished data. For 1995, see National Center for Health Statistics, "Death Rates for 72 Selected Causes, By 5-Year Age Groups, Race, and Sex: United States 1995," Table 210, unpublished data. For 1996, see National Center for Health Statistics, "Death Rates for 72 Selected Causes, By 5-Year Age Groups, Race, and Sex: United States 1996," Table 210, unpublished data.

Page 91. A Need to Consider.
For a discussion of prevention programs, see Centers for Disease Control, "Programs for the Prevention of Suicide Among Adolescents and Young Adults: Suicide Contagion and the Reporting of Suicide: Recommendations for a National Workshop," Morbidity and Mortality Weekly *Report,* vol. 43, no. RR-6 (Massachusetts Medical Society, April 22, 1994).

Health Care Coverage.

Page 92. "The number of people without health insurance is an important indicator of the adequacy". . . : The Center for National Health Program Studies, Harvard Medical School/The Cambridge Hospital; Physicians for a National Health Program; and the Public Citizen Health Research Group, *The Vanishing Health Care Safety Net: New Data on Uninsured Americans,* by David U. Himmelstein, Steffie Woolhandler, and Sidney M. Wolfe (Cambridge, Massachusetts, December 19, 1991), 2.

Page 93. Declining Benefits.
For a discussion of the effects of uninsurance, see, for example, *Economic Report of the President,* Transmitted to the Congress, February 1998, together with the Annual Report of the Council of Economic Advisors (Washington, D.C., February 1998), esp. Chapter 3: "The Economic Well-Being of Children"; The Henry J. Kaiser Foundation, "Uninsured in America: Straight Facts on Health Reform" (April 1994).

Percentage of people uninsured: For 1976-1986, estimated percentages are based on the number of uninsured from published and unpublished data from The Center for National Health Program Studies, Harvard Medical School/The Cambridge Hospital by David U. Himmelstein, Steffie Woolhandler, and Sidney M. Wolfe (Cambridge, Mass.), which are based on data from the U.S. Census Bureau, Current Population Survey and the National Health Interview Surveys, with correction factors, as a proportion of All Persons, U.S.; from U.S. Bureau of the Census, Current Population Reports, *Poverty in the United States: 1996,* P60-198, by Leatha Lamison-White (Washington, D.C., 1997); percentages calculated by the Fordham Institute for Innovation in Social Policy, Tarrytown, New York. For 1987-1995, see U.S. Bureau of the Census, *Health Insurance Historical Tables,* "Health Insurance Coverage Status and Type of Coverage by Sex, Race, and Hispanic Origin: 1987-1995," Table 1, internet download. For 1996, see U.S. Bureau of the Census, Current Population Reports, *Health Insurance Coverage: 1996,* P-60-199, by Robert Bennefield (Washington, D.C., September 1997).

For a calculation of rates slightly higher than those of the Census Bureau, see National Center for Health Statistics, *Health United States 1996-97 and Injury Chartbook* (Hyattsville, Maryland: National Center for Health Statistics, 1997).

See also: The Center for National Health Program Studies, Harvard Medical School/The Cambridge Hospital; Physicians for a National Health Program; and the Public Citizen Health Research Group, *The Growing Epidemic of Uninsurance,* by David U. Himmelstein, Steffie Woolhandler, James P. Lewontin, Terry Tang, and Sidney M. Wolfe (Cambridge, Mass., December 16, 1992).

Page 93. Who are the Uninsured?
Characteristics of the uninsured—all, age, race/ethnicity, poverty status, and income: U.S. Bureau of the Census, Current Population Reports, *Health Insurance Coverage: 1996,* P-60-199, by Robert Bennefield (Washington, D.C., September 1997).

Long-term analysis—one month or more during 1992-94: U.S. Bureau of the Census, Current Population Reports, *Who Loses Coverage and For How Long?,* Dynamics of Economic Well-Being: Health Insurance, 1992-1993, P70-54, by Robert Bennefield (Washington, D.C., May 1996).

Page 94. Underinsurance.
Estimates of the underinsured population: Karen Donelan, Robert J. Blendon, Craig A. Hill, Catherine Hoffman, Diane Rowland, Martin Frankel, Drew Altman, "Whatever Happened to the Health Insurance Crisis in the United States? Voices from a National Survey," *Journal of the American Medical Association,* vol. 276, no. 16 (October 23, 1996), 1346.

See also: Robert J. Blendon, Karen Donelan, Craig A. Hill, Woody Carter, Dennis Beatrice, Drew Altman, "Paying Medical Bills in the United States: Why Health Insurance Isn't Enough," *Journal of the American Medical Association,* vol. 271, no. 12 (March 23-30, 1994), 948.

Page 94. The Effect on Children.
Characteristics of uninsured children—all, poverty status, and race/ethnicity: U.S. Bureau of the Census, Current Population Reports, *Health Insurance Coverage: 1996,* P-60-199, by Robert Bennefield (Washington, D.C., September 1997).

Long-term analysis—one month or more during 1992-94: U.S. Bureau of the Census, Current Population Reports, *Who Loses Coverage and For How Long?,* Dynamics of Economic Well-Being: Health Insurance, 1992-1993, P70-54, by Robert Bennefield (Washington, D.C., May 1996).

Long-term analysis—one month or more during 1995-96: Updated estimate of the Survey of Income and Program Participation data, from Families USA. See, *One Out of Three: Kids Without Health Insurance 1995-1996,* A Report from Families U.S.A. (Washington, D.C., March 1997).

Page 95. Employee Coverage.
Health insurance employee coverage, total employer-financed, fully employer-financed, partly employer-financed: For 1980-1993 see: Employee Benefit Research Institute, *EBRI Databook on Employee Benefits,* 3rd ed. (Washington, D.C., 1995) Table 2.16 and Employee Benefit Research Institute, EBRI Databook on *Employee Benefits,* 4th ed. (Washington, D.C., 1997) Tables 4.1, 30.4. For 1995 see U.S. Department of Labor, "Employee Benefits in Medium and Large Private Establishments, 1997," USDL-99-02 (Washington D.C., January 7, 1999), Table 5. Note: 1997 data show a continuation of these trends.

Work status of the uninsured: Employee Benefit Research Institute, *Sources of Health Insurance and Characteristics of the Uninsured: Analysis of the March 1997 Current Population Survey,* by Paul Fronstein (Washington, D.C., December 1997), Table 3.

Page 96. States Vary.
Persons without health insurance, selected states, 1996: U.S. Bureau of the Census, "Health Insurance Coverage: 1996, Number of Persons Covered and Not Covered by Health Insurance by State in 1996," internet download.

See also: Centers for Disease Control, "Age- and State-Specific Prevalence Estimates of Insured and Uninsured Persons— United States, 1995-1996," Morbidity and Mortality Weekly *Report,* vol. 47, no. 25 (Massachusetts Medical Society, July 3, 1998) 529-32; U.S. Bureau of the Census, "Low Income Uninsured Children by State, Number and Percent of Children Under 18 Years of Age, at or Below 200 Percent Poverty, by State: Three Year Averages for 1993, 1994, 1995," internet download.

Page 97. A Problem Yet to be Addressed.
For a comparison of the U.S. to other industrial nations, see Jack Meyer and Diane H. Naughton, "Who's Saying No to Uninsured Kids?" *Business and Health,* vol. 15, no. 3 (March 1997), 33.

For a discussion of the expected expansion of Medicaid for children see: *Economic Report of the President,* Transmitted to the Congress, February 1998, together with the Annual Report of the Council of Economic Advisors (Washington, D.C., February 1998), esp. Chapter 3, "The Economic Well-Being of Children"; Center on Budget and Policy Priorities, "Reducing the Number of Uninsured Children. Building Upon Medicaid Coverage is a Better Approach Than Creating A New Block Grant to the States," by Andy Schneider (Washington, D.C., June 5, 1997).

For a discussion of the problems of portability of health insurance for workers, see *Economic Report of the President,* Transmitted to the Congress, February 1998, together with the Annual Report of the Council of Economic Advisors (Washington, D.C., February 1998), esp. Chapter 5, "Improving Economic Efficiency: Environment and Health Issues."

Wages.

Page 98. "Real wages, when adjusted for inflation".. : *Economic Report of the President,* Transmitted to the Congress, February 1997, together with the Annual Report of the Council of Economic Advisors (Washington, D.C., 1997), 144.

Page 99. How We Live.
"Wages and salaries make up approximately three-fourths": Lawrence Mishel and Jared Bernstein, *The State of Working America 1996-1997* (Washington, D.C.: Economic Policy Institute, 97), 131.

Average weekly earnings: "Average weekly earnings, total private, private nonagricultural industries, 1959-97, for production or nonsupervisory workers, 1982$," *Economic Report of the President,* Transmitted to the Congress, February 1998, together with the Annual Report of the Council of Economic Advisors (Washington, D.C., 1998).

Average hourly earnings: "Average hourly earnings, manufacturing, private nonagricultural industries, 1959-97, for production or nonsupervisory workers, 1982$," *Economic Report of the President,* Transmitted to the Congress, February 1998, together with the Annual Report of the Council of Economic Advisors (Washington, D.C., 1998).

Page 100. The Gender Wage Gap.
Male and female median earnings, 1996$: U.S. Bureau of the Census, *Historical Income Table-Persons,* "Year-Round, Full-Time Workers—Persons (All Races) 15 Years Old and Over by Median Earnings and Sex: 1960-1996," internet download. Women's earnings as a percentage of male: Calculations by the Fordham Institute for Innovation in Social Policy, Tarrytown, New York.

Page 100. Low Earnings of Full-Time Workers.
Low earnings, all, and by gender, education, and age: U.S. Bureau of the Census, March Current Population Surveys, "Percent distribution of Year-Round Full-time Workers by Ratio of Earnings to Low Earnings Threshold, Civilian Workers," unpublished data.

Page 101. Family Incomes Increase With Two Earners.
Median family income, all, wife in paid labor force, wife not in paid labor force: U.S. Bureau of the Census, *Historical Income Tables- Families,* "Type of Family—Families (All Races) by Median and Mean Income, 1947-1996," Table F-7, internet download.

Page 102. The Minimum Wage.
Value of the minimum wage: For 1970-1991, see Committee on Ways and Means, U.S. House of Representatives, *1993 Green Book, Overview of Entitlement Programs, Background Material and Data on Programs within the Jurisdiction of the Committee on Ways and Means,* July 7, 1993 (Washington, D.C., 1998). For 1996-1997, see "In Labor Day Bonus, U.S. Raises Minimum Wage," New *York Times* (August 31, 1997). Annual wage calculated by the Fordham Institute for Innovation in Social Policy, Tarrytown, New York.

Poverty thresholds: For 1970-1991, see *Social Security Bulletin,* Annual Statistical Supplement, 1992. For 1992, see U.S. Bureau of the Census, "Weighted Average Poverty Thresholds, 1992" (Washington, D.C. September 1993). For 1993, see "Weighted Average Poverty Threshold, 1993" (Washington, D.C., January, 1994). For 1994-1997, see U.S. Bureau of the Census, "Poverty Thresholds in [1994-1997] by Size of Family and Number of Related Children Under 18 Years Old," internet download.

Page 102. International Compensation Costs.
Hourly compensation costs: Bureau of Labor Statistics, "Indexes of hourly compensation costs for production workers in manufacturing, 29 countries or areas and selected economic groups, selected years, 1975-1996" [United States=100], internet download.

Page 103. Expectations for the Future.
For a general discussion of wages, see Lawrence Mishel and Jared Bernstein, T*he State of Working America, 1996-1997* (Washington, D.C.: Economic Policy Institute, 1997).

Inequality.

Page 104. "Families have been affected unevenly by recent income trends". . .: *Economic Report of the President,* Transmitted to the Congress, February 1998, together with the Annual Report of the Council of Economic Advisors (Washington, D.C., 1994), 115.

Page 106. Sharp Contrasts.
Gini Index of Inequality, 1947-1996, range from 0-1: U.S. Bureau of the Census, *Historical Income Tables—Families,* "Gini Ratios for Families, by Race and Hispanic Origin of Householder: 1947-1996," Table F-4, internet download.

See also: U.S. Bureau of the Census, Current Population Reports, "A Brief Look at Postwar U.S. Income Inequality," P60-191, by Daniel H. Weinberg (Washington, D.C., June 1996); "Rising Tide, Falling Boats, U.S. Income Separation Increases; Poorest Two-Fifths Fall Farther Behind Since Late 1970s," T*he Economist,* vol. 345, no. 8048 (December 20, 1997), 28.

Page 105. Different Shares.
Income shares of richest and poorest fifths, percent of aggregate family income: U.S. Bureau of the Census, *Historical Income Tables—Families*, "Share of Aggregate Income Received by Each Fifth and Top Five Percent of Families (All Races): 1947-1996," Table F-2, internet download.

Mean income, lowest fifth, top fifth, top 5 percent, 1996$: U.S. Bureau of the Census, *Historical Income Tables—Families,* "Mean Income Received by Each Fifth and Top 5 Percent of Families (All Races): 1966-1996," Table F-3, internet download.

See also: Center on Budget and Policy Priorities, "Unequal Shares: Recent Income Trends Among the Wealthy," by Isaac Shapiro, revised (November 22, 1995).

Page 106. What's Happening in the Middle?
Income share of middle three-fifths, percent of aggregate family income: U.S. Bureau of the Census, *Historical Income Tables—Families,* "Share of Aggregate Income Received by Each Fifth and Top Five Percent of Families (All Races): 1947-1996," Table F-2, internet download. See also: Center on Budget and Policy Priorities, "Poverty and Income Trends: 1996," by Lynette Rawlings (Washington, D.C., March 1998).

Income share of top fifth, percent of aggregate family income: U.S. Bureau of the Census, H*istorical Income Tables—Families,* "Share of Aggregate Income Received by Each Fifth and Top Five Percent of Families (All Races): 1947-1996," Table F-2, internet download.

See also: Charles Derber, "The End of the Middle Class," T*ikkun,* vol. 13, no. 1 (January-February 1998), 25.

Page 107. International Comparisons.
Inequality in OECD countries, Gini coefficient for equivalent disposable income, range 0-1, years: Timothy Smeeding and Peter Gottschalk, "The International Evidence on Income Distribution in Modern Economies," *Luxembourg Income Study,* Working Paper Series, No. 137, revised (Syracuse, New York, March 1996). Note: Years are variable, ranging from the oldest, Switzerland in 1982, to 1992 in Sweden, Belgium, and Denmark.

Page 108. Does Inequality Matter?
"The speed with which inequality has widened in the UK". . .: see Malcolm Dean, "Absolute Effects of Relative Poverty," *The Lancet,* vol. 344, no. 8920 (August 13, 1994), 463.

"widening health gap": "The Unhealthy Poor" *The Economist,* vol. 331, no. 7866 (June 4, 1994), 55.

See also: Frederick R. Strobel, "Britain Goes Down The Path of Income Inequality," *Challenge* (November-December 1995), 35.

Violent Crime.

Page 110. "From midyear 1996 through midyear 1997 the total population incarcerated in the country's jails"...: U.S. Department of Justice, "Nation's Prisons and Jails Hold More than 1.7 Million, Up Almost 100,000 in a Year," Advance for Release (Washington, D.C., January 18, 1998).

Page 111. Distrust in the Nation.
Homicide, second leading cause of death among 15-24 year olds, first leading cause of death among black youth, aged 15-24 years old, 1996: K. D. Peters, K. D. Kochanek, S. L. Murphy, *Deaths: Final Data for 1996,* National Vital Statistics Reports, vol. 47, no. 9 (Hyattsville, Maryland: National Center for Health Statistics, 1998).

Number and rates of violent crime per 100,000: For 1970-1972, see U.S. Department of Justice, Federal Bureau of Investigation, Uniform Crime Reports, *Crime in the United States, 1979* (Washington, D.C., 1980). For 1973-1976, see U.S. Department of Justice, Federal Bureau of Investigation, Uniform Crime Reports, *Crime in the United States 1991* (Washington, D.C., 1992). For 1977-1996, see U.S. Department of Justice, Federal Bureau of Investigation, Uniform Crime Reports, *Crime in the United States 1996* (Washington, D.C., 1997).

See also: Centers for Disease Control, "Trends in Rates of Homicide—United States, 1985-1994," Morbidity and Mortality Weekly *Report,* vol. 45, no. 22 (Massachusetts Medical Society, June 7, 1996) 460-464.

Page 112. Crime Patterns.
Rates for murder, rape, robbery, and aggravated assault: U.S. Department of Justice, Federal Bureau of Investigation, Uniform Crime Reports, *Crime in the United States 1996* (Washington, D.C., September 28, 1997). Calculation for rate of decline by the Fordham Institute for Innovation in Social Policy, Tarrytown, New York.

Crime Victimization Survey: Bureau of Justice Statistics, "National Crime Victimization Survey Crime Trends, 1973-1996, with 1973 to 1991 data adjusted to make data comparable to data after the redesign," internet download. Violent-crime rate includes murder, rape, robbery, aggravated assault, and simple assault; murder rates are from the FBI's Uniform Crime Reports.

Page 112. Among the Young.
Violent Crime Victimization by Age, per 1,000 population: U.S. Department of Justice, Office of Justice Programs, "Rates of Violent Crime and Personal Theft, by sex, age, race, and Hispanic Origin, 1996," in *Criminal Victimization 1996: Changes 1995-96 with Trends 1993-1996,* internet download.

"Young people also constitute a disproportionate share of arrests": U.S. Department of Justice, Federal Bureau of Investigation, Uniform Crime Reports, *Crime in the United States 1996* (Washington, D.C., 1997). Calculations by the Fordham Institute for Innovation in Social Policy, Tarrytown, New York.

See also: U.S. Department of Justice, Office of Justice Programs, Office of Juvenile Justice and Delinquency Prevention, *Juvenile Offenders and Victims: 1997 Update on Violence, Statistics Summary* (Washington, D.C., August 1997); "Gun Killings by Young Defy Drop in Homicides," National News Briefs, *New York Times* (January 3, 1998).

Page 112. Imprisonment.
State and federal prison populations, numbers and rates per 100,000,1926-1996, on December 31 each year: U.S. Department of Justice, Bureau of Justice Statistics, *Sourcebook of Criminal Justice Statistics 1997,* Kathleen Maguire and Ann L. Pastore, eds. (Washington, D.C., 1998), Table 6.21.

Jail population, per 100,000: U.S. Department of Justice, Office of Justice Programs, The Bureau of Justice Statistics, *Prison and Jail Inmates at Midyear 1996,* Bureau of Justice Statistics Bulletin, NCJ-1662843 (Washington, D.C., January 1997), see jail incarceration rate.

Total inmate rates, combining jails and state and federal prisons: U.S. Department of Justice, Office of Justice Programs, The Bureau of Justice Statistics, *Prison and Jail Inmates at Midyear 1997,* Bureau of Justice Statistics Bulletin, NCJ-167247, by

Darrell K. Gilliard and Allen J. Beck (Washington, D.C., January 1998). Note: The 1996 state and federal inmates, plus the 1996 jail inmates add up to slightly more than the total inmate rate because of a difference in measuring points in time.

See also: U.S. Department of Justice, Office of Justice Programs, Bureau of Justice Statistics, *Correctional Populations in the United States,* NCJ-163916 (Washington, D.C., 1997); U.S. Department of Justice, Office of Justice Programs, Bureau of Justice Statistics, *Profile of Jail Inmates, 1996,* Special Report, NCJ-164620 (Washington, D.C., April 1998).

Page 113. The Cost of Imprisonment.
Justice expenditures, total, federal, state, and local: U.S. Department of Justice, Bureau of Justice Statistics, *Sourcebook of Criminal Justice Statistics 1997,* Kathleen Maguire and Ann L. Pastore, eds., (Washington, D.C., 1998), Table 1.2.

A recent study conducted by the State University of New York's Center for the Study of the States: Fox Butterfield, "New Prisons Cast Shadow Over Higher Education," *New York Times* (April 12, 1995); see also, Steven D. Gold, *The Fiscal Crisis of the States: Lessons for the Future* (Washington, D.C.: Georgetown University Press, 1995).

See also: U.S. Department of Justice, Bureau of Justice Statistics, *Justice Expenditure and Employment Extracts: 1993*, NCJ-163068 (Washington, D.C., 1998).

Page 114. Imprisonment in the States.
Sentenced prisoners in state and federal institutions by state, 1996, per 100,000: U.S. Department of Justice, Bureau of Justice Statistics, *Sourcebook of Criminal Justice Statistics 1997,* Kathleen Maguire and Ann L. Pastore, eds., (Washington, D.C., 1998), Table 6.36.

See also: Fox Butterfield, "Southern Curse: Why America's Murder Rate is So High," *New York Times* (July 26, 1998).

Page 114. Leading the World.
Youth homicide rates, selected industrial nations, 1992-1995, deaths per 100,000, aged 15-24: World Health Organization, *1995 World Health Statistics Annual* (Geneva, 1997); and World Health Organization, *1996 World Health Statistics Annual* (Geneva, 1998).

Note: Nations included are those defined by UNICEF as "industrialized countries." See: UNICEF, *The State of the World's Children 1997* (New York: Oxford University Press, 1997), 101. Denmark omitted because data not available.

"The homicide rate for children in the United States . . .", twenty-six industrialized country study: Centers for Disease Control, "Rates of Homicide, Suicide, and Firearm-Related Death Among Children—26 Industrialized Countries," Morbidity and Mortality *Weekly Report,* vol. 46, no. 5 (Massachusetts Medical Society, February 7, 1997), 102.

Page 115. Good News Tempered.
For additional resources see, for example, Michael Tonry, ed., *The Handbook of Crime and Punishment* (New York: Oxford University Press, 1998); Franklin Zimring, *American Youth Violence* (New York: Oxford University Press, 1998); U.S. Department of Justice, Bureau of Justice Statistics, *Firearms, Crime, and Criminal Justice, Selected Findings, Guns Used in Crime,* NCJ-148201 (Washington, D.C., July, 1995); U.S. Department of Justice, Bureau of Justice Statistics, *Historical Corrections Statistics in the United States 1850-1984,* NCJ-102529 (Washington, D.C., December 1986).

Chapter Six: Indicators of Shifting Performance

Teenage Drug Use.

Page 118. "By their late twenties". . . : University of Michigan, National Institute on Drug Abuse, *National Survey Results on Drug Use from The Monitoring the Future Study, 1975-1995,* vol. 2, College Students and Young Adults (Washington, D.C.: U.S. Department of Health and Human Services, Public Health Service, National Institutes of Health, 1997), 25.

Page 119. Reemergence in the Nineties.
Drug use among twelfth graders, percent using any illicit drug in past twelve months: University of Michigan, National Institute on Drug Abuse, *National Survey Results on Drug Use from The Monitoring the Future Study, 1975-1997,* vol. 1, Second-

ary School Students (Washington, D.C.: U.S. Department of Health and Human Services, Public Health Service, National Institutes of Health, 1998).

Drug use among 12-17 year-olds, percent using any illicit drug in past twelve months: Department of Health and Human Services, Substance Abuse and Mental Health Services Administration, *National Household Survey On Drug Abuse, Main Findings 1996,* National Household Survey on Drug Abuse Series H-5 (Washington, D.C., April 1998).

Page 120. Increases Among the Very Young.
Drug use among eighth and tenth graders, percent using any illicit drug in past twelve months: University of Michigan, National Institute on Drug Abuse, *National Survey Results on Drug Use from The Monitoring the Future Study, 1975-1997,* vol. 1, Secondary School Students (Washington, D.C.: U.S. Department of Health and Human Services, Public Health Service, National Institutes of Health, 1998).

Page 120. College Age and Beyond.
Drug use among college students, percent using any illicit drug in past twelve months: University of Michigan, National Institute on Drug Abuse, *National Survey Results on Drug Use from The Monitoring the Future Study, 1975-1997,* vol. 2, College Students and Young Adults (Washington, D.C.: U.S. Department of Health and Human Services, Public Health Service, National Institutes of Health, 1998).

Drug use among 18-25 year olds, percent using any illicit drug in past twelve months: Department of Health and Human Services, Substance Abuse and Mental Health Services Administration, *National Household Survey On Drug Abuse, Main Findings 1996,* National Household Survey on Drug Abuse Series H-5 (Washington, D.C., April 1998).

Campus drug arrests: Kit Lively, "Campus Drug Arrests Increased 18 Percent in 1995: Reports of Other Crimes Fell," *Chronicle of Higher Education,* vol. 43, no. 28 (March 21, 1997), A44.

Page 121. Marijuana Use and Attitude Changes.
Marijuana use and perceived harm, percent use in past twelve months and perceived harm among twelfth graders: *National Survey Results on Drug Use from The Monitoring the Future Study, 1975-1997,* vol. 1, Secondary School Students (Washington, D.C.: U.S. Department of Health and Human Services, Public Health Service, National Institutes of Health, 1998).

See also: Jerald G. Bachman, Lloyd Johnston, Patrick M. O'Malley, "Explaining Recent Increases in Students' Marijuana Use: Impacts of Perceived Risks and Disapproval, 1976 through 1996," *American Journal of Public Health,* vol. 88, no. 6 (June 1998).

Page 122. International Concerns.
For a range of data on international youth drug use, see, "1998 Special Session on Drugs Recommended: Upsurge in Abuse of Stimulants, 33rd session of the UN Commission on Narcotic Drugs," *UN Chronicle,* vol. 33, no. 2 (Summer 1996), 77; Simon Elegant, "Dying for Attention: Lacking Parents' Counsel, Kids Turn to Crime, Drugs—Indonesian Youth Cover Story," *Far Eastern Economic Review,* vol. 159, no. 31 (August 1, 1996), 40; "High in the Gulf, Kuwait's Response to Growing Drug Problem," *The Economist,* vol. 346, no. 8057 (February 28, 1998), 51; Aileen O'Gorman, "Illicit Drug Use in Ireland: An Overview of the Problem and Policy Responses," *Journal of Drug Issues,* vol. 28, no. 1 (Winter 1998), 155; Rensselaer W. Lee, "Drug Abuse in Cuba," *Journal of Substance Abuse Treatment,* vol. 15, no. 2 (March-April 1998), 13; Editorial, "Illegal Drug Use in Australia," *Hecate,* vol. 23, no. 2 (October 1997), 4; Brian Palmer, "Criticize Opium and Methamphetamines Strongly, China's Anti-Drug Policy," *U.S. News and World Report,* vol. 122, no. 20 (May 26, 1997), 4; Aleksei Grishin, "Drugs Called a Threat to Russia's Society," *The Current Digest of the Post-Soviet Press,* vol. 50, no. 10. (April 8, 1998), 1; Sergei Mostovschikov, "Children on the Needle," The Current Digest of the Post-Soviet Press, vol. 47, no. 33 (September 13, 1995), 19; Michael Vatikiotis, "Social Climbers: Thai Youth Look for Kicks—And Status—In Bottles and Pills," *Far Eastern Economic Review,* vol. 58, no. 19 (May 11, 1995), 52; "Rural Daze, Rural Drug Problems in Britain," *The Economist,* vol. 347, no. 8066 (May 2, 1998), 53; Oonagh O'Brien and Luke Tierney, "The Irish Dimension to Drug Use and HIV in Britain," *Journal of Drug Issues,* vol. 28, no. 1 (Winter 1998), 167.

Page 123. Drug Use Implications.
"The nation does have the capacity". . .: University of Michigan, National Institute on Drug Abuse, *National Survey Results on Drug Use from The Monitoring the Future Study, 1975-1995,* vol. 1, Secondary School Students (Washington, D.C.: U.S. Department of Health and Human Services, Public Health Service, National Institutes of Health, 1997), 26-27.

"I hope that we have learned from the relapse"...: University of Michigan, Press Release (Ann Arbor, Michigan, December 18, 1997).

Teenage Births.

Page 124. "The children of adolescent parents". . .: Carnegie Corporation of New York, The Report of the Carnegie Task Force on Meeting the Needs of Young Children, *Starting Points: Meeting the Needs of Our Youngest Children* (New York, April 1994), 26.

Page 125. Family Redefined.
Average number of children per family, total fertility rates: For a discussion, see "Fertility Rate Crawls Back to Two Children Per Family," (Gannett News Service, May 8, 1990).

Teenage birth rates, birthrate per 1,000 women aged 15-19: For 1970-1996, see S. J. Ventura, J. A. Martin, S. C. Curtin, T. J. Matthews, *Report of Final Natality Statistics, 1996,* Monthly Vital Statistics Report, vol. 46, no. 11, supp. (Hyattsville, Maryland: National Center for Health Statistics, 1998). For 1960-1969, see National Center for Health Statistics, "Total Fertility Rates and Birth Rates, by Age of Mother and Race: United States, Specified Years 1940-55 and Each Year 1960-1991."

See also: T. J. Matthews, S. J. Ventura, J. A. Martin, S. C. Curtin, J. A. Martin, *Births of Hispanic Origin, 1989-1995,* Monthly Vital Statistics Report, vol. 46, no. 6, supp. (Hyattsville, Maryland: National Center for Health Statistics, 1998).

Page 126. Lingering Issues.
Number of births, by race/ethnicity, aged 15-19, 1996: S. J. Ventura, J. A. Martin, S. C. Curtin, T. J. Matthews, *Report of Final Natality Statistics, 1996,* Monthly Vital Statistics Report, vol. 46, no. 11, supp. (Hyattsville, Maryland: National Center for Health Statistics, 1998).

Teenage birth rate, by race/ethnicity, aged 15-19, birthrate per 1,000 women: For 1970-1979, see National Center for Health Statistics, "Total Fertility Rates and Birth Rates, by Age of Mother and Race: United States, Specified Years 1940-55 and Each Year 1960-1991." For 1980-1996, see S. J. Ventura, J. A. Martin, S. C. Curtin, T. J. Matthews, *Report of Final Natality Statistics, 1996,* Monthly Vital Statistics Report, vol. 46, no. 11, supp. (Hyattsville, Maryland: National Center for Health Statistics, 1998). Note: White and black rates in Table 6.6 differ from those in Appendix because of the additional breakdown by Hispanic origin.

Unwed parenthood, birthrate per 1,000 unmarried women, aged 15-19, 15-44, 1996: See S. J. Ventura, J. A. Martin, S. C. Curtin, T. J. Matthews, *Report of Final Natality Statistics, 1996,* Monthly Vital Statistics Report, vol. 46, no. 11, supp. (Hyattsville, Maryland: National Center for Health Statistics, 1998).

Page 127. Associated Problems.
Low birthweight by age: See S. J. Ventura, J. A. Martin, S. C. Curtin, T. J. Matthews, *Report of Final Natality Statistics, 1996,* Monthly Vital Statistics Report, vol. 46, no. 11, supp. (Hyattsville, Maryland: National Center for Health Statistics, 1998).

Dropout rates: National Educational Longitudinal Study, cited in *Facts at a Glance,* Child Trends, Inc. (Washington, D.C., October 1996).

Median income, all families, families 15-24: U.S. Bureau of the Census, *Historical Income Tables—Families,* "Age of Householder—Families by Median and Mean Income: 1947-1996," Table F-11, internet download.

Median income, married with children, female-headed families with children: U.S. Bureau of the Census, *Historical Income Tables—Families,* "Presence of Children Under 18 Years Old — Families by Median and Mean Income, and Type of Family: 1974-1996," Table F-10, internet download.

Poverty rates, married with children, female-headed families with children: U.S. Bureau of the Census, H*istorical Poverty Tables—Families,* "Poverty Status of Families, by Type of Family, Presence of Related Children, Race and Hispanic Origin: 1959-1996," Table 4, internet download.

Page 128. State Differences.
Teenage births, selected states, birthrate per 1,000 women aged 15-19, 1996: S. J. Ventura, J. A. Martin, S. C. Curtin, T. J. Matthews, *Report of Final Natality Statistics, 1996,* Monthly Vital Statistics Report, vol. 46, no. 11, supp. (Hyattsville, Maryland: National Center for Health Statistics, 1998).

See also: Centers for Disease Control, "State-Specific Birth Rates for Teenagers—United States, 1990-1996," Morbidity and Mortality Weekly *Report,* vol. 46, no. 36 (Massachusetts Medical Society, September 12, 1997); S. J. Ventura, S. C. Clarke, T. J. Matthews, "Recent Declines in Teenage Birth Rates in the United States: Variations by State, 1990-1994," Monthly Vital

Statistics Report, vol. 45, no. 5, supp. (Hyattsville, Maryland: National Center for Health Statistics, 1996); S. J. Ventura, S. C. Curtin, T. J. Matthews, _Teenage Births in the United States: National and State Trends, 1990-1996_ (Washington, D.C.: National Vital Statistics System, National Center for Health Statistics, 1998); S. J. Ventura, T. J. Matthews, S. C. Curtin, _Teenage Births in the United States: State Trends, 1991-1996, An Update,_ Monthly Vital Statistics Report, vol. 46, no. 11, supp. 2 (Hyattsville, Maryland: National Center for Health Statistics, 1998).

Page 128. International Differences.
Percent of women 20-24 who gave birth before age 18, in Niger, Bangladesh, Cameroon, United States, Great Britain, France, Poland, Germany, and Japan: Alan Guttmacher Institute, _Into a New World: Young Women's Sexual and Reproductive Lives_ (New York, 1998).

Page 129. Causes or Consequences.
"there is little difference in levels of sexual activity". . .: Alan Guttmacher Institute, Issue Brief, _Teenage Pregnancy and the Welfare Reform Debate_ (New York, 1995).

"a product of 'early disadvantage" . . . : Jacqueline Darroch Forrest, Vice President of Research, Alan Guttmacher Institute, cited in "Teen Pregnancy Rate Splits Along Class Lines, Studies Show" (Gannett News Service, June 7, 1994).

For a general discussion of teenage pregnancy, see Alan Guttmacher Institute, _Sex and America's Teenagers_ (New York, 1994).

Alcohol-Related Traffic Fatalities.

Page 130. "About three in every ten Americans". . .: U.S. Department of Transportation, National Highway Traffic Safety Administration, National Center for Statistics and Analysis, _Traffic Safety Facts 1996: Alcohol_ (Washington, D.C.).

Page 131. Nearly A Decade of Improvement.
Traffic accidents are the leading cause of death among people aged 1-24: Centers for Disease Control, "Alcohol-Related Traffic Fatalities Involving Children—United States, 1985-1996," Morbidity and Mortality Weekly _Report,_ vol. 46, no. 48 (Massachusetts Medical Society, December 5, 1997), 1130-33.

"...the fourth leading cause of death among adults aged 25-44" . . .: K. D. Peters, K. D. Kochanek, S. L. Murphy, _Deaths: Final Data for 1996,_ National Vital Statistics Reports, vol. 47, no. 9 (Hyattsville, Maryland: National Center for Health Statistics, 1998).

Alcohol-related traffic fatalities, percent of all traffic fatalities which are alcohol-related (AEDS): CSR, Inc., and the Division of Biometry and Epidemiology, National Institute on Alcohol Abuse and Alcoholism, Alcohol Epidemiological Data System, U.S. Department of Health and Human Services, Public Health Service, National Institutes of Health, Surveillance Report #42, _Trends in Alcohol-Related Fatal Traffic Crashes, United States, 1977-1995_ (Washington, D.C., December 1997).

See also: U.S. Department of Transportation, National Highway Traffic Safety Administration, National Center for Statistics and Analysis, _Traffic Safety Facts 1996: Overview_ (Washington, D.C.); Centers for Disease Control, "Involvement by Young Drivers in Fatal Motor-Vehicle Crashes—United States, 1988-1995," Morbidity and Mortality Weekly _Report,_ vol. 45, no. 48 (Massachusetts Medical Society, December 6, 1996), 1049-53; Centers for Disease Control, "Alcohol-Related Traffic Crashes and Fatalities Among Youth and Young Adults—United States, 1982-1994," _Morbidity and Mortality Weekly Report,_ vol. 44, no. 47 (Massachusetts Medical Society, December 1, 1995), 869-74.

Page 131. Fatal Accident Reporting System.
Alcohol-related traffic fatalities, percent of all traffic fatalities which are alcohol-related (FARS): U.S. Department of Transportation, National Highway Traffic Safety Administration, National Center for Statistics and Analysis, _Traffic Safety Facts 1996: Alcohol_; and unpublished data, National Highway Traffic Safety Administration, Office of Alcohol and State Programs, NTS-20 (Washington, D.C.).

"The National Safety Council has warned" . . .: See, for example, Matthew L. Wald, "Safety Group Reports Rise in Fatalities on Highways," _New York Times_ (October 10, 1996), A24; Matthew l. Wald, "Repeal of U.S. Speed Limit Is Found to Raise Highway Deaths," _New York Times_ (October 12, 1997), 36.

Page 132. Deaths Are Still High, Injuries Severe.
Number of alcohol-related traffic fatalities (AEDS): CSR, Inc., and the Division of Biometry and Epidemiology, National In-

stitute on Alcohol Abuse and Alcoholism, Alcohol Epidemiological Data System, U.S. Department of Health and Human Services, Public Health Service, National Institutes of Health, Surveillance Report #42, *Trends in Alcohol-Related Fatal Traffic Crashes, United States, 1977-1995* (Washington, D.C., December 1997).

Number of alcohol-related traffic fatalities (FARS), "one every thirty-one minutes" . . .: U.S. Department of Transportation, National Highway Traffic Safety Administration, National Center for Statistics and Analysis, *Traffic Safety Facts 1996: Alcohol* (Washington, D.C.).

Number of alcohol-related traffic injuries (FARS), "one every two minutes" . . .: U.S. Department of Transportation, National Highway Traffic Safety Administration, National Center for Statistics and Analysis, *Traffic Safety Facts 1996: Alcohol* (Washington, D.C.).

Page 133. Who and When?
Alcohol-related traffic fatalities by age, gender, time, and day: U.S. Department of Transportation, National Highway Traffic Safety Administration, National Center for Statistics and Analysis, *Traffic Safety Facts 1996: Alcohol* (Washington, D.C.).

See also: U.S. Department of Transportation, National Highway Traffic Safety Administration, National Center for Statistics and Analysis, *1995 Youth Fatal Crash and Alcohol Facts,* DOT HS 808 525 (Washington, D.C., February 1997).

Page 134. State Differences.
Alcohol-related traffic fatalities, selected states, 1996: U.S. Department of Transportation, National Highway Traffic Safety Administration, National Center for Statistics and Analysis, *Traffic Safety Facts 1996: Alcohol* (Washington, D.C.).

See also: U.S. Department of Transportation, National Highway Traffic Safety Administration, National Center for Statistics and Analysis, *Traffic Safety Facts 1996: State Alcohol Estimates* (Washington, D.C.).

Page 134. Saving Lives.
Cumulative estimated lives saved by minimum-drinking-age laws: U.S. Department of Transportation, National Highway Traffic Safety Administration, National Center for Statistics and Analysis, *Traffic Safety Facts 1996: Alcohol* (Washington, D.C.).

"advocates for safe driving believe their message is no longer being heard" . . . : See, for example, Matthew L. Wald, "A Fading Drumbeat Against Drunk Driving," *New York Times* (December 15, 1996), Week in Review, 5.

Page 135. Future Gains?
For a discussion of future trends, see American Public Health Association, "Incentive Grants Encourage States to Enact 0.08 BAC Laws" and American Public Health Association, "DWI Deaths Reach Historic Low," *The Nation's* Health (October 1998), 4.

Affordable Housing.

Page 136. "The Congress hereby declares that the general welfare". . .: *The Housing Act of 1949,* July 15, 1949, S. 1070, Public Law 171, "Declaration of Housing Policy."

Page 137. The American Dream.
Housing Affordability Index, twenty percent downpayment on median priced home as a percent of median family income, all buyers: For 1970-1990, see National Association of Realtors, *Home Sales Yearbook: 1990, Statistical Summary of Existing Home Sales* (Washington, D.C., 1991). For 1991-1993, see National Association of Realtors, *Real Estate Outlook* (June 1994). For 1994-1996, see National Association of Realtors, *Real Estate Outlook* (April 1997).

Page 138. Homeownership Rates.
Home ownership rates, U.S., all: For 1973, 1976, 1980, see Joint Center for Housing Studies, Harvard University, *The State of the Nation's Housing, 1993* (Cambridge, Mass.). For 1982-1996, see U.S. Bureau of the Census, "Homeownership Rates for the United States, by Age of Householder and by Family Status 1992-1997," internet download.

Homeownership rates by race and ethnicity: For 1973, 1976, 1980, 1983, 1987, 1989, 1992, see Joint Center for Housing Studies, Harvard University, *The State of the Nation's Housing, 1993* (Cambridge, Mass.). For 1991, 1993, 1995, see Joint Center for Housing Studies, Harvard University, *The State of the Nation's Housing, 1996* (Cambridge, Mass.). For 1994, see Joint Center for Housing Studies, Harvard University, *The State of the Nation's Housing, 1998* (Cambridge, Mass.). For 1996, see Joint Center for Housing Studies, Harvard University, *The State of the Nation's Housing, 1997* (Cambridge, Mass.).

Page 138. For the Young.
Homeownership by age: Joint Center for Housing Studies, Harvard University, *The State of the Nation's Housing, 1996* (Cambridge, Mass.).

Page 139. Among Renters,
"The number of renter households with incomes of $10,000 or less has grown". . . : Joint Center for Housing Studies, Harvard University, *The State of the Nation's Housing, 1996* (Cambridge, Mass.).

Contract and gross rent as percent of income: Joint Center for Housing Studies, Harvard University, *The State of the Nation's Housing, 1998* (Cambridge, Mass.).

See also: Tracy L. Kaufman, *Out of Reach: Can America Pay the Rent?* (Washington, D.C.: National Low Income Housing Coalition, May 1996); Tracy L. Kaufman, *Out of Reach: Rental Housing At What Cost?* (Washington, D.C.: National Low Income Housing Coalition, September 1997).

Page 139. Worst Case Needs.
"Despite robust economic growth between 1993 and 1995," the number of worst case needs remained at an "all time high" of 5.3 million households: U.S. Department of Housing and Urban Development, Office of Policy Development and Research, *Rental Housing Assistance—The Crisis Continues, The 1997 Report to Congress on Worst Case Housing Needs* (Washington, D.C., April 1998), Letter of Transmittal.

Numbers of elderly, children, and people with disabilities with worst case needs: U.S. Department of Housing and Urban Development, Office of Policy Development and Research, *Rental Housing Assistance—The Crisis Continues, The 1997 Report to Congress on Worst Case Housing Needs* (Washington, D.C., April 1998).

Worst case needs among working households, suburbs, and as a percentage of the nation's population: U.S. Department of Housing and Urban Development, Office of Policy Development and Research, *Rental Housing Assistance—The Crisis Continues, The 1997 Report to Congress on Worst Case Housing Needs* (Washington D.C., April 1998).

Page 140. Low-Cost Housing Availability.
"According to the Center on Budget and Policy Priorities, in 1970 there was a surplus of 300,000 units. There were 6.2 million low-income renters". . . : Center on Budget and Policy Priorities, *In Search of Shelter: The Growing Shortage of Affordable Rental Housing* (Washington, D.C., July 15, 1998).

"The Department of Housing and Urban Development reports that between 1993 and 1995 alone, the supply of low-cost housing declined by 9 percent": U.S. Department of Housing and Urban Development, Office of Policy Development and Research, *Rental Housing Assistance—The Crisis Continues, The 1997 Report to Congress on Worst Case Housing Needs* (Washington, D.C., April 1998).

See also: Center on Budget and Policy Priorities, *In Short Supply The Growing Affordable Housing Gap* (Washington, D.C., July 1995).

Page 141. Homelessness.
Varying definitions and estimates: See National Coalition for the Homeless, "How Many People Experience Homelessness," NCH Fact Sheet #2, internet download.

"HUD cites estimates that families with children now exceed 30 percent of the homeless population" . . . : U.S. Department of Housing and Urban Development, *The State of the Cities, 1998* (Washington, D.C. June 1998).

See also: The United States Conference of Mayors, *A Status Report on Hunger and Homelessness in America's Cities: 1996, A 29 City Survey* (Washington, D.C., December 1996); Homes for the Homeless and the Institute for Children and Poverty, *A Snapshot of Family Homelessness Across America: Ten Cities, 1997-1998* (New York, 1998); Bruce G. Link, et al., "Lifetime and Five-Year Prevalence of Homelessness in the United States," *American Journal of Public Health,* vol. 84, no. 12 (December, 1994), 1907-12; Jon Erikson and Charles Wilhelm, eds., H*ousing the Homeless* (New Brunswick, N.J.: Center for Urban Policy Research, 1986).

Page 141. A Decent Home For Every American.
See for example: Harvard University, Joint Center for Housing Studies, *Housing in America 1970-2000,* by William C. Apgar,

George Masnick, and Nancy McArdle (Cambridge, Mass., Spring 1998); National Low Income Housing Coalition, *Federal Policy in Transition: A National Briefing Book on Housing, Economic and Community Development* (Washington, D.C., June 1996); Jeanne Macklin, "Housing Costs Burdensome for Some Groups," *Human Ecology Forum,* vol. 24, no. 1 (Winter 1996); National Coalition for the Homeless, *Homelessness in America* (Phoenix, Ariz.: Oryx Press, 1996).

Unemployment.

Page 142. "The Congress hereby declares that it is the continuing policy". . . : *The Unemployment Act of 1946,* S380, Public Law 304, Section 2.

Page 143. Work in America.
Unemployment rates: *Economic Report of the President,* Transmitted to the Congress, February 1998, together with the Annual Report of the Council of Economic Advisors (Washington, D.C., February 1998).

Periods of recession: U.S. Bureau of the Census, Current Population Reports, *Money Income in the United States: 1996* (with separate data on valuation of non cash benefits), P60-197 (Washington, D.C. 1997).

Page 143. Inching Up over Time.
Average unemployment rates per decade: Annual rates from *Economic Report of the President,* Transmitted to the Congress, February 1998, together with the Annual Report of the Council of Economic Advisors (Washington, D.C., February 1998). Calculations by the Fordham Institute for Innovation in Social Policy, Tarrytown, New York.

Page 144. Still Struggling.
Black and Hispanic unemployment rates: *Economic Report of the President,* Transmitted to the Congress, February 1998, together with the Annual Report of the Council of Economic Advisors (Washington, D.C., February 1998).

Page 144. Unemployment Insurance.
"Changes in the economy". . .: *Economic Report of the President,* Transmitted to the Congress, February 1997, together with the Annual Report of the Council of Economic Advisors (Washington, D.C., February 1997).

Insured unemployment as a percentage of total unemployment, by month, 1967-1996, annual averages: U.S. House of Representatives, Committee on Ways and Means, *1998 Green Book, Background Material and Data on Programs within the Jurisdiction of the Committee on Ways and Means, May 19, 1998* (Washington, D.C. 1998).

Page 145. Unemployment Duration.
Duration of unemployment, Average (mean) duration in weeks: *Economic Report of the President,* Transmitted to the Congress, February 1998, together with the Annual Report of the Council of Economic Advisors (Washington, D.C., February 1998).

For a discussion of the proportion of unemployed, twenty-seven weeks or longer, see Randy E. Ilg and Angela Clinton, "Strong Job Growth Continues, Unemployment Declines in 1997," *Monthly Labor Review,* vol. 121, no. 2 (February 1998), 48: "The feature of unemployment in which the current and previous expansions have differed most significantly is long-term unemployment. In more recent years, the proportion of the unemployed who had been looking for work for 27 weeks or longer has continued to be substantially higher than in similar phases of the 1983-90 expansion. In fact, during the 1996 and 1997, long-term unemployment as a percentage of total unemployment ranged from 2-7 percentage points higher than it had at similar points in the business cycle expansion of the late 1980s."

Page 146. Variations by State.
1996 state unemployment rates: Bureau of Labor Statistics, "State and Regional Unemployment 1997 [and 1996] Annual Averages," internet download.

Page 146. The Contingent Economy.
"29 percent of the work force in nonstandard or contingent jobs": Arne Kalleberg, et al., *Nonstandard Work, Substandard Jobs: Flexible Work Arrangements in the U.S.* (Washington, D.C.: Economic Policy Institute and the Women's Research and Education Institute, 1997).

See also: Richard Belous, *The Contingent Economy: The Growth of the Temporary, Part-time and Subcontracted Workforce* (Washington, D.C.: National Planning Association, 1989); Chris Benner, *Shock Absorbers in the Flexible Economy: The Rise of Contingent Employment in Silicon Valley* (San Jose, Ca.: Working Partnerships USA, May 1996).

Page 146. International Rankings.
Unemployment rates, selected nations: Bureau of Labor Statistics, Comparative Civilian Labor Force Statistics, Civilian Unemployment, Approximating U.S. Concepts Series, internet download.

Page 147. When the Cycle Shifts.
See for example: Thomas S. Moore, *The Disposable Work Force: Worker Displacement and Employment Instability in
America* (New York: Aldine de Gruyter, 1996).

Chapter Seven: Judging the Nation's Social Performance

Page 150. "Given its pattern of performance over time, is it likely that such progress will occur in the future?": The category of
future potential is intended to be merely suggestive. The future behavior of these indicators will be determined by a variety of
factors, many of which are unpredictable. A systematic analysis of past performance, however, can at least provide a beginning understanding of what might occur. In general, the extent to which the indicator has shown significantly more years of
improvement than decline indicates its potential for past improvement and, if the trends remain consistent, may tell us something about the future. Also if the yearly average improvement is higher than the yearly average decline, it may be revealing as
well. Judged by this standard, the prospects for indicators such as infant mortality or life expectancy seem far better than child
poverty or child abuse. But, of course, predicting the future from the past, presumes all things are equal, and they rarely are.
These very tentative categories can be refined, and their accuracy tested as new data become available.

Page 151. "Chart 7.1 shows that several indicators now stand at their best point since the 1970s—a performance score of 100
percent.": Note that the best performance for each indicator can be reached in any year between 1970 and 1996. The years in
which each indicator achieved its best performance are as follows: Improving Indicators: Infant Mortality 1996; Life Expectancy 1996; Poverty Ages 65 and Over 1995; High School Dropouts 1992; Worsening Indicators: Violent Crime 1970; Child
Poverty 1973; Youth Suicide 1970; Inequality 1970;Wages 1972; Health Insurance Coverage 1976; Child Abuse 1976; Shifting Indicators: Alcohol-related traffic fatalities 1996; Unemployment 1970; Teenage Births 1986; Affordable Housing 1972;
Teen Drug Use 1992.

Page 151. "Chart 7.2 provides a closer look at the performance of each indicator." We anticipate that in the future this table
will be updated annually with each projection reviewed and revised as new data become available. It is also worth noting that
if data were available each quarter, a far more frequent and precise picture could be reported.

Part Three: Pursuing a Practical Vision

Chapter Eight: Advancing the Field

Page 159. "We have learned—perhaps it is our greatest achievement—to envisage the economy as a whole composed of
many parts". . .:Wesley C. Mitchell, "Empirical Research and the Development of Economic Science," *Economic Research
and the Development of Economic Science and Public Policy* (New York: National Bureau of Economic Research, June 6-7
1946), 7-8.

New Concepts and Ideas

Page 160. "All fields of knowledge, in order to advance". . .: Thomas Kuhn, *The Structure of Scientific Revolutions* (Chicago:
University of Chicago Press, 1970).

Page 161. "To advance the work, Wesley C. Mitchell, the economist". . .: Wesley C. Mitchell, *Business Cycles,* (Berkeley:
University of California Press, 1913); Philip A. Klein and Geoffrey H. Moore, *Monitoring Growth Cycles in Market Oriented
Countries: Developing and Using International Economic Indicators,* National Bureau of Economic Research, Studies in
Business Cycles, No. 26 (Cambridge, Mass.: Ballinger, 1985); T. Koomans, "Measurement without Theory," *Review of Eco-
nomics and Statistics* (1947), 24, 161-92.

Key Questions.

Page 162. "Alex Kotlowitz's book". . .: Alex Kotlowitz, *There are No Children Here, The Story of Two Boys Growing Up in the Other America* (New York: Anchor, 1991); Jonathan Kozol, *Savage Inequalities: Children in America's Schools* (New York: Crown, 1991).

New Tools

A National Social Survey.

Page 163. "The first report of these surveys was issued in 1997 by Eurostat". . .: Joachim Vogel, Statistics Sweden, *Living Conditions and Inequality in the European Union* (European Commission, 1997), 8.

Page 163. "Existing surveys, the Eurostat report observes". . .: Joachim Vogel, Statistics Sweden, *Living Conditions and Inequality in the European Union* (European Commission, 1997), 8.

A National Social Report.

Page 165. "It is the national acknowledgment of the importance of a social health perspective". . .: Progress toward this end has been achieved at the state level. The Connecticut legislature, in 1997, passed a law requiring an annual index of social health and an annual report of the social health of the state. See Note for page 26 for further detail.

Chapter Nine: The Tasks of Visibility: A New Direction for Social Reporting

The Federal Government: The Most Important Source.

Page 170. "According to Franz Rothenbacher, in his review of international social reporting". . .: Franz Rothenbacher, "National and International Approaches to Social Reporting," *Social Indicators Research,* vol. 29 (1993), 28.

Page 171. "Such questions are meant to suggest paths" . . . Others who have suggested needed changes for the current social indicators movement include: Kenneth Land, "Social Indicators and the Quality-of-Life: Where Do We Stand in the Mid-1990s?" *SINET* (February 1996), 5-8; Hazel Henderson, *Paradigms in Progress: Life Beyond Economics,* (Indianapolis: Knowledge Systems, 1991).

Index